Other titles in the Jossey-Bass Nonprofit and Public Management Series:

Strategic Planning for Public and Nonprofit Organizations, Revised Edition, *John M. Bryson*

Handbook of Public Administration, Second Edition, *James L. Perry*

Creating and Implementing Your Strategic Plan Workbook, *John M. Bryson, Farnum K. Alston*

Handbook of Practical Program Evaluation, *Joseph S. Wholey, Harry P. Hatry, Kathryn E. Newcomer*

Handbook of Training and Development for the Public Sector, *Montgomery Van Wart, N. Joseph Cayer, Steve Cook*

Strategic Management of Public and Third Sector Organizations, *Paul C. Nutt, Robert W. Backoff*

The Search Conference, *Merrelyn Emery, Ronald E. Purser*

Seamless Government, *Russell M. Linden*

Authentic Leadership, *Robert W. Terry*

Planners on Planning, *Bruce W. McClendon, Anthony James Catanese*

Benchmarking for Best Practices in the Public Sector, *Patricia Keehley, Steven Medlin, Sue MacBride, Laura Longmire*

Transforming Government, *Patricia Ingraham, Ronald Sanders, and James Thompson, editors*

Transforming Public Policy, *Nancy C. Roberts, Paula J. King*

The Spirit of Public Administration, *H. George Frederickson*

Understanding and Managing Public Organizations, Second Edition, *Hal G. Rainey*

New Strategies for Public Pay, *Howard Risher, Charles Fay*

Grassroots Leaders for a New Economy, *Douglas Henton, John Melville, Kimberly Walesh*

Human Resources Management for Public and Nonprofit Organizations, *Joan E. Pynes*

How Do Public Managers Manage? *Carolyn Ban*

Catalytic Leadership

Catalytic Leadership

Strategies for an
Interconnected World

Jeffrey S. Luke

Jossey-Bass Publishers • San Francisco

Substantial discounts on bulk quantities of Jossey-Bass books are available to corporations, professional associations, and other organizations. For details and discount information, contact the special sales department at Jossey-Bass Inc., Publishers (415) 433–1740; Fax (800) 605–2665.

For sales outside the United States, please contact your local Simon & Schuster International Office.

Jossey-Bass Web address: http://www.josseybass.com

Library of Congress Cataloging-in-Publication Data

Luke, Jeffrey Scott.
    Catalytic leadership : strategies for an interconnected world /Jeffrey S. Luke.
  — 1st ed.
      p. cm. — (The Jossey-Bass nonprofit and public management series)
    Includes bibliographical references and index.
    ISBN 0–7879–0917–3 (acid-free paper)
    1. Political planning—United States. 2. Political leadership—United States. I. Title.
  II. Series.
  JK468.P64.L85 1998
  320.973—dc21   97–21085

FIRST EDITION
HB Printing 10 9 8 7 6 5 4 3 2 1

The Jossey-Bass
Nonprofit and Public Management Series

Contents

Preface   xi

The Author   xxiii

Part One: The Challenge Facing Public Leaders   1

1   The Interconnected Nature of Public Problems   3

2   Defining Public Leadership   22

Part Two: The Catalytic Tasks of Public Leadership   37

3   Raising Awareness: Focusing Public Attention on
    the Issue   41

4   Forming Working Groups: Bringing People
    Together to Address the Problem   67

5   Creating Strategies: Stimulating Multiple
    Strategies and Options for Action   89

6   Sustaining Action: Implementing Strategies and
    Maintaining Momentum   123

Part Three: The Foundational Skills for Catalytic Leaders   149

7   Thinking and Acting Strategically   151

8   Facilitating Productive Working Groups   185

9   Leading from Personal Passion and Strength
    of Character   218

Appendix: Establishing Criteria Based on
Desired Outcomes   241

Bibliography   245

Index   263

*This book is dedicated to the alumni of the Pacific Program,
energetic and spirited catalysts in the public interest.*

Preface

For the first time in human history, we now exist in a truly inter-connected world. Whether we exclaim or bemoan this condition, our behaviors and approaches to solving public problems have not adapted to the change. How do we provide effective leadership to address interconnected public problems with a reduction of fiscal resources, a lack of consensus on options, and the involvement of many diverse, independent-minded stakeholders? This question has driven my consulting and public service since the mid-1980s.

Most of my first clients were local, state, and federal agencies. I attempted to help them think and act more strategically around the public problems they were responsible for addressing, and this perplexing question kept surfacing. Unfortunately, modern theories and strategies for leading in an interconnected context have lagged. Bookstores are stocked with titles purporting the latest strategies in organizational leadership, but these books provided little practical relevance for me or my clients.

In 1985, we researched how to reduce homelessness in Douglas County, Nebraska, the metropolitan area of Omaha. We found multiple causes of homelessness; none were amenable to a simple solution or quick fix, and all would involve multiple agencies if any concerted action were to be taken. Next we assisted in the economic development of several Midwest communities. The region faced increasing unemployment, caused in part by a dying agricultural base. In the process of helping the communities to diversify their economies strategically, we found that successful action required commitment by numerous public and private sector agencies, many of which had not worked together before.

After moving to Oregon in 1987, I continued to work in economic development. Completing projects with more than a dozen communities, we discovered that no matter how strategic their planning was, sufficient leadership to stimulate concerted or collective action was often missing. What became apparent was that the leadership needed was not the type currently popular—visionary leadership that grabbed the reins and took charge. Successful leadership around community and economic development was more catalytic and collaborative than charismatic and controlling. (See Chapter Eleven of Luke, Ventriss, Reed, and Reed, 1988, for our initial insights on catalytic leadership.)

By the early 1990s the challenges of interconnected problems became more serious and we started analyzing successful and unsuccessful catalytic efforts across a much broader set of policy issues. We developed a case analysis of the start of the Applegate Partnership, a nationally recognized joint effort by environmentalists and the logging industry in southern Oregon. Stephanie Buffum drafted a case study of Applegate's beginnings. In the study we found that heated controversies did not always end up in gridlock and that there were effective ways to bring together diverse, polarized stakeholders to address a common problem. A case analysis of the Partners for Human Investment (PHI) was drafted by Todd Barnhart and funded by the Oregon Progress Board. PHI sought to be a catalyst to help Oregon communities improve the quality of their local workforce. This analysis captured some of the common difficulties in attempting to make things happen in a policy domain that was fragmented and suspicious of competing interests.

Another case study in Oregon took a close look at Tillamook County's success at reducing teenage pregnancies by 75 percent in five years. Funded by the U.S. Dept. of Health and Human Services, and with the help of Katie Neville, Ruth Daron, and Becky Lamoureux, we interviewed more than sixty community leaders and held six focus groups with teens to assess what approaches and programs worked best. The answer was surprising yet simple. The most effective methods were multiple strategies by multiple agencies, stimulated by several catalysts with no particular central control or coordination. It was a unique catalytic effort that stimulated many "self-organizing" efforts all aimed at the same outcome: the reduction of teen pregnancies.

The Tillamook experience became the model for the Oregon Option, another innovation in addressing interconnected public issues. The Oregon Option is a nationally known effort to develop new federal, state, and local intergovernmental partnerships with targeted, agreed-upon benchmarks or outcomes. Other successful catalytic efforts were also studied: at the federal level, the Education 2000 initiative; at the state level, the Oregon Progress Board and the Oregon Benchmarks; at the local level, the Josephine County Coalition for Kids.

In 1996 we organized the Oregon Leadership Summit to draw lessons from a decade of experience. With the support of the Annie E. Casey Foundation, the summit convened more than forty of Oregon's community, civic, and elected leaders to help "mine" the successful projects and to further develop public leadership capacities. The gathering was held at Mt. Hood's Timberline Lodge, an ideal place for such a gathering of leaders.

Analysis of the case studies and the results of the summit provided valuable insights. To create strategic action on urgent public problems, federal, state, and local agencies and communities had to reach out beyond their boundaries and engage a much wider set of individuals, agencies, and stakeholders. Tackling public problems required unusual and dynamic partnerships between government agencies, nonprofit service providers, business enterprises, neighborhood groups, sovereign tribal nations, and educational institutions. For most public leaders this was new and unexplored territory. Many of the issues requiring attention, such as teenage pregnancy, homelessness, and economic development, were so complex that old solutions seldom helped and sometimes even worsened the situation. Emerging challenges, complex and interconnected, required new forms of collective action across traditional agency lines and jurisdictional boundaries. Elected officials, appointed public managers, civic leaders, and community volunteers needed new public leadership skills and practices.

The purpose of *Catalytic Leadership* is to summarize the lessons learned over the past decade around this question: How do you provide effective leadership to address difficult and interconnected public problems? Public leadership is an activity engaged in by citizens of all walks of life: elected and appointed, public and private, paid and volunteer, urban and rural. This book is written for them. We hope they will realize that they are not alone in facing these new challenges. Local community leaders frequently commented to us that they felt they were odd, different, and often isolated in their attempts to stimulate action in a very interconnected system. Because they found no examples or models to show how this kind of catalytic work was done, they felt they had to invent them. Our case studies located many examples of successful catalytic work by nonheroic public leaders and identified common threads among them. The Oregon Leadership Summit highlighted the common themes and began to build and nurture a statewide network of catalytic leaders.

We hope this book illuminates the common themes and details how the successful tasks work. By providing a framework from which custom-tailored strategies can be devised, the book can help those who are just beginning to get active and who want to be catalysts for positive change. The book can also aid seasoned public leaders to improve their effectiveness. Many individuals already engage in many of these activities, if only intuitively. This book can help them to be more aware of their successful practices and to refine their skills at solving urgent public issues.

Summary of Contents

When we think of leadership, we often conjure up pictures of corporate leaders such as Chrysler's Lee Iaccoca or GTE's Jack Welch, who transformed their staid organizations into high-performing corporations. Visionary and charismatic, such leaders breathe new life into organizations so they can better compete in a complex marketplace.

Leadership to address such public problems as economic development and teenage pregnancies is different, however. Public problems are interconnected, they cross organizational and jurisdictional boundaries, and they are interorganizational. No single agency, organization, jurisdiction, or sector has enough authority, influence, or resources to dictate visionary solutions. Thus, contemporary strategies for organizational leadership are less effective in addressing public problems in an interconnected world. Public leadership faces a different set of challenges. The chapters in Part One of the book address the unique challenges facing public leaders.

Chapter One, "The Interconnected Nature of Public Problems," emphasizes that there are seldom, if ever, quick fixes or silver bullets. Urgent problems are intertwined with other issues, they cross traditional boundaries, and they are difficult to define, analyze, and permanently solve. Not only are the problems interconnected, but the problem-solving activity occurs in a context of fragmentation and shared power. No one organization, jurisdiction, or sector has enough power to dictate solutions unilaterally.

Chapter Two, "Defining Public Leadership," highlights the differences among contemporary forms of corporate leadership. These popular approaches often prescribe a set of skills that help executives to pursue organizational excellence, take charge, stimulate extraordinary performance by employees, or change an organization's internal culture by being transformational. Because these approaches are fundamentally based on hierarchical authority, they cannot be transferred easily to the interconnected and nonhierarchical contexts of public problems. Public leadership is different from traditional organizational leadership. It emerges from citizens of all walks of life who seek to generate new jobs, improve the water system or roads, improve their schools, or protect unique natural resources. It involves public officials; individuals from the private, nonprofit, and education sectors; community activists; and volunteers. Leadership in this environment demands different roles, tasks, and skills than those required in the corporate world.

Understanding effective public leadership requires more than the attitude of "we'll know it when we see it." It involves four specific, interrelated tasks. The exercise of each task alone can have an individual catalytic effect. Together the four tasks can amplify their catalytic impact on addressing public problems and improving the quality of the human condition. The four tasks are

1. Focus attention by elevating the issue to the public and policy agendas.
2. Engage people in the effort by convening the diverse set of people, agencies, and interests needed to address the issue.
3. Stimulate multiple strategies and options for action.
4. Sustain action and maintain momentum by managing the interconnections through appropriate institutionalization and rapid information sharing and feedback.

Each essential task summarizes a complex set of activities and processes found in successful efforts to address public problems in an interconnected world. The catalytic leadership process is not a formal, linear model. The four tasks are more organic and artistic than mechanical and sequential. Public leaders commonly spiral back to earlier tasks as the need arises.

Part Two focuses on these four catalytic tasks and the roles of public leaders when pursuing something in the public interest. Each chapter in the section elaborates on a particular task.

Chapter Three, "Raising Awareness: Focusing Public Attention on the Issue," explains how public leaders direct attention toward a pressing issue. Because the list of potential problems is vast and resources are limited, public leaders need to be advocates to ensure that a particular issue or problem is seen as more important and urgent than competing issues. Leaders attempt to get others to believe that an issue is urgent or important enough to invest their time and energy in it.

Chapter Four, "Forming Working Groups: Bringing People Together to Address the Problem," shows how public leaders can include diverse factions to address a problem, urgent issue, or emerging opportunity. They identify key stakeholders and knowledgeholders and invite them to address the issue. Acting as catalysts, public leaders use their knowledge of the particular problem, their knowledge of stakeholders' interests, their personal contacts in related networks, and their personal charm and available authority to convince key individuals that the issue is worthy of their involvement.

Chapter Five, "Creating Strategies: Stimulating Multiple Strategies and Options for Action," explains how public leaders act as catalysts to create the conditions necessary for a working group or network to develop and commit to multiple strategies to address the targeted problem. Leaders help to create a core of committed and motivated group members with sufficient skills and knowledge who do not relinquish their organizational autonomy or institutional independence when joining a working group or network. They help to formulate a unifying purpose based on desired outcomes or results they hope to achieve. Public leaders act as process champions by facilitating an interactive group process that enhances mutual learning, stimulates shared leadership, and builds trust. They help the working group or network to design a structured, credible process of decision making and action planning, a process that gives confidence to those involved that something positive will result from their time and effort.

Chapter Six, "Sustaining Action: Implementing Strategies and Maintaining Momentum," shows the difficulty in sustaining attention and effort by the numerous and diverse individuals and agencies, most of whom are independent of each other. Public leaders act as catalysts to gain support and legitimacy for the multiple strategies. They network to ensure that supportive coalitions will advocate and champion continued implementation. They keep focused on the ultimate goal, outcome, or desired result. They also help to develop an outcome-based information system to monitor progress and to ensure that successes and "small wins" are recognized and acknowledged.

For public leadership to effectively address interconnected public problems, individuals must step forward and act as catalysts. With a diverse group of individuals, they must forge sustainable agreements on action strategies, set in motion multiple strategies, and sustain momentum over time. Such catalytic leadership requires a set of analytical skills and interpersonal competencies and is characterized by a common set of attitudes, traits, and habits.

The three chapters in Part Three, "The Foundational Skills for Catalytic Leaders," elaborate on the crucial analytical and interpersonal skills that cut across the four public leadership tasks. These skills must be learned through experience and trial and error. The core set of analytical skills involves thinking strategically, while the core group of interpersonal skills clusters around an individual's ability to facilitate and mediate within working groups and networks. A strong character, rather than a strong personality, provides the foundation for the core skills.

Chapter Seven, "Thinking and Acting Strategically," emphasizes that to address interconnected problems, strategic analysis is required. This type of analysis raises an issue to public attention, identifies common and conflicting interests of key stakeholders, and illuminates linkages and interconnections. Strategic thinking involves framing and reframing issues and their strategic responses; identifying and defining end outcomes or desired results; assessing stakeholder interests to discover common and complementary interests; and thinking systemically to reveal interconnections and strategic leverage points. Catalytic leaders must think strategically and they must encourage and nurture key stakeholders to do so, too. Failure to engage in strategic thinking commonly prevents working groups from making significant progress on some of our most pressing public problems. A wide variety of analytical techniques and tools are discussed that have proven successful in stimulating work group members and other key stakeholders to engage in strategic thinking.

Public leaders must also be catalysts for their productive working group, assisting it in reaching durable and sustainable agreements on strategies aimed at a particular outcome. Chapter Eight, "Facilitating Productive Working Groups," focuses on the interpersonal skills necessary for facilitating a productive working group or network. Public leaders use a repertoire of process skills to understand the multiple points of view and stakes in the particular issue, to draw truth out of poorly stated positions, and to synthesize statements and actively integrate varied interests. Encouraging and stimulating a productive working group process with diverse stakeholders, with varying and often opposing views, requires a strong set of facilitation, negotiation, and mediation skills. These process skills essentially involve four distinct challenges: generating fresh ideas and new insights, coping with conflict, getting a group unstuck and moving forward, and forging agreements.

Such public leadership is more than a set of analytical skills and interpersonal competencies. Chapter Nine, "Leading from Personal Passion and Strength of Character," outlines the underlying character of successful catalysts in an interconnected world. Character is the spirit and intent of one's leadership actions to make a difference. Character undergirds and infuses energy into the specific tasks and skills discussed in earlier chapters and is characterized by a common set of attitudes, traits, and habits. Rather than having a strong personality, successful catalysts exhibit strength of character. This trait establishes their credibility to convene diverse groups, builds confidence to facilitate and mediate difficult agreements, and develops a long-term perspective to focus and refocus attention when faced with minor defeats. Character lies behind one's conduct and encompasses the "inner" side: one's will, dispositions, and inclinations. What distinguishes catalytic leadership is the strength of character based on three key habits: a passion for results, a sense of connectedness and relatedness, and exemplary personal integrity.

Acknowledgments

I am deeply indebted to hundreds of individuals who seldom seek recognition but who must be acknowledged here. First, I am grateful to the scholars who built the earlier foundations of public leadership—in particular, John Bryson and Barbara Crosby, for their breakthrough *Leadership for the Common Good* (1992). Personal discussions with John and Barbara provided inspiration and a foundation. Barbara Gray's *Collaboration* (1989) and her 1991 symposium in the *Journal of Applied Behavioral Sciences* provided me with a conceptual framework to which I continuously returned. The late Herbert Shepard provided considerable wisdom and insights on catalytic power and group facilitation that are woven throughout the book. His creative ideas continue to be catalysts for me and my work. Paul Nutt's research on decision making and his collaborative work with Bob Backoff on strategic management further enriched my understanding of strategic thinking and acting. Ron Hiefetz's *Leadership Without Easy Answers* (1995), *Collaborative Leadership* by David Chrislip and Chris Larson (1995), and *Grassroots Leaders for a New Economy* by Henton and others (1997) were three other important sources that provided critical insights and illuminating examples. These works built a foundation on which I tried to build. Personal discussions with Paul Slovic at the University of Oregon considerably deepened my understanding of underlying psychological dynamics, and e-mail conversations with George Richardson at SUNY-Albany greatly helped in clarifying the strengths and weaknesses in systems modeling for interconnected problems. These influences are cited numerously throughout the book; I hope I have accurately noted them while not burdening the reader with too many citations.

I am indebted to a wide range of elected officials; public managers at the federal, state, and local levels; and nonprofit administrators, civic leaders, and community activists who were interviewed, observed, and analyzed to figure out what made them successful public leaders. All were gracious about sharing their stories with me. Special thanks to Beverly Stein, chair of the Multnomah

County (Oregon) Board of Commissioners and former state legislator, for being candid and open as I studied her catalytic traits and skills for more than five years. (After several years of being observed and studied by me, she once introduced herself at a public meeting as "Jeff Luke's guinea pig.") Other Oregon leaders I closely followed included Randy Franke, Marion County commissioner and former president of the National Association of County Officials (NACO); Laurie Swanson-Gribskov, Eugene city councilor and former executive director of the Southern Willamette Private Industry Council; Sue Cameron, Tillamook County commissioner and formerly the director of the Tillamook County Health Department; and Duncan Wyse, president of the Oregon Business Council and founding director of the Oregon Progress Board. In addition, I worked closely with Rural Development Initiatives, Inc. (RDI), a nationally recognized nonprofit agency that helps to build leadership capacities in rural communities. RDI staff, particularly Lynn Youngbar, Bruce Boggs, and Jenn Pratt, were extremely helpful in testing and refining initial ideas regarding catalytic leadership. I must also thank Zoë Johnson and Deirdre Molander of the Oregon Progress Board for their continuing help and support.

The 1996 Oregon Leadership Summit provided considerable insights on the practice of public leadership that are woven throughout the book. Participants included Candace Bartow, Lennie Bjornsen, Jo Ann Bowman, Sue Cameron, Mary Coacher, Molly Cooley, Pat Corcoran, Kathleen Cornett, Don Coyhis, Bill Flood, Janice Flowers, Randy Franke, Larry Griffith, Guadalupe Guajardo, Jono Hildner, Cliff Jones, Hal Jones, Michael Jordan, Brett KenCairn, Skip Knight, Carolyn Kohn, Jim Kuntz, Bob Landauer, Judy-Ellen Low, Mimi Maduro, Doug Morgan, John Morgan, Gina Mulford, Chris Neilsen, Jan Oliver, Ginny Peckinpaugh, Mike Peterson, Connie Revell, Ethan Seltzer, Jim Seymour, Beverly Stein, Scott Taylor, Mary Unruh, Barbara Willer, Ernest Woodson, and Lynn Youngbar. Quotes in the book that are not cited, such as those that begin chapters, are personal insights of summit participants.

I wish to thank many of my students at the University of Oregon. Beginning in 1993, I conducted an annual advanced graduate seminar on public leadership in which students critiqued, challenged, and refined many of the ideas that reached this final version. Students in the seminars included Margaret Allison, Leer

Bao, Todd Barnhart, Marshall Billick, Teresa Bishow, Susan Brengelman, Ronald Britt, Stephanie Buffum, Lori Bumgardner, Elizabeth Burke, Nicholas Calkins, Matthew Crook, John Darnell, Ruth Daron, Mary Gautreaux, Geoffrey Gaydos, Amy Gould, Laurie Swanson-Gribskov, Eileen Johnson, Maria Johnson, Jeanne Kowalewski, Edward Morris, Katherine Richardson, Gena Salvatore, Vicki Shives, Jana Sorenson, Amelia Thomas, Martin Tusler, Lawrence Vasquez, and Carmen White. Others who provided helpful comments on earlier drafts include Skip Laitner, Mimi Maduro, Tony Mounts, Charlene Phipps, and Georgia Robertson. I am thankful to each of them for their encouragement and enthusiasm.

I also must thank Mary Black and Vicki Shives. Vicki edited my first draft and made many helpful suggestions to tighten and weave together the three parts; Mary painstakingly interpreted Vicki's and my scribbles and word-processed the final versions of the book. I am extremely grateful to both of them for helping to complete this important project. In addition, Peggy Luke provided encouragement and emotional support that sustained my energy throughout the project. Finally, I owe a special thanks to my two teenage daughters, Mona and Tori, who were extremely patient and understanding with me when I was too busy writing to drive them to the mall.

Eugene, Oregon   JEFFREY S. LUKE
August 1997

The Author

JEFFREY S. LUKE is director of the Pacific Program for State and Local Government and Nonprofit Executives, and associate professor in the Department of Planning, Public Policy, and Management at the University of Oregon. He received his B.A. (1972), M.P.A. (1974), and Ph.D. (1982) degrees, all in public administration, from the University of Southern California.

Luke's main research interests are in public leadership, ethics, and public management. He is coauthor of *Management Training Strategies in Third World Countries* (1987, with J. Kerrigan) and *Managing Economic Development: A Guide for State and Local Government Leadership Strategies* (1988, with C. Ventriss, B. J. Reed, and C. Reed). He has published more than twenty articles, papers, and chapters on public leadership, strategic planning, and ethics. His public management experience in Scottsdale, Arizona, and Monterey County, California, and his consulting work for numerous federal, state, and local governments have provided the foundations for much of his research. In addition, his writing and research are greatly tempered by his community volunteer experience, particularly as a member of the board of directors of Head Start of Lane County, Oregon, and as chair of the Lane County Commission on Children and Families.

Catalytic Leadership

Part One

The Challenge Facing Public Leaders

When we think of leadership, we often conjure up pictures of corporate leaders such as Chrysler's Lee Iaccoca or GTE's Jack Welch, who transformed their staid organizations into high-performing corporations. Visionary and charismatic, such leaders breathe new life into organizations so they can better compete in a complex environment.

Leadership to address such public problems as economic development and teenage pregnancies is different. Public problems are interconnected, they cross organizational and jurisdictional boundaries, and they are interorganizational. No single agency, organization, jurisdiction, or sector has enough authority, influence, or resources to dictate visionary solutions. Thus, contemporary strategies for organizational leadership are less effective in addressing public problems in an interconnected world. Public leadership faces a different set of challenges.

Chapter One, "The Interconnected Nature of Public Problems," emphasizes that there are seldom, if ever, quick fixes or silver bullets. Urgent problems are intertwined with other issues, they cross traditional boundaries, and they are difficult to define, analyze, and permanently solve. Not only are the problems interconnected, but the problem-solving activity occurs in a context of fragmentation and shared power.

Chapter Two, "Defining Public Leadership," highlights the differences among contemporary forms of corporate leadership.

These popular approaches often prescribe a set of skills that help executives to pursue organizational excellence, take charge, stimulate extraordinary performance by employees, or change an organization's internal culture by being transformational. However, because these approaches are fundamentally based on hierarchical authority, they cannot be transferred easily to the interconnected and nonhierarchical contexts of public problems.

Chapter One

The Interconnected Nature of Public Problems

As we approach the twenty-first century, educational levels in the United States are the highest ever. The economy continues to grow, doubling since the 1960s alone, and the United States leads the world in economic competitiveness (International Institute for Management Development, 1996). Yet nagging public problems continue to capture the headlines. The United States has the highest teen birthrate among all the industrialized countries (Guttmacher Institute, 1996), and it also leads the world in the number of children killed by gunfire (Centers for Disease Control and Prevention, 1996). In urban areas such as New York City, Salt Lake City, and Seattle, gang violence threatens lives, teenagers find employment and self-esteem in the illegal drug trade, transportation congestion drives away growing business enterprises, and air pollution continues to raise health concerns. Rural areas have not escaped serious economic and social problems either. They are troubled with a dramatic loss of jobs in traditional industries, such as agriculture and timber, and a lack of opportunities for youth. Many inhabitants of small towns feel a general sense of helplessness.

Scores of problems demand attention; people are hungry for immediate solutions. Why is it so difficult to solve anything? How can one individual make a significant difference? What type of leadership works in addressing these difficult public problems? Case studies of successful efforts to improve the quality of life, reduce social problems, and stimulate job generation reveal several common leadership tasks. Most interesting is that the type of leadership required is different than what we would normally imagine.

The traditional "take charge" kind of leader is not successful with the complex problems facing the country. A different type of leadership has emerged in small rural towns that are trying to diversify their economies, in urban areas that are trying to increase public safety in their streets, and in metropolitan regions that are trying to clear up their air basins. In this form of leadership—catalytic leadership—individuals and groups convene multiple stakeholder groups and facilitate and mediate agreement around tough issues. They think systemically and strategically about short- and long-term actions and their impacts. Individuals are passionate about reaching a particular outcome, yet are flexible and inclusive on strategies to reach the desired results. We live in a world of complex interconnections in which take-charge leaders are less successful than individuals and groups who provide the spark or catalyst that truly makes a difference.

Emerging public leadership tasks are best understood, however, by illuminating the context in which we find ourselves at the end of the twentieth century. Today's public problems are interconnected—crossing jurisdictional, organizational, functional, and generational boundaries—and are intertwined with other public problems. The authority to solve public problems is fragmented and disbursed over an ever-tightening web of constraints. No single person, agency, or jurisdiction has sufficient power to develop and implement solutions unilaterally (Bryson and Crosby, 1992).

Emphasizing Public Leadership, Not Public Sector Leadership

Institutionalizing more government leadership does not work. Public organizations are often sluggish, are hampered by constraints, and have short time frames—usually election to election. The problems most troubling to communities, regions, states, and the nation—those problems that are high on the public agenda—seem largely immune to intervention by government alone. Governance in the United States is characterized by a dynamic interplay among government agencies, nonprofit service providers, business enterprises, multinational corporations, neighborhood groups, special-interest and advocacy groups, labor unions, academia, the media, and many other formal and informal associations that attempt to influence the public agenda.

Although books and theories on leadership offer a plethora of approaches, few focus on leadership for solving public problems with diverse, interconnected groups. Contemporary organizational approaches to leadership do not work well for leaders attempting to address persistent public problems in an interconnected context. This type of leadership must focus attention and mobilize sustained action by multiple and diverse stakeholders to address issues usually defined in terms of desired outcomes or results. This form of leadership is pursued not only by elected officials and appointed public administrators but also by individuals in the private, educational, and nonprofit sectors, including civic leaders and community volunteers. To address pressing social, economic, and environmental problems, we need public leadership, not public sector leadership.

Successful public leadership has the difficult challenge of solving complex, boundariless public problems in highly interconnected political and interorganizational contexts in which authority is shared and power is fragmented. Such leadership is essentially nonhierarchical and occurs outside organizational boundaries. This intergovernmental and intersectoral leadership faces constraints and challenges that are substantially different than those facing contemporary organizational leadership.

The Interconnected Web for Public Leadership

In the last twenty years, a quiet crystallization of interdependencies has set in that has changed the way we engage in public action. We are now tied into multiple webs of interconnections never before witnessed in human history. Public and corporate executives have mistakenly focused on complexity while lamenting the increased turbulence and unpredictability in which they are forced to manage and lead. The cause of this turbulence and complexity, however, is an underlying interdependence and interconnectedness that creates unforeseeable and unintended consequences on organizations and agencies. This web inextricably ties together historically separate economic, social, and environmental problems. Global, regional, and local interdependencies are connecting political and economic fortunes of communities, states, and national governments more closely than ever before.

Interconnections and interdependencies did not develop slowly, in a linear fashion, one step at a time. Rather, their emergence is similar to the process of crystallization—instantaneous connections forming to link and bind historically separate and autonomous agencies, organizations, and institutions. Evolutionary biologists call such a quick shift in a species' environment an *anagenesis*—a rather sudden, qualitative shift in evolutionary development. As a result of this social anagenesis, public leadership has changed fundamentally at the local, state, national, and global levels, leaving little resemblance to the context for self-governance that has existed during the two hundred years of American history. There are no precedents for us to follow because no human society so interconnected has previously existed.

The problems confronting communities, regions, states, and the nation are so interwoven that new skills and strategies are required to lead effectively in the public interest. This requires a fundamentally new way of viewing public problems and new strategies for acting in the public interest. The major challenge facing elected officials, public administrators, business leaders, nonprofit executives, community activists, and citizens is not managing complexity and turbulence. Rather, the challenge is how to address critical public problems successfully in a highly interdependent and interconnected world. This interconnectedness stems from two fundamentally new characteristics: the boundariless nature of public problems, and the existence of shared power and fragmented authority in the public arena.

Teenage Pregnancy: A Practical Example

Although the subject of considerable debate, the root cause of teenage pregnancy is impossible to pinpoint. While adolescent mothers share several common characteristics, no single cause can be clearly attributed to adolescent pregnancy. Generally, it has as much to do with a history of childhood sexual abuse or molestation, dysfunctional family circumstances, drug and alcohol abuse, low school achievement, low self-esteem, and lack of hope as it does with early onset of adolescent sexual activity, lack of contraceptive knowledge, and lack of access to family planning services. It is a multifaceted issue with no root cause. It requires multiple strategies and concerted action by several groups for addressing it: educational strategies in schools to encourage abstinence and reproductive understanding; plentiful alternative recreational opportunities; child-abuse prevention and counseling programs to prevent sexual maladjustment; and easy access to counseling and contraceptives for sexually active teens.

Similar difficulties in defining and solving public problems occur whether leaders focus on increasing the number of high-tech jobs, improving the quality of a regional workforce, reducing teenage drug abuse, or decreasing air pollution in metropolitan areas. These issues defy easy solutions because they are essentially interconnected problems. They have several characteristics that differentiate them from the traditional kinds of problems that public leaders and citizens have historically confronted.

The Interconnecting and Boundary-Crossing Nature of Public Problems

Public problems are essentially discrepancies or gaps between a current situation or condition and a desired condition or situation. The problems that confronted public leaders in the past were often simple engineering-type problems, such as how governments could build roads and ports to meet expanding vehicle usage, how school districts could plan for growth in school-age populations, and how communities could build a physical infrastructure for attracting industries. The problems facing us today, such as diversifying the local economy in a global setting or preventing alcohol and drug abuse among high school students, are much more difficult to define, analyze, and solve because they are intertwined with other related problems. Table 1.1 summarizes the characteristics of interconnected problems and their impacts on public leadership.

The most troubling public problems cross jurisdictional, organizational, functional, and generational boundaries. The world is shrinking, drawn together by an increasingly interdependent, globalized web. Interdependencies involve "mutual dependence," where actions of one individual or agency influence or constrain actions of another. High-cost, very important mutual dependencies, or interdependencies, can be distinguished from low-cost, relatively unimportant mutual dependencies, or interconnections (Keohane and Nye, 1977).

Table 1.1. The Interconnected Nature of Public Problems.

Characteristics of Interconnected Problems	Impact on Public Leadership
Problems cross traditional boundaries:	*Requires cross-boundary thinking and action:*
Problems cross organizational and jurisdictional boundaries	Interorganizational arrangements required to address the problem
Issues are often "cross-cutting," transcending functional boundaries	Cross-functional teams required
Problems cross temporal and generational boundaries	Must consider intergenerational impacts
Involved in interrelated web of other problems; "wicked" or nontame; caught in "swamp"	Extremely difficult to untangle cause-and-effect relationships; difficult to find just one "cause"
Problems are socially constructed:	*No natural consensus on problem definition:*
Range of problem representations, depending on one's cognitive and emotional biases	Multiplicity of conflicting problem definitions; public leader influences definition process
Strategies emerge from one's definition of problem and "mental model" of causes and effects	Agreement on problem definition is critical for concerted action
No optimal solutions:	*No quick fixes or easy remedies:*
Problems are intractable and never entirely solved	Seek improvements in conditions or outcomes, rather than problem elimination
Technical remedies ineffective; real progress requires deeper systemic changes	Multiple strategies needed, a "portfolio of strategies" rather than the one, right solution

Geographical, Functional, and Generational Interdependencies

The most common form of interconnectedness is geographical. Pollution has no geographical boundaries. Air and water currents carry wastes and toxic substances far beyond their original sources. Similarly, drug abuse, juvenile crime, and teenage gangs cannot be contained within a particular geographical area.

Geographic interconnections are blurring historical distinctions between what is "global" and what is "local," with a considerable number of issues now crossing national, state, and local government boundaries. Acid rain is a tangible example, in which industrial emissions of sulfur dioxide mix in the atmosphere to create toxic rain. At least 50 percent of the acid rain falling in Canada originates in the United States, creating an environmental and economic problem that transcends geographical boundaries (Peach, 1991).

This is the type of interconnected policy problem that public leaders increasingly face. For example, an aggressive campaign to reduce the number of "street people" in downtown San Francisco, prompted by complaints from local businesses that panhandlers were scaring off customers, resulted in a dramatic increase in the homelessness problem across the San Francisco Bay, in Berkeley. Homelessness does not recognize political borders. Effective public leadership requires understanding that public problems are interconnected and that they cross geographical and political boundaries.

Blurring geographical boundaries means that actions in one part of a state, region, or globe have consequences in other areas. Costs and benefits of any action or policy are seldom evenly distributed. "Turning Brazilian jungles into orange groves may be good news for the food processor in Sao Paulo, the Dutch company that owns the tank ships, the juice distributor in Newark, the Tokyo banker who managed the project, and those of us who like cheap o.j.; but it is bad news for the Brazilian Indians, Florida orange growers, and environmentalists" (Council of State Planning Agencies, 1989, p. 6).

Functional Interdependence

Issues such as job creation, educational reform, teenage pregnancies, and affordable housing require efforts from a variety of functional areas of expertise. In state and local economic development job creation is significantly influenced by the quality of K–12 education, access to post-secondary education, the quality of natural resource amenities, and the availability of an electronic infrastructure to facilitate high-speed communications. Yet there is considerable functional fragmentation in solving public problems. When the federal government mandated that the City of Los Angeles stop disposing treated sewage into the Pacific Ocean, alternative disposal strategies were anticipated to have serious negative ripple effects in other areas of quality of life. For instance, they would worsen air quality, increase traffic congestion, and expand landfill usage (Kirlin, 1991). Addressing such cross-functional issues requires joint, collaborative efforts among many distinct government agencies and between the public and private sectors.

Intergenerational Boundaries

Major problems and issues confronting public leaders also have intergenerational significance. The consequences of our actions and policy decisions are often known only long after the fact (and even then with some ambiguity). Decisions made by earlier generations directly shape the policy issues we face today, and policy choices that respond to current problems can have significant influences on the quality of life and the capacity to govern for future generations. Past, present, and future generations are now interdependent, a temporal interconnection that ties together society in ways seldom considered in solving public problems.

Causes and Effects of Interconnected Problems

Although issues each have a unique history, interconnected problems are characteristically intertwined with related problems. Public problems are nested in a complex of other problems, and their multiple consequences "ripple out" unexpectedly. Problems are not separate issues but are intertwined with other related problems in an ongoing dynamic process. For every problem there is a whole constellation of other problems. For example, many of those imprisoned in state and federal correctional institutions have had trouble with alcohol and other drugs or were physically, mentally, or emotionally abused. As one correctional officer stated: "It's all connected."

It is not that an interconnected problem "contains" other prob-lems; rather, it is "involved" with other problems. Interconnected problems are frequently, if not always, both a symptom and a cause of other problems. Poverty, for example, is linked to other social and economic problems as both cause and an effect. It cannot be narrowed down to one specific cause or one specific consequence. To separate one problem out of its systemic context is much like pulling a live insect out of a big clump of soft bubble gum. There may be no absence of information regarding a problem; yet, our understanding and knowledge of the multiple causes and effects are limited to such a degree that it becomes extremely hard to untangle and pinpoint root causes.

Ripple-Effect Stakeholders

With interconnected problems, stakeholders do not exist in isola-tion from one another (Mitroff, 1983). The ripple effects expand to include people and organizations that may never meet. A poignant example exists in the Pacific Northwest, where fishers, fisheries, and leaders of small fishing communities are joining envi-ronmentalists to stop existing patterns of timber harvesting. Fish habitats such as the salmon spawning grounds are being slowly destroyed by the increased silting of mountain streams due to the clear-cutting of timber along stream beds. Logging practices dis-tant from ocean fishing grounds can create such ripple effects as a significant decline in salmon stock, a reduced fish catch, and a deteriorating local coastal economy more than five hundred miles away from the timber harvest.

Socially Constructed Definitions of Problems

Defining a problem is increasingly difficult. In interconnected problems, with few obvious definitions and no clear boundaries, social and psychological factors play a significant role in defining the problem. A problem's definition has far less to do with data and scientific analysis than with values, traditions, and internalized mental models.

The fundamental cause or the source of a problem is difficult to isolate. Cause-and-effect relationships are difficult to untangle because multiple causes influence the problem. Simple "bounded problems" have easily discernible cause-and-effect trails and have a finite set of workable solutions (Mitroff and Linstone, 1993). A problem boundary separates one issue from other issues and delineates an existence independent from other problems. Today's public problems are "unbounded problems" with malleable and often invisible boundaries that make it nearly impossible to separate them from other problems. With no distinct or natural boundaries, it is very difficult to locate the exact cause of the problem, that is, to find where it is in the interconnected web that the trouble originates. Teenage pregnancies are clearly related to at least three other issues: personal self-esteem, school achievement, and child abuse at an earlier age. What is the cause and what is the effect?

Mental Models of Problems

To understand complex, intertwined problems, individuals develop and carry a "mental model," or internalized picture, of what a problem is, what is causing it, and how to solve it. Mental models are networks of familiar facts, ideas, and concepts with specific yet simplified cause-and-effect relationships. The mental images assert "causal responsibility," a belief about the sequence of causes that factually accounts for the existence of the problem. Individuals typically focus attention on information that is most salient to and that supports their internalized assumptions or mental model. Information inconsistent with one's mental model is ignored, either unconsciously or consciously.

Interconnected and boundariless problems involve a multiplicity of stakeholders, and each sees the problem from a unique perspective. Because the causes of problems are not clear-cut, conflicting formulations and definitions of any particular public problem are very likely. Interconnected problems have a range of representations, which vary depending on one's mental model of each issue. For example, homelessness is simultaneously an affordable housing problem, an alcohol and drug abuse problem, an employment problem, a mental health problem, a spousal abuse problem, and an immigration problem. Any environmental, social, or economic problem could be similarly analyzed. Economic development is simultaneously a workforce quality problem, a financial capital problem, a regional collaboration issue, a property tax issue, and an infrastructure problem.

Because it is hard to determine what the "real" problem is, there is seldom one correct solution upon which a consensus naturally or effortlessly emerges. Interconnected problems are not only extraordinarily difficult to define, they do not lend themselves easily to technical remedies or quick fixes. Resources are always limited. Further, with the multiplicity and diversity of stakeholder groups, each with a well-defined set of preferences, there is a natural competition for the "right" solution.

A multiplicity of stakeholders and affected parties are involved with each public problem. They see the problem and its best solution from their own perspective or mental model. Among the affected parties, specific, objective criteria for sorting through potentially successful strategies and identifying the "best" solution often are in conflict. There is also little incentive for leaders to sponsor pilot efforts to test the effectiveness of risky interventions, because resources can seldom be devoted to experimental or demonstration projects. Even on those rare occasions when there is a pilot program, it is extremely difficult to separate and isolate the effects of the experimental program from those of outside influences. With several equally promising solutions emerging, "good" strategies are differentiated from "bad" strategies according to an individual's personal preferences, interests, and political or ideological biases.

The reality that problems have multiple definitions is not trivial. The way a situation or problem is defined guides and frames solutions. The choice of how to define the problem determines the kind of data, facts, and analyses developed to explain the issue. It also determines the nature of the recommended problem resolution. How the problem is defined has a very powerful influence on the strategies, actions, and interventions that seem appropriate to narrow the gap of what is and what ought to be.

With complex, interconnected problems, short-term fixes are alluring. Unfortunately, there are no easy cures for interconnected public problems. For example, a recent newspaper editorial on reducing gang violence begins with the exclamation: "It's guns. It's the culture. It's gangs. It's values. It's peer pressure." The editorial ends with a call to action, not by proposing one particular solution but by emphasizing that any effective response must target the kids, the parents, the schools, and the community in a multifaceted effort. Although the newspaper editorial board takes a risk by not recommending one particular solution or silver bullet, multilevel interventions are now soundly backed by empirical research.

Realistic View of Problem Solving

Problems may be temporarily reduced, but if the interrelated issues are left unresolved or unaddressed, the problem will quickly reemerge. Public problems have multiple causes, and one specific policy or strategy alone cannot eradicate the problem. The targeted issue or problem is imbedded and intertwined with long-standing issues. As long as these linkages are unaddressed, new directions or changes are unlikely to be sustained. Attracting high-tech industries with high-paying jobs cannot be accomplished by merely promoting a high-tech industrial park with easy access to transportation. A workforce trained and educated in new skills is also needed, as well as a local network of similar companies, good schools, clean air, and low crime that will attract and retain the executives and managers of such industries. Heroin addiction, a more wrenching example, cannot be completely solved without dealing with the constellation of related problems: underlying psychological factors, housing, job training, and education. Treating the addiction alone is insufficient.

The last distinguishing feature of interconnected problems is that they are never totally solved. There is no "stopping rule," or natural termination of a problem (Rittel and Webber, 1973). Consequences of policy choices take a long time to become clear, and the background noise of interrelated problems and policies easily overwhelms our ability to track the impacts of selected strategies (Mitroff and Linstone, 1993). In addition, there are seldom any objective criteria or outcome measurements that clearly and unambiguously signify that an optimal solution has been reached. For example, at what level or frequency do we say that teenage drug abuse is solved? When only 10 percent are abusing? Five percent? Zero percent? And air pollution: When is it solved? When smog alerts occur only seven days a year? Three days a year? When ozone readings are 120 parts per billion or 10 parts per billion?

Finally, public problems often need to be addressed repeatedly over time. At different times, the same problem or issue may require a different answer. As a result, they are often felt to be intractable. Rather, they may be re-solved, perhaps repeatedly, or reduced through successive small wins that push the issue closer to satisfactory levels.

The Expanding Web of Constraints: The Problem of "Many Hands"

Public problems not only are interconnected and intertwined with other issues, but they also exist in a governance context in which no one organization or jurisdiction is in charge of or contains an important problem or issue. Often, many different and independent agencies are involved and affected, and have only partial responsibility to address problems that spill into their boundaries. This creates a shared-power world in which everything depends on and has an impact on everything else. The power to stimulate or resist action on a particular problem is dispersed to and shared by a multiplicity of jurisdictions, organizations, and organized interests (Bryson and Einsweiler, 1991; Bryson and Crosby, 1992).

Fragmented Authority

Shared power does not automatically imply coherence. Too often it results in divided and fragmented public authority. The United States is unique in its division of governmental authority, with power shared among legislative, executive, and judicial branches. Formal authority for policymaking is disbursed among federal, state, county, and city governments, as well as the thousands of special districts and authorities that control such local activities as transit companies, air quality, and ports. The fragmentation has significantly increased simultaneously with the increasing interconnectedness of public problems. A striking example is a landfill in Southern California, which by 1996 was regulated by eleven state agencies and three regional agencies. None had absolute authority, but all sought to achieve state and federal environmental policy goals in the Southern California region (Kirlin, 1991).

Proliferation of Stakeholders and Knowledgeholders

For each issue or problem, there is a community of interests: problem "elites," opinion leaders, government and university experts, engaged corporate leaders, activists, specific clients or consumers, and fragmented legitimate authorities. In the last decade there has been an explosive growth in the number and diversity of non-governmental groups in the development of public policy. These stakeholders and knowledgeholders are increasingly active in for-mulating responses to public problems. Stakeholders are organized groups, clients, and institutions who hold a stake in the issue and are key to getting solutions accepted and implemented. As the def-inition implies, stakeholders and knowledgeholders both exert a hold on an issue.

There are many explanations for this increase in stakeholders and knowledgeholders. Advances in communication technologies have lowered costs of direct-mail solicitation and have created new forms of inexpensive access, such as electronic bulletin boards, thus greatly speeding the efficient distribution of data and infor-mation. Because of the information revolution, many more citi-zen groups feel compelled to get directly involved in the resolution of burning issues. In addition, access to public agen-cies is now more widely distributed, beyond the select privileged groups of business executives and corporations that historically had enjoyed access. Although wealthy, elite groups still have con-siderable access and influence on particular policy areas, they are now only one of many special interests that attempt to influence public policy.

The number of knowledgeholders has also grown and includes university experts, government specialists, industry researchers, and activists who hold important information regard-ing the multiple dimensions characterizing interconnected prob-lems. High-status knowledge, once guarded by officials, is more easily accessed and distributed because of the proliferation of elec-tronic information exchange. New, specialized policy issue net-works are causing a radical change in the structure of external pressure on solving public problems. By replacing historical party politics with policy issue networks, the channels in which influ-ence is exerted have multiplied. The expanding web of individu-als and organizations that significantly address issues, combined with the country's continuing fragmentation of authority, have resulted in a dissipation of the traditional power structure (Dahl, 1994; Wilson, 1989).

Diminished Influence of Special-Interest Groups

Although the variety of conflicting and substantially independent special-interest groups and the intensity of their lobbying continues to increase, their influence is diminishing for three reasons. First, the proliferation of special-interest groups is matched by the political organization of neighborhood and citizens' groups and the expanded involvement of knowledgeholders and ripple-effect stakeholders. Local, regional, and national citizens' groups, for example, have increased their capacity to organize for effective action. They have become more active and sophisticated in communicating their concerns. As their skill in working with the media increases, the media are increasingly responsive. The media amplifies their concerns, magnifying a group's impact through short stories and sound bites on national and local news networks. The cumulative effect is a thinning of power traditionally held by special-interest groups (Dahl, 1994; Thomas and Hrebenar, 1994).

Second, civic power has thinned within communities in the last several decades. This coincides with the downsizing and restructuring of large corporations and the growing influence of small businesses. Once clout and authority were wielded by a few businesspersons. Now local influence is spread among many nonbusiness leaders. As a local leader in Cleveland explained, "There was a time in this community when four people could decide to do something, and then just do it" (Henton and others, 1997).

Third, the sheer numbers of diverse groups result in political stalemates, with each group advocating for its preferred solution and fighting over declining governmental resources. Traditional interest groups are having more difficulty maintaining their strong positions due to "hyper-pluralism"—more groups advocating and competing for declining resources (Thomas and Hrebenar, 1994). This leads to a policy gridlock or "demosclerosis," in which organized groups have multiplied to the point that they clog the arteries of democracy (Rauch, 1994). This inhibits the ability of any one individual, agency, or group to secure broad-based agreement and to mobilize people and resources effectively to address a public problem.

Addressing public problems today requires the interaction of many diverse groups and individuals. Interconnected problems do not lend themselves to easy cures by independent agencies acting alone. Proposed actions affect an increasingly large number of stakeholders on any particular issue, and perceived adverse effects can evoke widespread resistance. The result is that large-scale, systemic, or comprehensive solutions that attempt to get at the roots of a public problem are often considered too far-reaching and radical by some and will likely be vocally opposed.

Constraints of Public Distrust

In addition to fragmented authority, a further complicating factor is the diminished public confidence in government's ability to address difficult problems. The public feels strongly about the issues facing them and their families (Harwood Group, 1993a). However, there is an equally strong distrust that government agencies can solve these problems. That distrust has been rising for the last two decades. A variety of complex governance issues have fed this lack of trust, from the Vietnam War and the Watergate scandal in the 1970s, to the Reagan era of the 1980s, which consistently blamed government for many of the country's failures (Lipset and Schneider, 1987). Consequently, the public has lost faith in major governmental initiatives that attempt to address serious problems.

The public's perception that the government cannot solve problems leads to strong frustration with government leaders. Not only do people distrust and disrespect "bureaucrats," but they feel dissatisfaction with elected officials who are seen as not telling the truth about or not taking responsibility for serious problems. Problems appear to be getting bigger, not smaller, while taxes continue to go up. One can point to the decline of American education, the rise of health care costs, the decay of physical infrastructure, the inability to site long-term nuclear waste facilities, or the continual and chronic urban and rural unemployment. Citizens perceive a severe disconnect with the taxes they are paying and the results they are seeing. Thus government is often seen as an obstacle rather than as a problem solver. Distrust can be so strong that hostility can be a common reaction when someone suggests that government play a stronger role in addressing an issue.

Even as our problems become more serious, citizens do not necessarily want one individual to save them. Although individuals may feel compelled to find a leader who can "work magic" or "do battle for us" on a particular problem (Heifetz and Sinder, 1988), there is simultaneously a great suspicion of leaders in our country. Bryson and Crosby (1992, p. 34) note that this "love-hate" attitude toward leadership reflects a unique tendency for Americans "to admire the heroic, charismatic individual who can lead troops or organizations to great victories yet at the same time, they distrust great concentrations of power and authority." Even though the public tends to look to individual leaders for answers, today's declining trust and confidence in the government significantly constrains traditional forms of leadership. This wariness is symptomatic of a longer-term decline in social trust and civic engagement in America over the last twenty-five years (Putnam, 1993).

Addressing Public Problems with Public Leadership

Governmental problem solving no longer means directly funding services. Distrust in government, dwindling revenue sources, thinning of traditional interest groups, and interconnected public problems frustrate those who wish to make a difference. Individuals easily feel overwhelmed. Common statements include: "It's just too big for one person to solve." "It's so complex. I just don't know where to start." "It will take more time than I have to solve this."

Yet large numbers of individuals do get involved in problem solving, so many, at times, that any action seems impossible. Out of frustration, one is tempted to go it alone and work on the problem with a very small, select group. Unfortunately, that approach does not work either. Problems are so complex and interconnected, and power to solve the problem is so shared and disbursed, that one person or agency has little power or authority to develop and implement solutions unilaterally. A seasoned city manager explains that "this is new turf for those of us in the professional urban management business. . . . We must diligently work behind the scenes to bring together the diverse interests that confront us on virtually every public meeting agenda" (Blumbaugh, 1987, p. 9).

Addressing interconnected problems does not yield readily to single efforts and is beyond the capacity of any one agency or jurisdiction. Authority and responsibility to solve the problem require diverse, independent stakeholders to come together around a common interest, mobilizing or galvanizing collective action. In addition, responses to interconnected problems cannot be dictated from one public agency. What is needed is concerted action by multiple and diverse groups.

There are many examples of effective public leadership stimulating concerted action within this unique web of constraints. In 1985, Tillamook County's teen pregnancy rate was the second highest in Oregon and higher than the national average. This fact went unnoticed by this small coastal community until a proposal for school-based health clinics was soundly defeated. Community leaders realized that their teenage pregnancy rate was second only to that of the state's largest and most urban county containing Portland. That shocking realization stimulated multiple actions to curb teenage pregnancy. Early community efforts included a local teen parenting program and a Healthy Start program aimed at reducing second pregnancies among teens. The efforts then sharpened toward early prevention. The local YMCA sponsored teen girls' recreation programs, schools added self-esteem and sexuality education to their curriculum, and churches taught refusal skills and abstinence within their teen groups. The local public health department significantly expanded its outreach to teens to include one-on-one counseling within forty-eight hours of the teen's first inquiry. By 1994, Tillamook County reduced its teen pregnancy rate 75 percent, from 24 per 1,000 females to the state's lowest rate of 7 per 1,000 (Luke and Neville, 1996).

In San Mateo County, California, on the southern part of the San Francisco Bay, several cities realized that East Palo Alto, a neighboring city, had the highest per capita homicide rate in the country. They also realized that its crime and drug problems were spilling into adjacent areas and that East Palo Alto lacked the resources to fight the problem effectively alone. Neighboring cities and the county joined with East Palo Alto in a concerted effort to address the problem. East Palo Alto witnessed an 86 percent decline in its homicide rate and a 60 percent reduction in other violent crimes without corresponding increases in neighboring jurisdictions (Bellone, 1994).

There are hundreds of similar examples of this type of public leadership across the country: affordable housing in West Garfield Park, Chicago, and Northeast Portland, Oregon; revitalized economies in Silicon Valley and Cleveland. Communities, states, and regions that are successfully addressing public problems realize they must work across traditional boundaries, creating partnerships and alliances among historically separate business, government, and education sectors. They are following a different kind of leadership process than prescribed in many organizational descriptions of contemporary leadership.

This type of leadership does not make the headlines. Rather, it provides a more quiet catalytic effect. It elevates the issue to the public agenda, convenes critical stakeholders, stimulates multiple initiatives to achieve goals, and sustains action over the long term. The primary role for public leadership is that of a catalyst—thinking about problems in a systemic or interconnected way, fostering dialogue and concerted action toward solving problems, and sustaining momentum over time. Unfortunately, guidance offered by contemporary organizational approaches to leadership has limited applicability to the nonhierarchical webs in which nagging public problems exist. Contemporary approaches to leadership focus on managing organizations and small-group leadership within organizations, not in solving complex public problems. Public leadership thus requires a redefinition of leadership to illuminate the unique tasks, strategies, and skills necessary to lead in the public interest in an interconnected world.

Chapter Two

Defining Public Leadership

Traditional models of organizational leadership prescribe a set of skills or steps that helps executives either to pursue organizational excellence, to take charge, to stimulate extraordinary performance by employees, or to change an organization's internal culture by being transformational. (For examples, see Bennis and Nanus, 1985; Peters and Waterman, 1982; Peters and Austin, 1985) However, these models do not focus on leadership that can address interconnected, boundariless public problems in a context of fragmented authority and expanding webs of stakeholders.

Organizational leadership models have several things in common. They are based on distinct differences between leaders and followers. They seek to identify ways to get more out of individuals in the workplace. They emphasize the importance of a vision that is clearly articulated throughout the organization and that guides employees' actions. Extreme characterizations of leadership emphasize the leadership-followership dichotomy. As Sherman writes in *Fortune*, a leader's job is "to get people to follow you voluntarily" (1995, p. 92).

Because contemporary organizational leadership models are based on hierarchical authority, they cannot be transferred easily to the nonhierarchical contexts in which public problems exist today. A former senior vice president for Boeing, after working to establish a regional collaboration in Wichita, Kansas, to stimulate economic development, noted how traditional organizational leadership approaches seldom work in addressing interconnected problems: "There are multiple jurisdictions with multiple personalities, and you can't just say 'follow me, let's go this way' and have people follow. You must get people to work together. This is the most complex equation as a businessperson that I have ever had to work with" (Henton and others, 1997, p. 57).

Leadership is one of the most studied concepts in the world today. Popular approaches to leadership stress the importance of being transformational, visionary, or charismatic. Unfortunately, attempts at defining leadership outside an organization too often adopt an organization-focused definition. They merely substitute references to *employees* with references to *citizens*.

A different framework is necessary, one that is more relevant to the political and interorganizational realities of societal problem solving. An individual attempting to take a leadership role to address a public problem must stimulate collective action toward a particular outcome. In today's world, no single agency or jurisdiction has enough power—resources, influence, or authority— to dictate solutions unilaterally. Pursuing a set of multiple, smaller strategies across jurisdictions, agencies, and individuals entails mobilizing resources and support from diverse stakeholders and stimulating concerted action based on shared interests in certain policy outcomes. Thus, public leadership occurs when an individual or group focuses attention on an issue or problem and elevates it to the public agenda, stimulates concerted action among diverse stakeholders to address the issue, and ensures sustained action during implementation. Public leaders act as catalysts in a collective effort to achieve a desired result or outcome. This, of course, requires a different approach to leadership than the traditional "take-charge" kind of organizational leader often typified in contemporary leadership books (see Table 2.1).

Reviewing Contemporary Organizational Approaches to Leadership

Historically, leadership research has focused on leadership of groups or teams in organizations by people in positions of organizational authority. During World War II, for example, submarine crews and bomber teams were intensively studied to improve their effectiveness, with group leadership identified as a significant variable in group productivity and morale. In the post-war era, growing interest in business and industry productivity sparked

Table 2.1. A Required Shift in Leadership Approaches.

From Organizational Leadership	To Public Leadership
Hierarchical	Nonhierarchical and interorganizational
Evokes followership	Evokes collaboration and concerted action
Takes charge; seizes the reins of an organization	Provides the necessary catalyst or spark for action
Takes responsibility for moving followers in certain directions	Takes responsibility for convening stakeholders and facilitates agreements for collective action
Heroic; provides the right answers	Facilitative; asks the right questions
Has a stake in a particular solution or strategy	Has a stake in getting to agreed-upon outcomes, but encourages divergent ways to reach them

continued and expanded research on supervisory leadership, employee motivation, and small-group dynamics. Consequently, supervisory or managerial leadership was initially defined as a process of influence by one individual who steers or motivates other individuals or group members toward a predetermined goal, particularly on matters of organizational relevance.

Supervisory and small-group leadership theories evolved to theories on how to lead the entire organization. A barrage of books and articles in the 1980s extolled the leadership talents of "folk heroes" such as Chrysler's Lee Iacocca, who saved a failing corporation from the threat of bankruptcy. New leadership models focused on leading an organization rather than on providing small-group leadership within an organization (Bryman, 1992). The historical focus on small-group leadership was no longer the crux of leadership. The focus shifted to leading the organization as a whole and changing and adapting members to perform better in a complex global market. While analysis of organizational leadership has evolved, there continues to be a gap in understanding the process of leadership within networks of organizations. A brief review of the three most contemporary theories provides insights from which a more relevant approach to public leadership can be crafted.

Transformational Leadership

A wide-ranging and historical analysis of political and social leadership by James MacGregor Burns (1978) identified two forms of leadership throughout history: transformational and transactional. Transactional leadership involves an exchange between the leader and follower: wages, gifts, votes, prestige, advancement, or other valued things are exchanged for the individual following the leader's wishes or meeting the leader's objectives. The exchange can be economic, political, or even psychological. Other than exchanging things of value, the bargainers have no enduring purpose that holds them together. Transactional leaders develop explicit or implicit agreements or exchanges with their followers, with followers receiving rewards for good performance, and threats or discipline for poor performance (Bass, 1990b).

In contrast, transformational leadership involves a leader drawing followers out of a narrow, parochial interest into a "higher" purpose. Transformational leaders choose goals that, although latent or unexpressed, are native to the community or society. A leader engages followers by tapping their existing and potential motives and aspirations. Through the leader's inspiring, teaching, and modeling, the followers' motives and aspirations are transformed into higher-order needs and visions to achieve intended change. Leadership, Burns explains, is the act of "leaders inducing followers to act for certain goals that represent the values and the motivations—the wants and needs, the aspirations and expectations—of both leaders and followers" (1978, p. 381).

At the organizational level, transformational leaders change the outlooks and behaviors of followers. They stir followers to broaden and elevate their personal self-interests to incorporate the larger purposes of a group or organization. Two descriptions of transformational leadership have emerged in organizational settings. The first approach targets transforming employee performance. In this approach, a leader raises a follower's interest and ability to perform in ways that exceed expectations, not by granting large wages or rewards but by addressing a follower's higher-order psychological needs and by stimulating a follower to transcend self-interest for the good of the team or organization. Bass provides the most researched description of this approach. He explains that although there are different transformational leadership styles, each includes four common characteristics (Bass, 1990b; Howell and Avolio, 1992; Bass and Avolio, 1990):

1. *Charisma.* The leader creates a sense of excitement, an emotional arousal that incites and propels employees to exceed expectations, by providing vision and instilling a deeper sense of purpose and mission, and by gaining the respect and trust of followers to overcome uncertainties.

2. *Inspiration.* By acting as a model for followers, the leader manifests a higher purpose; by following a variety of communication techniques, the leader uses symbols to focus efforts and to express the vision in simple ways.

3. *Individualized consideration.* The leader gives individual attention to followers regarding their interests, issues, and concerns, and builds mutual trust and respect in the leader-follower relationship; the employee's personal and professional development are encouraged through coaching, delegating challenging tasks, and increasing employee responsibility.

4. *Intellectual stimulation.* Transformational leaders stimulate followers to be innovative problem solvers within a given "vision." Stimulating followers intellectually leads to increased employee creativity and higher levels of performance. A leader provides a rich flow of new ideas that challenges employees' normal ways of thinking. In addition, a leader encourages followers to question tried and true ways and to develop new perspectives for accomplishing organizational goals.

The second transformational approach aims at transforming organizations rather than employees. Tichy and Devanna (1986) analyzed twelve CEOs involved in major organizational transformations, including Lee Iacocca of Chrysler and Jack Welch of General Electric. The researchers identified three strategies, called "acts," that corporate leaders use in transforming their organizations to respond to new markets and to increase competitiveness.

In Act 1, transformational leaders recognize and highlight things that trigger the need for change and organizational transformation. They create a "felt need" for change within the organization, deal with resistance to change, and fight to avoid the quick fix. They also facilitate a sense of "endings" for organizational members by disengaging from the past.

Act 2 entails creating a motivating vision that mobilizes employee commitment to transform. The vision provides direction and new values that challenge conceptual road maps for action. At the individual level, the transformational leader assists employees through the often painful transition process by using techniques and strategies that focus on endings and new beginnings.

During Act 3, changes are institutionalized, and new organizational structures and managerial systems are designed to align the organization with its vision. The transformational leader creatively destroys the old structure and then reassembles it in a fashion congruent with the new vision. Personnel systems, such as appraisal and reward systems, are also altered, as is the underlying culture of the organization. This reweaving of the social fabric focuses new organizational energy toward the inspiring vision articulated in Act 2.

Visionary Leadership

Having a compelling vision is central in transformational leadership. Other leadership approaches similarly highlight the importance of visionary leadership—leaders who create a vision for the organization that expresses a set of common values and goals and that excite followers (Berlew, 1974). In the mid-1980s, attention turned to the need for a compelling, persuasive vision.

The central ingredient of visionary leadership is the articulation of a compelling vision that attracts, excites, and animates followers in pursuit of a common organizational cause. After a detailed study of ninety successful corporate and public sector leaders, Bennis and Nanus identified four strategies that exemplify visionary leadership. The first is to manage and guide the attention of the organization through the development of a compelling vision. The vision—"vague as a dream or as precise as a goal or mission statement"—creates a focus, shared by members of the organization, that gives a sense of direction (1985, p. 89).

Visionary leaders communicate the vision in a way that permeates the organization. The vision establishes a set of shared meanings that clearly defines roles and authority. The communication style and method, however, varied significantly among the leaders studied.

A climate of trust in the leader and the vision is required to implement the vision effectively. Once the leader has chosen a direction—a vision that is innovative, challenging, but credible—he or she sticks with it. A leader's actions and words clearly exemplify the ideals of the vision. Through constancy and reliability while pursuing the vision, called "courageous patience," an atmosphere of mutual trust can be created that reduces suspicions, empowers employees, and enhances implementation.

The final strategy is the creative deployment of self, by understanding and using one's strengths, understanding and compensating for one's weaknesses, and continually learning and reflecting on one's experiences to improve one's ability to lead. Positive self-regard is the foundation of this strategy and grows from several personal actions by the leader: recognizing strengths and weaknesses, using self-discipline to nurture and develop skills, and discerning the fit between one's skills (and weaknesses) and the organization's needs.

Charismatic Leadership

The notion of *charisma,* Greek for "divine gift," has recently been revived and has produced a third approach to understanding leadership today. Traditionally, a charismatic leader had considerable emotional power over followers, particularly in times of crisis that required strong direction. The followers' bond was highly emotional, and the leader relied on this power to influence followers' actions.

More recently, charismatic leadership is characterized by a leader-follower bond wherein the leader attracts followers with a specific vision for action or by other means than merely emotional appeals to survive a crisis. A charismatic leader has a strong vision or mission and produces high levels of personal loyalty and commitment to his or her vision or mission. The leader is perceived as exceptional and extraordinary, and enjoys the personal devotion of a large portion of the organizational membership. (Bryman, 1992, provides a thorough review of the decades of research on charismatic leadership.)

Charismatic leadership is often equated with or described as a part of transformational leadership and visionary leadership. There are only small differences among the three; the differences, however, are a matter of emphasis. Charismatic organizational leaders lead by virtue of their personal qualities. They have a high level of self-confidence, a strong conviction in their beliefs and purpose, and a tendency to dominate and influence others (House, 1977). Conger and Kanungo (1987) identify a set of behaviors that commonly define a charismatic leader in an organization, implying that charisma can be learned and is not necessarily a mystical quality inherent in only a few special people. The behaviors include having an idealized goal or vision; taking risks and using unconventional methods to achieve the goal; portraying the status quo as inadequate and offering a viable alternative; using personal power rather than positional power to influence and guide others; and taking advantage of strategic opportunities when they emerge to further the implementation of their vision.

Common Themes in Contemporary Definitions of Leadership

To become an effective leader within an organization, these three approaches offer common strategies for success, with only minor differences and emphases. Each approach recognizes that a leader is an instrument of change and prescribes a core set of skills or actions necessary to implement organizational improvements successfully (Bryman, 1992), including

- Creating an inspiring and challenging vision, and infusing that vision in a compelling way that motivates employees to extraordinary performance in organizationally directed ways
- Enlisting followers in the leader's vision to stimulate extra effort to achieve the organizational vision
- Aligning the organizational structure, culture, and other management systems to facilitate employee performance toward the organizational vision

Two underlying assumptions—unidirectional flow of influence and clear distinctions between leaders and followers—further highlight the differences between organizational and public leadership.

Unidirectional Flow of Influence

The common elements for transformational, visionary, or charismatic leadership involve a process that is active but unidirectional from superior authority to subordinate authority. This has even been characterized as a hypodermic needle approach where the medicine (the vision) is loaded into the hypodermic syringe (words, symbols, and other rhetorical strategies) and then injected into the patient (the followers) to increase employee performance, to stimulate organizational change, or to improve organizational health (Westley and Mintzberg, 1989).

This image of visionary leadership is not new. Chester Barnard, one of the founders of modern management in the 1930s, argued that the leader's responsibility is to "bind the wills of men to the accomplishment of purposes beyond their immediate ends" (1938, p. 283). However, this exercise of authority and direct control is less popular today. Contemporary theories suggest that effective organizational leadership requires such elements of influence as shared vision and increased reliance on persuasion to induce extra effort, rather than the imposition of control by formal authority and the allocation of rewards.

Visions can be jointly developed and strategies can be devised collaboratively by the executive team. Nevertheless, organizational leadership is still based on the formal and informal influence of one person of position or prominence over another to pursue organizationally relevant goals. Although organizational visions can be generated collaboratively through interaction and discussion with subordinates and key stakeholders, when push comes to shove, they are unilaterally imposed from a higher authority (Howell and Avolio, 1992). After the vision is formulated and sanctioned by the top executives, unidirectional influence from superior to subordinate transfers the vision to others and enlists their contributions to ensure action toward its accomplishment. Organizational leaders use their hierarchical authority to redesign the organization's architecture—structure, incentives, and reward system—and to reshape its culture, values, assumptions, rites, and ceremonies

(Bass, 1985). Although the visionary approach advocates empowering followers in pursuit of the vision, it is a transfer of power from a higher level of authority to a lower level of authority. Visionary and transformational organizational leaders rely on the status and authority inherent in their hierarchical positions to leverage appropriate follower behavior.

There is nothing inherently wrong with unidirectional flow of influence. Power over others is inevitable in organizations. However, it is not effective in the interconnected context in which most public problems are embedded today. Problems cross organizational and jurisdictional boundaries, and growing numbers of stakeholders have legitimate interests and rights to insert themselves in problem solving. In addition, there is little trust by followers in leaders' abilities to solve the critical problems facing society. To be a leader in such a context requires different tasks, skills, and personal characteristics than are required for effective organizational leadership.

Clear Distinctions Between Leaders and Followers

In the past, most leaders studied were supervisors and other lower-level managers in organizations. Contemporary leadership focuses on senior-level organizational leaders and executives. Consequently, there is a strong tendency to focus on top-level executives, individuals at the apex of an organizational hierarchy who empower subordinates or convert followers in lower parts of the organization. Charismatic leadership produces strong personal devotion to the leader by the led. Visionary leadership uses communication to align the followers' goals to the leader's vision so that organizational members can bring the vision to fruition. Nevertheless, the transformational, visionary, and charismatic theories of leadership imply that leaders single-handedly improve the performance of their organizations. Because of this distinction between leader and follower, the "team" is seldom considered as an instrument of vision and implementation (Greiner and Bhambri, 1989; Child and Smith, 1987.)

Organizational leadership assumes that one top-level individual is the leader who mobilizes followers to act. In an interconnected world, this model is simply inaccurate. One individual may be the leader who galvanizes and stimulates initial action. Then other leaders and autonomous stakeholders will refine the initial burst of vision, agree on directions for action, and pursue specific initiatives aimed at solving the problem. Public leadership does not engage followers; rather, it involves collaborations, audiences, and other self-organizing groups. In pursuing the public interest, effective leaders are forced to become "leader-followers" simultaneously. Public leadership shifts, changes, and is shared at different times by different people in different organizations.

Examining Leadership in an Interconnected World

Clearly, organizational leadership models do not adequately address the unique environment in which public problems thrive. Leadership that targets solving complex public problems in highly interconnected policy arenas is less well understood and much less researched. In this context,

- Problems cross jurisdictional and functional boundaries and are interconnected with other problems.
- An increasing number and diversity of impassioned activists, special-interest groups, and legitimate stakeholders demand involvement on each issue.
- No one is in charge, and no single agency has sufficient power to achieve objectives unilaterally.

Shared power and authority in public policy arenas blur the types of distinctions between leaders and followers made in organizational and corporate hierarchies. A compelling vision articulated by a chief administrative or elected official is seldom sufficient to mobilize diverse stakeholders or to generate enough collective action to solve a perplexing social issue. Stakeholders naturally have diverse perspectives on what causes the problem and how to resolve it. Leadership strategies that attempt to evoke followership not only are unsuccessful in interconnected contexts, but they can even be destructive to effective problem solving. Often, the more one pushes a particular solution, the more independent stakeholders resist or push back, creating what has been popularly called "policy gridlock." A convincing vision, no matter how popular in corporate circles, can seldom break such gridlocks.

Public leadership is essentially a transorganizational leadership process of focusing attention and mobilizing or catalyzing a diverse set of individuals and agencies to address a public problem. It is a type of leadership that evokes collaboration and concerted action among diverse and often competing groups toward a shared outcome. A leadership that evokes collaboration rather than followership can create a critical mass of action that has long-term impact on addressing public problems. This type of public leadership can be characterized as catalytic rather than heroic or visionary. While corporate leadership hinges on influencing followers over whom one has legitimate authority, catalytic leadership stimulates action among people over whom one has little or no authority. Just as in chemistry, where a catalyst causes or increases a reaction, a catalytic leader in the public realm provides a spark that can create a critical mass of action with a long-term impact. Catalytic leaders are collaborative and strategic, but do not dominate. They are found in the middle of a group rather than in front or on top.

Effective public leadership in today's interconnected world—catalytic leadership—involves four specific, interrelated tasks. The exercise of each task alone can have an individual catalytic effect. Together, the four tasks can amplify the catalytic impact on addressing public problems and improving the quality of life. The four essential catalytic tasks are

1. Focus attention by elevating the issue to the public and policy agendas.
2. Engage people in the effort by convening the diverse set of people, agencies, and interests needed to address the issue.
3. Stimulate multiple strategies and options for action.
4. Sustain action and maintain momentum by managing the interconnections through appropriate institutionalization and rapid information sharing and feedback.

Each of the four essential tasks summarizes a more complex set or pattern of activities and processes commonly found in successful efforts to address public problems. The catalytic leadership process is not a formal, linear model. The four tasks are more organic and artistic and less mechanical and sequential than other types of change models.

The specific exercise of each task differs depending on the local and cultural context, the life cycle of the particular issue being targeted, and the level of critical mass energized or required. Thus, each task needs to be custom-tailored and implemented according to the particular circumstances. Being a catalyst at the federal level in the United States on health care or education reform requires different strategies within each of the four tasks than would the economic revitalization of a small rural downtown. Although each task is relevant, the specific leadership strategies within each task must be adapted.

The four tasks are not a simple, unitary set of stages in a sequential order. Although many efforts follow this four-stage order, all four tasks are not necessary to create a catalytic effect. A leader can complete any one of the tasks and have a catalytic impact. Alternatively, several tasks can be completed, but in a different order. Examples in subsequent chapters show that it is a "teleological process," with each task, regardless of order, moving toward the betterment of a specific social condition on a permanent basis.

Although fueled by individual acts in the beginning, catalytic leadership shifts among individuals and organizations. No one person or single organization can take the lead role in all four tasks; the issues are too interconnected and complex for one person or agency alone to achieve results. Catalytic leadership is not a leaderless model; rather, it is a "leader-full" approach where leadership evolves and is shared. An individual can move in and out of the leadership role without the group feeling abandoned and without forward motion coming to a complete stop, as is too often the case when a charismatic or heroic leader steps down. Because each task requires considerable energy and a wide array of interpersonal and conceptual skills, a shared or shifting leadership model is critical for sustaining efforts.

The problem or issue gets redefined during each task. As events move forward, an accumulation of new information and a mixing of individual perspectives keeps refocusing the issue as initially presented and defined. Reformulations of the problem are inevitable as each catalytic task is approached. Such ongoing attempts to find where the particular trouble originated are key to finding meaningful solutions and strategies.

The actions, interventions, and solutions considered appropriate also change and evolve. At the beginning of each catalytic task, individuals naturally have implicit and explicit assumptions about the right programs or policies to deal with the issue. Issues that emerge on the public agenda often have what are perceived as appropriate solutions attached to them, so-called "quick fixes." Individuals and special interests invited to help address the problem bring with them these preconceived solutions. The "problem-solution pairs" go through a reformulation during the catalytic leadership process (Bryson and Crosby, 1992). The most profound insight from observing catalytic efforts is that within each separate task there is a continuous reiteration of both the problem-defining and problem-solving phases. As the four catalytic tasks unfold, the predominant focus shifts from problem defining to problem solving. Nevertheless, each task captures both so that problem redefinition often continues even after strategies are being implemented and sustained. The four catalytic leadership tasks are discussed further in the next four chapters.

Part Two

The Catalytic Tasks of Public Leadership

Public leadership involves public officials; individuals from private, nonprofit, and education sectors; community activists; and volunteers. Leadership in this environment demands roles, tasks, and skills different from those required in the corporate world.

Understanding effective public leadership requires more than the attitude of "we'll know it when we see it." It involves four specific, interrelated tasks. The exercise of each task alone can have an individual catalytic effect. Together, the four tasks can amplify the catalytic impact on addressing public problems and improving the quality of the human condition. The four tasks are

1. Focus attention by elevating the issue to the public and policy agendas.
2. Engage people in the effort by convening the diverse set of people, agencies, and interests needed to address the issue.
3. Stimulate multiple strategies and options for action.
4. Sustain action and maintain momentum by managing the interconnections through appropriate institutionalization and rapid information sharing and feedback.

Each essential task summarizes a complex set of activities and processes found in successful efforts to address public problems in an interconnected world. The catalytic leadership process is not a formal, linear model. The four tasks are more organic and artistic than mechanical and sequential. Public leaders commonly spiral back to earlier tasks as the need arises.

The chapters in Part Two focus on the four catalytic tasks and the roles of public leaders when pursuing something in the public interest. Each chapter elaborates on a particular task.

Chapter Three, "Raising Awareness: Focusing Public Attention on the Issue," explains how public leaders direct attention toward a pressing issue. Because the list of potential problems is vast and resources are limited, public leaders need to be advocates to ensure that a particular issue or problem is seen as more important and urgent than competing issues. Leaders attempt to get others to believe an issue is urgent or important enough to invest their time and energy in it.

Chapter Four, "Forming Working Groups: Bringing People Together to Address the Problem," shows how public leaders can include diverse factions to address a problem, urgent issue, or emerging opportunity. They identify key stakeholders and knowledgeholders and invite them to address the issue. Acting as catalysts, public leaders use their knowledge of the particular problem, their knowledge of stakeholders' interests, their personal contacts in related networks, and their personal charm and available authority to convince key individuals that the issue is worthy of their involvement.

Chapter Five, "Creating Strategies: Stimulating Multiple Strategies and Options for Action," explains how public leaders act as catalysts to create the conditions necessary for a working group or network to develop and commit to multiple strategies to address the targeted problem. Leaders help to create a core of committed and motivated group members with sufficient skills and knowledge who do not relinquish their organizational autonomy or institutional independence when joining a working group or network. They help to formulate a unifying purpose based on desired outcomes or results they hope to achieve. Public leaders act as process champions by facilitating an interactive group process that enhances mutual learning, stimulates shared leadership, and builds trust. They help the working group or network to design a structured, credible process of decision making and action planning, a process that gives confidence to those involved that something positive will result from their time and effort.

Chapter Six, "Sustaining Action: Implementing Strategies and Maintaining Momentum," shows the difficulty in sustaining attention and effort by the numerous and diverse individuals and agencies, most of whom are independent of each other. Public leaders act as catalysts to gain support and legitimacy for the multiple strategies. They network to ensure that supportive coalitions will advocate and champion continued implementation. They keep focused on the ultimate goal, outcome, or desired result. They also help to develop an outcome-based information system to monitor progress and to ensure that successes and "small wins" are recognized and acknowledged.

Chapter Three

Raising Awareness
Focusing Public Attention on the Issue

*Sometimes the most important thing you can do is give 'em
a "wake-up call."*

Effective public leaders act as a catalyst, focusing attention toward
an issue or problem area, and initially defining a situation in ways
that stir others' interests and mobilize them to search for responses.
Through the strategic use of stories, anecdotes, and data, they create a "wake-up call" that directs attention to an emerging opportunity or that demonstrates that a problem or condition is urgent. By
putting a spotlight on an issue, they increase the likelihood that key
stakeholders will either be recruited or attracted to address it.

As catalysts, effective public leaders do not necessarily promote
solutions; they promote problems. Thus, they are advocates for
issue emergence, but not necessarily strong advocates for a particular solution or policy position. They get others not only to focus
on the issue or problem, but to embrace it as a priority. They evoke
a sense of urgency that stimulates people to invest their time and
energy. Because public problems and issues are numerous and
resources are limited, public leaders may become an issue champion. They try to ensure that a particular issue is more concrete,
visible, and urgent than other potential issues that may be competing for attention and resources. They champion an issue by promoting it to higher prominence or by getting people to see or feel
an old problem in a new way.

Public leaders who have visibility, access to the media, and
prominent positions are strategically placed to stimulate interest

in an issue. However, having a position of prominence is not a prerequisite. Citizens in all walks of life can step into the public leadership process and be catalysts to focus attention on urgent public problems. To do this, individuals first raise the public's consciousness about a particular social condition so it is perceived as a salient issue—concrete and visible. They arouse strategic discomfort toward the problem or a strategic opportunity for action, generating strong concern or broad enthusiasm so it becomes an attention-demanding priority. They often have a broad understanding of the agenda-setting process and use a variety of attentional triggers to capture the public's attention and to move the issue to a high-priority status. They define an issue so that it galvanizes attention and expands others' interest and concern for the issue. They also create a sense of hope—a sense that the issue can be addressed and that efforts are not futile.

Catalytic leaders are not necessarily focused on crises. They often target issues before they reach a crisis stage. Some examples include the warning of a dramatic increase in teenage pregnancies in a community, the closing or relocation of an industry vital to a region, or the increasing numbers of individuals who lack health insurance in the nation.

Agenda setting is a prelude to public action, and there always exists sets of agendas: the long list of ongoing problems and a smaller set of priority issues. The *public agenda* is the larger set of problems or societal concerns to which the general public is paying serious attention at any given time. The *policy agenda* includes a much smaller set of issues, alternatives, and policy choices to which key policymakers pay serious attention.

Issue Attention Cycles

No single factor can place an issue or problem high on the public or policy agendas. Public problems generally go through an "issue attention cycle," from a latent concern, to the public agenda, to the policy agenda (Coates, 1991; Downs, 1972.) The movement of a public problem through these phases seldom proceeds in a tidy linear or sequential fashion. Kingdon (1984) notes separate, independent streams of activities, issues, and solutions that happen simultaneously but separately on a wide variety of related problems.

At a critical point or succession of points, a catalytic effect occurs, pushing one problem higher on the agenda and displacing other issues from prominence. An issue often leaps into the public view, captures center stage for a period of time, and becomes a problem in common currency. It may then emerge as a salient issue worth investing time, attention, and resources. Then it gradually fades into the background (resolved or unresolved) and is replaced by more burning issues (Schön, 1971; Downs, 1972; Coates, 1991; Bryson and Crosby, 1992.)

Public problems often start as a condition or a latent concern, then rise to the public's attention as a problem, and finally become an issue that is seen as urgent and pressing and that displaces other problems from the public agenda (see Figure 3.1). They do not necessarily proceed through these phases in a linear, sequential fashion, however. Some problems may skip phases, particularly when a crisis evokes immediate policy responses. Even after an issue has reached the policy agenda, attention does not remain sharply focused over a long period of time. The issue will eventually fade from public attention, even if largely unresolved, and will be replaced by another pressing and urgent issue. Thus public leadership involves moving a particular condition to problem status, and then to priority issue status, so that it attracts the attention of the general public and other key decision makers and leaders and stimulates the search for responses. As a result, effective catalysts must be mindful of where the issue is in the issue attention cycle.

Capturing Public Attention: Transforming a Condition into a Problem

Not every unwanted or undesirable social, environmental, or economic condition will become defined as a problem. Until 1980, for example, the existence of transients was not seen as an issue of public concern. After 1980, the condition jumped onto the public agenda as a problem of homelessness. Drunken driving and alcoholism killed thousands annually, but didn't emerge as matters of public concern until the 1980s. Serious conditions may exist, but unless they capture the attention or interest of the public, they remain latent problems. They exist as impersonal trends or statistics, are dismissed as unimportant, or are ignored altogether.

Figure 3.1. The Issue Attention Cycle.

A *"condition"*		A *"problem"*		A *"priority issue"*
(an existing situation or latent problem)	→	(a problem captures the public's attention)	→	(an issue rises to priority status of key decision makers)
Not every condition will surface as a problem or be defined as a problem.		A societal concern becomes salient and important, and thus captures public attention through increasing awareness, visibility and emotional concern		The issue is felt as urgent and pressing, coupled with some optimism that it can be addressed, and thus displaces other problems on the policy agenda.

A condition is judged as negative and labeled a problem only within the context of one's value system (Etzioni, 1966). A condition must challenge what the community or society thinks "ought to be." It must confront and tug at some image of what "should be" before it can be taken seriously. No one trigger or strategy can cause this to occur. Several factors or events come together, on both intellectual and emotional levels, before people feel "something should be done about this!"

How do public leaders create a salient problem from a latent, problematic condition? How do social conditions become social problems? How are conditions raised to the public's consciousness, bringing them to the notice of important stakeholders? Examining the issue cycles of major public issues, such as health care (Kingdon, 1984), AIDS (Yankelovich, 1991), and the greenhouse effect (Yankelovich, 1991), and of less-visible issues, such as radon (Scheberle, 1994), asbestos (Scheberle, 1994), and thalidomide (McKinley, 1981), researchers found that issues reach the public agenda or the public consciousness in different ways. Transforming latent concerns into public problems can take just a few minutes, or it can take decades. Although the time factor varies considerably, common features required for an issue to reach the public agenda include

- One or more key focusing events that forcefully dramatize an issue
- Concreteness and clarity of the issue to the general public and applicability to one's self
- Credibility and legitimacy of the sources of information the public receives
- Sustained media presence or a dramatic spike in media attention
- Issue networks or groups that form around the issue
- Connections to possible or actual policy options

Catalysts capture public attention first by raising awareness of the problem (an intellectual dimension) and then by arousing interest and concern (an emotional or moral dimension) that something should be done. Individuals must have a sense that the condition is worsening or is of such magnitude that it is recognized as an immediate or impending threat or danger.

Increased Awareness and Visibility of the Condition

Countable problems are more easily recognized than less countable ones. Available data can highlight warning signals; however, a reference point is necessary to interpret whether a current condition is better or worse. For example, it is difficult to know if a teenage pregnancy rate of 9 per 1,000 girls is good or bad without a frame of reference in which to compare and contrast.

One approach catalysts employ is to show a worsening trend by comparing current data with past data. In 1992, the U.S. Department of Education found that literacy skills for people ages twenty-one to twenty-five had declined significantly during the previous seven years. Giving this issue a time reference provides a stronger mental impact than stating an absolute number (90 million adults are illiterate) or by using a population percentage (20 percent of the adult population is illiterate).

Another approach is using data to identify troubling comparisons. Consider again the rural community of Tillamook County, Oregon. The issue of teenage pregnancies was raised to public attention (and embarrassment) when data were released indicating the county's teenage pregnancy rate was second only to that of Oregon's most populous and urban county. In another example, the U.S. Advisory Board on Child Abuse and Neglect found that more babies and young children die at the hands of their parents than in car accidents, house fires, falls, or drownings. Similarly, antismoking advocates argue that the number of smoking-related deaths in the country is equal to two 747s crashing every day of the year.

How the facts are arrayed obviously has a significant impact on arousing concern. It is clear, however, that merely giving the public "the facts" doesn't work for several reasons (Covello, von Winterfeldt, and Slovic, 1986):

• The numbers may be too large and unfathomable, as in whether the global population will level off toward the middle of the twenty-first century at 8.3 billion or 12 billion, which could dramatically impact the quality of life for future generations.

• The numbers may not be believable. The facts are often suspect if provided by a government source, such as the "real size" of the federal budget deficit, or if provided by a special-interest group, such as the $3 trillion estimate of infrastructure and public works needs in America identified by the Associated General Contractors of America (1983), which makes its money by building roads.

• The numbers may be too technical and highly complex, as in the chemical composition or size of particulate matter in air pollution.

• The numbers may be ignored when the data appear to contradict strongly held personal beliefs. A good example is the findings on indigenous, small business development—that 80 percent of all new U.S. jobs are created by small business enterprises while only 10 percent are generally created by the attraction of industries from one region to another (Birch, 1979).

It is difficult for conditions to gain placement on the public agenda without supportive data. Yet the acceptance of information regarding a condition or risk is highly dependent on the confidence in the source of information. Who provides the information and analysis becomes a critical question. The last two decades witnessed a decreased public willingness to defer to and to trust in the judgment of scientists, private industries, and governmental institutions (Laird, 1989; Slovic, 1993).

An analysis of national polls over several years found that attempts to promote energy conservation and a national energy policy were seriously undermined in the 1970s because of the public's deep mistrust in the oil companies and the federal government. In contrast, national data related to AIDS create less suspicion because they are generated by the Center for Disease Control and Prevention, which is more closely allied with the medical profession than with the government (Yankelovich, 1991). If trust is lacking, no amount of data will be effective. Trust and credibility in the sources of information are crucial elements in generating and promoting a condition to be recognized and labeled as a public problem (Slovic, 1993).

Increased Salience of an Issue

Worsening trends, troubling comparisons, and other indicators provide the intellectual foundation for recognizing that a serious condition exists. The condition, however, must be concrete, acquiring a degree of salience before it rises to the public agenda. Providing the best, credible data is not enough. Sometimes the proverbial "writing on the wall" can't be read or does not impact people if they have no personal experience with the issue.

Salience occurs when a condition is viewed as real, personal, and tangible. For many, personal experiences and anecdotes provide more salience than statistics, data, and other forms of "proof." Trend data, indicators, and other sources of information can be important sources of energy and catalysts for action, but they are not sufficient to make a social, economic, or environmental condition become a salient problem. Interest and concern are difficult to stimulate if a condition seems remote from personal life, no matter how countable or measurable. People naturally respond more easily to vivid information than to dull statistics (Nutt and Backoff, 1992). Raising the condition to the public's attention often depends on people's ability to apply the condition or situation to their lives or those close to them. Individuals pay more attention to problems relevant to their lives than to those that seem far away.

Stories and Personal Anecdotes

People's primary sources of information on social and economic conditions—and what they feel and remember about problems—are what they hear from their neighbors and family members, what they discuss with folks at the office, and what they see in the news. As a result, one's initial recognition and understanding of a problem may not be guided by trend analysis or reasoned judgment, but by what is personally observed or discussed anecdotally.

Direct personal experience significantly enhances the recognition and salience of conditions and problems. For example, people's estimates of the causes and risks of death are not guided by statistical probability. They are strongly influenced by subjective factors: the number of individuals one knows who have suffered those particular misfortunes, such as knowing several women who have died of breast cancer, and the amount of media coverage devoted to the deaths (Fischoff, 1985). Providing direct or personal experience—for example, using stories, pictures, and anecdotes—heightens the salience of a particular condition or problem.

Planned or unplanned personal experiences also increase the salience of conditions and can dramatize the impacts. One famous story involves a Seattle pediatrician concerned about the dangers of flammable children's clothes. He brought Warren Magnuson, at the time a U.S. senator from Washington, to a local hospital where he was shown the impact and severity of the burn cases. The senator was struck by the suffering he saw and pursued efforts to raise this issue to the attentions of the public and the U.S. Congress (Kingdon, 1984).

Stories and word-of-mouth communication are extremely influential in problem recognition. Mount St. Helens erupted in 1980, spewing thousands of tons of volcanic ash from the crater eastward toward Spokane, Washington. Although radio and television aired warnings as the ash was carried by the winds, more than half of the Spokane citizens first found out about the danger from a friend or relative, on the phone, in line at the market, or at the office. Similarly, policy agendas for locally elected mayors are guided by personal stories and anecdotes from friends, rather than by academic studies and analyses (Nalbandian, 1994). Stories and anecdotes from those one trusts are powerful ways to demonstrate convincingly and personally that the condition is unacceptable and must be attended to.

Images

Photographs are powerful catalysts. Pictures dramatically document a condition that needs attention when data can leave it unreal and distant. In the 1930s, a group of government photographers played a significant role in stimulating national attention on the hidden sufferings of rural dislocation due to the Depression. Dorothea Lange and other professional photographers, employees of the Resettlement Administration's Information Bureau, documented the plight of homeless migrant families, creating in the public mind "images of hope as well as the reflection of guilt" that aroused public consciousness. One federal administrator later noted that "Lange's photographs had an extremely powerful effect on those who were unaware of the severity of the dislocation problem in the West" (Gawthrop, 1993, p. 513).

With technological advances that include digital photography, color copying, and enhanced imaging processes, visual techniques are increasingly used to document conditions and to draw attention. Federal auditors have now begun to use color photographs to highlight conditions they find in their audits. Auditors from the Inspector General's Office of the U.S. Department of Health and Human Services (1993) inspected 149 licensed day care, foster care, and Head Start programs in six states, which served more than 6,600 children. In the official report, color photographs graphically revealed what their inspections found: children exposed to raw sewage, household chemicals, and toxic cleaning supplies; and kitchen floors with dead cockroaches and other insect infestations.

Increased Emotional Concern

Raising an issue to the public agenda thus requires more than intellectual awareness. Providing credible documentation that there is a problematic condition or trend is not enough to generate concern or enthusiasm. The public and the key policymakers must care about the particular condition. Emotions play an important motivational role in focusing attention. The more subjective side of emotions and values also plays a critical role in raising an issue to the agenda. Emotional concern is aroused, stimulating serious discussion and the public will to change a societal condition.

Conditions are more likely to arouse emotional interest when there is either a perceived threat or risk to oneself or others, or a moral gap between the current situation and "what ought to be." Both intellectual awareness and emotional dissatisfaction about a current condition must be stimulated or there simply will not be enough energy and motivation to address the situation. Catalysts, therefore, arouse the public's attention by revealing the threat or opportunity or by identifying and amplifying a moral discrepancy. They elevate a sense of moral awareness or ethical responsibility for the condition, creating strategic discomfort, intolerance, or a sense of injustice for the discrepancy.

Threats and Opportunities

Seeing a condition as a threat or risk can stimulate personal interest sufficiently to encourage one pay closer attention. A threat or risk exists when a loss might occur that is irreversible, is dreaded (with unknown but potentially significant negative impacts), or has negative long-term consequences on one or more stakeholder groups. Conditions can also be framed as opportunities, engaging individuals' interests in a positive way, such as John F. Kennedy's goal to "put a man on the moon" to respond to the threat of the Soviet Union's growing strength in space technology. Opportunities are expected or unexpected situations that can be taken advantage of to reach a particular goal.

Conditions framed as opportunities, however, seem to have less of an emotional impact than those framed as threats. Although many people are motivated to respond to a situation perceived as an opportunity, they place less value on the potential for gaining something than on the avoidance of losing something. Psychological research shows that people will risk less to gain a particular amount and will risk more to avoid the loss of the same amount. When avoiding a loss, individuals have a larger "response magnitude" and will risk larger amounts of money than with an opportunity for a potential gain (Tversky and Kahneman, 1981).

A Moral Gap

Arousing emotional concern does not require being personally threatened or seeing a dreaded risk. If a condition conflicts with closely held values—a gap between what is and what ought to be—emotions are aroused. There is, as one community leader noted, "a refusal of the status quo." The trend could worsen or the situation could fall below what is felt as acceptable or satisfactory, thus provoking attention. Or conditions could become visible problems because of an upward movement in people's expectations. Although the situation doesn't change, people's values, standards, or expectations do. For example, public school dropouts weren't a problem at the turn of the century when high school graduation was rare, but became unacceptable in the 1960s when a new standard emerged because a majority of kids were graduating. Dumping sewage and waste into rivers, a common practice historically, is now seen as an unacceptable health and environmental hazard. Similarly, smoking in public places is increasingly intolerable—not because more people are smoking, but because of changing beliefs and attitudes about the health risks of secondhand smoke.

The resulting gap between what is and what should be generates a natural tension that arouses attention and stimulates a need for action. Thus, public problems are defined within a context of social values and aspirations. Conditions normally tolerated or even ignored become problems when enough people believe that the situation is no longer acceptable and that something should be done to eliminate, resolve, or remedy it.

Moving a Public Problem to a Priority Issue Status

Public recognition of a pressing problem is not enough to make it a priority issue for key policymakers. Public problems get attention only when they move onto the shorter set of issues—the policy agenda—displacing other issues from priority focus. Often, a staggering number and variety of problems demand attention at any given time. Public agendas are growing and becoming more intense as fiscal resources tighten. Problems compete for attention and must be viewed as urgent and needing attention before any significant action can occur. In this context, effective public leaders act as catalysts by creating urgency (but not necessarily a crisis) and by instilling hope and optimism that there are potential solutions.

Creating Urgency

Interpreting problems as urgent is a continual responsibility of public leadership. The public can recognize that a problem exists, but if there is little urgency about it, it won't be able to compete successfully for attention by key decision makers. It is not necessarily that people are too short-sighted to pay serious attention to anything that lacks immediacy. Rather, we are too distracted or too busy to focus on every problem that deserves attention. A problem needs to be sufficiently compelling and pressing before it can crowd out less-pressing issues from the public agenda. A jolt of urgency is needed both to disrupt the current set of issues being actively considered and to overcome resistance or objections of an entrenched or vocal stakeholder group that fears potential disruption of the status quo.

Although urgency can be defined in a variety of ways, urgent action must be implied. It is tempting to stimulate a sense of urgency by declaring that the problem is a crisis. At the federal government level, conditions sometimes must deteriorate to crisis proportions before a problem achieves national attention. This may especially be true in less-visible policy areas, such as national transportation and economic policy. Although defining a problem as a crisis to mobilize attention may shake people up and create the prerequisite emotions or a "felt need" for change, two things commonly happen. First, a hurried attempt is made to solve the crisis immediately, perhaps to save lives, which often results in quick fixes and stopgap measures. Second, hurried crisis resolution inhibits the development of more comprehensive options and longer-term strategies that may be necessary. Once the crisis is over, people's attention too quickly turns elsewhere.

Establishing urgency is different from responding to a crisis. Problem-related arousal is kept at modest intensities so that problem diagnostic capabilities and complex problem-solving skills are used. With increasing levels of arousal, performance first improves and then declines. When a problem is truly experienced as a crisis, it generates not only arousal, but also anxiety, frustration, and even hopelessness, which diminishes thought and action. Highly aroused individuals—those experiencing what they would consider a real crisis—find it difficult to brainstorm, to concentrate for any length of time, to consider new or novel ideas, or to think in complex, long-term, or highly abstract, systemic ways (Weick, 1984; Holsti, 1978). They feel pressure to react quickly and pick a solution from a narrower set of preexisting options. Thus, defining a problem as a crisis may be appropriate to propel a problem past public ignorance. However, further problem diagnosis and direction setting occur more effectively when emotional arousal mobilizes attention but does not inhibit or narrowly focus option generation. Furthermore, the looming crisis must be real, or the catalyst will lose credibility, not to mention the trust of key stakeholders for this and future efforts.

Instilling Hope and Optimism

Sounding the proverbial alarm is not sufficient to move a recognized problem to priority issue status. It must also be perceived as "action-able" or "do-able." Individuals not only must be troubled by the problem, but also must have hope that it can be addressed. Hopelessness emerges when there are no viable options, when alternatives are too expensive, or when the inherent value conflicts seem so interminable that no alternatives are available. Hopelessness leads to personal withdrawal and acceptance of the status quo. The mayor of a Northwest timber-dependent town spoke with resigned despair about the closing of the region's largest lumber mill. "It would hurt a substantial portion of our local economy, but it would not be the end of the world. We'd learn to adjust. It would be like cutting off a boy's arm or leg in surgery—we'd learn to live with it" (Hibbard, 1986, p. 192).

Optimism often exists when one or more options might address the problem. Problems thus gain a priority position on the policy agenda when associated with at least one potential strategy or option. (See particularly Bryson and Crosby, 1992, for a thorough discussion of this "problem-solution" coupling.) This optimism, however, must not prematurely fasten solutions to problems. A broad portfolio of strategies and actions by a diverse set of stakeholders is ultimately needed to address interconnected problems (see Chapter Five).

Common Catalytic Strategies

Issues rise to priority in the policy agenda due to the convergence of four elements, which do not necessarily occur in a predictable time frame or sequential order. The four elements are

1. Intellectual awareness of a worsening condition or troubling comparison
2. Emotional arousal and concern regarding the condition
3. Sense that the problem is urgent
4. Belief that the problem can be addressed

Policymakers do not notice all the problems facing them, however. Which problems get attention and are identified as priority issues is fairly unpredictable. The obstacles for a problem becoming a priority issue and generating strategic responses are often formidable.

Public leadership thus involves moving a problem through the three stages of agenda setting: from a condition or latent problem, to a recognizable and visible problem capturing public attention, to a priority issue being considered by relevant policymakers. Some issues arrive quickly on the policy agenda, while others recycle several times through the process before being considered truly a high priority. Three general catalytic strategies are commonly used in the public leadership process: take advantage of attentional triggers, use media strategically, and frame and reframe the problem.

Attentional Triggers

In the corporate world, organizations seldom experience dramatic change until a trigger stimulates action—a new competitor in the market, unexpected revenue losses, an eroding market share, SEC audits, or dramatically shrinking sales. These triggers focus the attention of organizational members on existing conditions, problems, or issues (Dumaine, 1993). Public problems also have triggers that focus attention and increase problem salience and urgency (Cobb and Elder, 1983). The need for change must be made dramatically clear for a condition to be elevated from a free-floating concern to a priority issue.

Nothing advances a problem as forcefully as a dramatic event or series of events that highlights a disturbing condition. As seasoned pollster Daniel Yankelovich (1991) emphasizes, nothing retards a problem more than the lack of such triggers. Three general kinds of triggers serve as catalysts that raise the awareness and salience of public problems: accidents, disasters, and other dramatic events; intentional focusing events; and the release of major studies, reports, or evaluations.

Attentional triggers provide both the intellectual awareness of the problem and the emotional push that stimulates action. The strength of an attentional trigger is determined not by any number or statistic, however, but by what it signals or portends. This is obvious when examining disasters as triggers.

Accidents and Disasters

Accidents, disasters, and other dramatic events underscore the seriousness of a condition and provide signals that something needs to be done before further harm occurs. Calamities awaken us to the seriousness and potential impacts of certain conditions. Several airplane crashes in a row push forward air safety as a critical public problem. The back-to-back assassinations of the Rev. Martin Luther King, Jr., and Robert Kennedy significantly influenced gun control legislation in 1968. The accident at the Three Mile Island nuclear reactor in 1979 riveted attention to the regulation and operation of reactors worldwide. The deaths of famous actors and athletes to AIDS-related illnesses drove home the effect of the HIV virus. As these examples show, accidents, disasters, and other events provide a catalytic effect or "trigger mechanism" necessary for creating priority issues.

Absolute numbers are not as crucial as emotional impact. It's not the number of people killed or the amount of property damaged, but rather the perception of what the tragedy signals or portends for the future. The resulting emotional concern, or "signal potential," is directly related to the potential short- and long-term impacts. Internationally recognized risk expert Slovic (1987) notes that a train accident that takes many lives can produce relatively little concern beyond that felt by the victims' families and friends because it occurs as part of a familiar and well-understood transportation system. However, a small accident in a highly advanced technological system that is unfamiliar to the public, such as an accident in a recombinant DNA laboratory, can elicit tremendous public emotion because it is seen as a harbinger of future problems and possibly catastrophic consequences. Arousal and emotional concern are heightened the more unfamiliar or poorly understood the condition or situation is and the more "dreaded" the potential impact of the accident or disaster. The disaster or accident has more attentional impact if it is seen as symptomatic of larger dangers.

However, issues rarely rise on the agenda solely because of dramatic and unforeseen events. Credible data is also critical to emphasize and reinforce the events. Without data, such events can be dismissed as an exception or denied as a fluke, reducing the willingness for individuals to expend time and energy addressing the issue.

Intentional Focusing Events

Unlike dramatic events, focusing events are planned attentional triggers. Focusing events include community forums, special national conferences, and policy summits. Public events such as town hall meetings on teenage pregnancy reduction or marches to eliminate hate crimes also act as attentional triggers. The purpose is to raise public consciousness and generate a sense of both urgency and "do-ability." They are typically nonroutine gatherings that galvanize attention and media publicity toward specific conditions requiring action. Unlike unplanned dramatic events, focusing events can also generate initial solutions or proposals and a process for continual refinement of and advocacy for those proposals.

Most communities provide opportunities at city council or county board hearings in which to air grievances and to advocate causes. Fewer communities provide forums where people can seriously deliberate the critical problems and issues facing the whole community. As early as 1633, community forums were used in the American British colonies to identify local problems, foster serious talk, and set directions on critical issues. More common today are citizen surveys, public opinion polls, and focus groups that can produce information about the community, reveal where perceptions and interests converge and diverge, clarify interrelationships among urgent issues, and articulate underlying community values. Today, forums are conducted all over the country and are sponsored by a variety of agencies and persons acting as catalysts, such as city governments, community organizations, school districts, libraries, chambers of commerce, local colleges, legislators, and other public officials.

According to the Kettering Foundation, a nonprofit agency that conducts community forums throughout the country:

> Anyone can organize a forum, but not any kind of meeting can be a genuine public forum. Debates, lectures, and panel presentations are all useful, but they are not forums. What makes a forum a forum is lateral communication, people interacting with those around them. The deliberations have to be so direct and vital that no one is unaffected. They have to move toward making choices in an environment that is impartial and open. People also have to listen in order to understand the reasons that others have for positions contrary to their own. Moral posturing has to give way to a shared, moral struggle. People have to go beyond being reasonable to learn to reason together. Most of all, they have to appreciate that working through issues takes time (Mathews and McAfee, 1995, p. 30).

Unlike community forums, national summits typically take on a more issue-specific focus, with invited guests and speakers discussing urgent and serious issues within a particular policy area, such as economic growth, urban violence, aging, or small business development. In 1994, for example, the American Medical Association (AMA) sponsored a four-day National Conference on Family Violence that targeted such topics as violence in the media, elder abuse, child physical and sexual abuse, spousal abuse, and the intergenerational nature of family violence. The conference ended with the AMA establishing a set of working groups in specific issue areas to fight violence in the home.

Highly competitive funding opportunities can produce a galvanizing effect that raises issues to prominence. The chance to compete for federal funds for school-based health clinics always generates community discussions on the appropriate services to be provided to students by public schools, particularly around issues of teen pregnancy. In economic development, interstate competitions to locate industrial plants or major corporate headquarters similarly raise the issue of jobs and stimulate diverse groups to meet to discuss ways to take advantage of these potential opportunities.

Reports and Evaluations

Reports, studies, evaluations, and strategic plans can highlight troubling comparisons, worsening conditions, unmet needs, and performance deficiencies. Some are commissioned, while others are produced as part of ongoing studies and news reporting. In 1986, *Washington Post* columnist Neal Pierce was commissioned to analyze urban issues in Phoenix and to produce a "fresh and untinted view" of the city's urban problems and opportunities. His analysis, called the "Pierce Report," was published in the city's major newspapers in 1987. It generated broad concern and "stirred the community to write an agenda for action" for better managing growth (Hall and Weschler, 1991, p. 141). In many communities, regions, and states, studies are commissioned to diagnose their economy's strengths and weaknesses and to assess their positioning for future growth in a global economy. Arizona's *Redefining Economic Development for the 1990s,* Oregon's groundbreaking *Oregon Shines,* and Silicon Valley's *An Economy at Risk* called attention to new problems and opportunities and sparked major changes in their region's economic development policies and strategies.

Data from credible sources, packaged in ways that can be easily understood, can have high catalytic value because they amplify weak signals that can be used as triggering devices. They point to a need for action instead of allowing denial or inaction to precipitate a more serious crisis. The Urban Strategies Council of Oakland (USCO) used statistical information from numerous databases on low-birth-weight babies to galvanize neighborhood action. USCO convened a broad range of agencies, each holding different pieces of the relevant data, mapped the information on transparent overlays, and identified areas with the most concentrated problems in the community. The combined information, documented in a report called *Changing the Odds,* was used to attract resources and energy among fragmented agencies to develop a more comprehensive program for early childhood development.

New or original findings produced by the academic community, often first seen in unpublished monographs or in scientific and professional journals, can focus attention on particular problems or concerns. An excellent example is David Birch's classic analysis of job generation and economic development. In 1979 his national study revealed that 80 percent of the generation of new jobs through the 1970s occurred by the introduction and expansion of small businesses. Only 10 percent of job growth in any state was due to the attraction of industries relocating to new regions. His analysis was extremely controversial because the data directly contradicted the popular notion of industrial recruitment. Initially it was available only in mimeographed form from his MIT department. He later published a summary of his findings in a popular intellectual journal, *The Public Interest*. By 1985 his findings were included in President Reagan's State of the Union Address. This one study, although hotly debated during the 1980s, was a catalyst for serious evaluation and redirection of economic development strategies nationwide.

Changes in specific indicators in regularly published reports also provide important warning signals. An annual survey conducted and published by the National Institute on Drug Abuse since 1975 showed that illegal drug use by teenagers increased significantly in 1993, reversing a downward trend that began in 1981. This created what Donna Shalala, secretary of Health and Human Services, called an "urgent alarm that we must heed at once." Other common sources of indicator data and trend analysis are national think tanks and policy-planning groups, such as the American Enterprise Institute, the Brookings Institution, the Business Roundtable, the Center for Policy Priorities, and the Committee for Economic Development. Although each has discernible political leanings, the groups generate unique data and access other basic data sources, synthesizing and highlighting social, economic, and fiscal trends and framing appropriate policy responses.

Local, state, and national evaluation studies can highlight deficiencies or gaps that stimulate increased attention on an existing condition. As mentioned earlier, a national evaluation of children in day-care centers and foster care homes, conducted by the inspector general of the U.S. Department of Health and Human Services, found that some children were exposed to deplorable conditions. The review was conducted to determine whether child-care providers that receive federal funding comply with federal, state, and local health and safety standards. The chair of the

U.S. House of Representatives small business subcommittee on regulation stated: "I am now convinced that significant numbers of kids under five may be in day care facilities that are unsanitary, unsafe, and possibly dangerous."

National and state advocacy groups provide provocative "report cards" in various issue areas and promote a framework for assessing and highlighting related gaps or deficiencies. The Corporation for Enterprise Development annually publishes *Making the Grade: The Development Report Card for the States,* which provides state-by-state comparisons on seventy-eight factors that have a direct influence on economic growth and vitality. It grades states on four general areas—economic performance, business vitality, economic capacity (such as human investments and infrastructure), and policy strength—and identifies for each category where each state is strong or deficient. The Annie E. Casey Foundation annually publishes *Kids Count,* which documents data and ranks the states on such children and families issues as child abuse, teenage pregnancy, and school dropout rates. These evaluations can provide credible and objective data on troubling comparisons and worsening trends, triggering public attention and policy action.

Federal, state, and local mandates also stimulate action. The Clean Air Act of 1970 promulgated air-quality standards. The act prompted related scientific and technical data collection and strategy development for measurably improving air quality. Although the standards are still far from being met, the act has spurred considerable progress toward reducing pollution from stationary sources and vehicle emissions in many urban areas. With both standards and deadlines, mandates can influence how quickly an issue gets on the state or local agenda and how urgent the problem is perceived.

Another example of an externally produced trigger event happened in Cleveland in 1979, when the city become the first large urban setting since the Depression to default legally on its loans. The default was a deliberate choice by AmeriTrust Bank, which decided to call in the loan, creating an urgency that pulled together diverse business leaders and government officials. Interviews with community leaders indicated the default was not required from a monetary standpoint. However, it was necessary to arouse emotional concern and to break the business community out of its other preoccupations and its denial that there was a serious fiscal problem in city government (Henton and others, 1997).

Issue Windows and Timing

Much of the impact of attentional triggers—dramatic events, focusing events, and published studies—stems from the wide publicity generated and the increased salience of the issue to both the general population and those who are directly involved in the event. The publicity needs to create an awareness and a concern that something needs to be done. Dramatic events, such as disasters and accidents, can stimulate danger signals. Focusing events have a further advantage because they also generate a sense of "do-ability" by identifying potential action responses or proposals that can be considered. Published reports provide the necessary supporting data and historical context for dramatic and focusing events. They can also reveal new and surprising findings that motivate people to focus attention. Attentional triggers have different impacts, and one is not inherently better than another. Seldom is just one trigger sufficient. Multiple events or a mix of triggers are needed to generate attention to mobilize energy.

One needs more than an urgent problem and potential actions; one must be sensitive to timing and the unique attentional rhythms of issues. The emergence of policy windows or issue windows often provides the opportunity to focus attention on a particular problem or issue. Windows occur following a dramatic event, a focusing event, or the release of a report or study. Attentional triggers can shake up the status quo, breaking the inertia of the existing system and providing the chance to push a problem into the spotlight. Typically, windows are small and do not stay open for long. Windows that follow dramatic events are, of course, unpredictable. However, if an issue has been circulating in appropriate circles and is ripe, it can more quickly capture interest and concern, gaining the urgency and optimism needed to move forward.

Strategic Use of the Media

There are several sources of publicity, each with a unique emphasis, influence on the issue life cycle, and targeted readership. Undesired conditions and latent problems are first noted in statistical documents, academic research, and highly technical and specialized literature. As the condition becomes more visible and a matter of broad public interest, magazines and journals typically focus articles and feature stories in ways that make the issue more personally relevant, better understood, and salient. If there is a sense of urgency, it can then become politicized, or turned into a common item in the mass media and a matter of instantaneous media coverage. Although different sources of information emerge as more important during each one of the phases, the news media plays an important role throughout in raising attention and arousing interest.

The media's impact on actually shaping public opinion continues to be debated (Koren and Klein, 1991). At the federal policy level the media is less important in generating new issues and is more important in amplifying those issues generated elsewhere, such as by dramatic events, focusing events, interest groups, and published research and evaluations. Although it is hard to gauge the media's catalytic effect on the agenda-setting process, the media does focus attention in two specific ways. First, the media is quick to highlight crises, conflicts, and controversies. Often it targets negative events. Conflict is an important media criterion for news worthiness. The news media can easily increase urgency and salience of a public problem by giving greater emphasis and attention to the dramatic, the sensational, and the negative aspects of a problem or issue. For example, when covering two published studies examining the link between radiation exposure and cancer (one showing no increase in cancer and the other showing an increased risk of leukemia), newspaper coverage was significantly higher for the study with the negative results (Koren and Klein, 1991).

Second, how an issue is reported has a significant impact on how the problem is initially characterized or framed. Once an issue has been described in one way early in the issue attention cycle, it is difficult for individuals to reframe the issue to a different perspective.

Particularly in the early phases, catalysts who ignore the media will typically encounter "trouble down the road" (Linsky, 1986). Successful public leaders view the media as opportunities to focus attention on issues rather than as adversaries to be avoided. They use a variety of media in strategic and deliberative ways early in the agenda-setting process. Sometimes public leaders go directly to television stations to get an issue out. When the goal is to reach the opinion makers, the message is taken to print by going to the editorial boards and using established relationships with reporters (Walters, 1994). Radio, particularly talk radio, is increasingly used to raise issues locally. A study of twenty-nine nonprofit agencies and twenty-four talk-show producers on the East and West coasts revealed that talk radio is relatively inexpensive, broadens the base of policy discussions, legitimizes local issues of concern, and acts as a catalyst for political action. A variety of issue "campaigns" on talk-show radio can be used successfully as part of a larger media strategy, such as the "Heal the Bay" effort in Los Angeles to address pollution concerns in the Santa Monica Bay (Aufderheide and Chester, 1990).

Framing and Reframing the Problem

Multiple sources of publicity and media attention are necessary to raise public awareness and concern. Yet the quantity of publicity is not all that counts. Priority issues must be defined or framed in ways that capture and hold broad interest. Problem framing determines whether or not it will receive sufficient attention to reach the policy agenda. Framing should simplify a complex issue, making it more understandable and highlighting one salient element of an interconnected problem over another. Simply put, framing provides a succinct label, metaphor, or way a thinking about a problem, such as the "homeless," "small business incubators," and "elder abuse," which can then crystallize thinking, focus attention, and stimulate discussion.

Framing problems is an important catalytic task. A single problem can be defined various ways by diverse stakeholders, each reflecting a unique perspective and an internalized mental model. Public leaders understand that problems are socially constructed. Individuals view and interpret the same problematic situation in different ways, thus paying particular attention to different aspects of the same problem. Some see the problem of teenage pregnancy as one of poor sex education or the lack of available birth control. Others believe it's due to inadequate parenting by the teen's parents or poor moral development. Education provides another excellent example of how framing highlights different facets and perspectives of a problem. Some educational experts see the country's educational problem as a skill deficit, with schools lacking rigorous curriculum and academic standards. Many parents view the problem as a moral deficit, blaming teachers who do not impose enough discipline. Public officials often describe educational problems as systemic, blaming a sluggish school system bureaucracy. Teachers' unions argue that the real issues are low wages and not enough school days in a school year. Each has a unique perspective and underlying interest, which shades how the issue is defined and interpreted.

Public leadership requires great strategic sensitivity to how a condition, problem, or issue is initially framed, because framing directly influences whether or not individuals will feel that the condition, problem, or issue is urgent and worthy of attention or merely one of a myriad of other current problems. (For more details on strategic framing and reframing, see Chapter Seven.) Further, if the problem is framed in a way that feels overwhelming or unsolvable, it will not generate the requisite sense of optimism or "do-ability." Problem framing has several other impacts.

- It influences how fast the problem gets recognized and reaches the policy agenda.
- It influences who sees this condition as a compelling or urgent problem or opportunity.
- It influences who will be naturally drawn to discussions on the issue, ultimately widening or narrowing who will join in the efforts to address the issue.
- It shapes and directs the generation of options for action.

The media is a very integral part of how a problem is defined and framed. The media formulates the meaning of problems and issues by selecting, screening, and even distorting the flow of information (Lowery and De Fleur, 1988). Once the media has framed an issue in a particular way, it is difficult to alter or change the perspective. Research in cognitive psychology and decision making confirms this. When people are first confronted with a complex issue, their perspective is more malleable. At this early stage, the media has a great impact on shaping how someone defines a problem. As a result, one's later analysis and understanding of an issue are directly shaped by how the issue was initially framed (Fischoff, 1983).

Being thoughtful in framing issues can raise attention and urgency. Child abuse provides an interesting example of the influential nature of a particular label or framing of a social problem. Dr. C. Henry Kempe, a pediatrician conducting funded research from the Children's Bureau, wanted to draw attention to the increasing incidences of physical injuries to children. He designed a seminar for other doctors using the title of "physical abuse," which to many emphasized legally liable and socially deviant behavior. He then renamed the seminar "Battered-Child Syndrome," which downplayed the criminal aspects while highlighting the medical aspects. In 1962 Kempe published a classic article in the *Journal of the American Medical Association* under the same title. Mass media snagged the phrase and the issue became nationally hot. As a result, a model battered-child reporting statute was proposed in 1963, and by 1967 every state in the country had passed a reporting law.

Public Leadership Summary

Elevating a Public Problem to the Policy Agenda

- Stimulate an awareness and emotional concern that a problem or opportunity exists.
- Elevate the problem to priority status by creating a sense of urgency and "do-ability."
- Use attentional triggers and other catalytic mechanisms to expand the number of people who are aware of and concerned about the issue.

Public leaders direct attention toward an urgent problem or opportunity (and away from others) by initially defining a situation in ways that mobilize people in the search for responses. They act as a catalyst, focusing attention of the public, independent organizations and agencies, and the broader community. To more effectively mobilize attention, the following questions are asked.

- Is the issue on the public agenda already? Has it been on the agenda before? If so, why hasn't this stimulated sufficient action already?
- What are the data on the problem? Is there a worsening condition or a troubling comparison?
- Does it need more visibility? How can the project become more real or salient to the public and key decision makers?
- How can the media best be engaged?
- How can the issue be defined or framed to expand the number of those interested and concerned?

Catalysts help others not only to focus on the issue or problem but also to embrace it as a priority. They attempt to get others to see and feel that it is urgent or important enough to warrant investing time and energy. They reveal worsening trends or troubling comparisons with credible data, and use pictures, stories, and anecdotes to make the problematic situation more real and salient. Catalysts take advantage of attentional triggers that propel an issue to front stage. Because the full list of potential problems and issues requiring public attention is vast, and because resources to address each problem are limited, catalytic leaders ensure that a particular issue is more salient, important, and urgent than other potential issues that may be competing for attention and resources.

Using a variety of attentional triggers, the media, and thoughtful framing, catalytic leaders promote a public problem to higher prominence. They focus attention on an urgent issue, expanding public awareness and arousing concern and hope to move a public problem to priority status. Catalysts attempt to frame a problematic situation in ways that capture the attention of key decision makers and the larger population. They try to arouse concern in ways that stimulate the search for responses. No matter how dramatic the focusing events, how revealing the academic studies, or how creative the framing, merely raising the issue to the attention of the public and key decision makers does not solve a public problem. It does, however, provide the rallying point or catalyst around which key stakeholder groups can then be engaged.

Chapter Four

Forming Working Groups
Bringing People Together to Address the Problem

We needed to think beyond the usual suspects.

The types of problems facing public leaders today are interconnected and consequently are immune from technical remedies and quick fixes by any one individual or agency. Public problems cross organizational and jurisdictional boundaries. Successfully addressing them requires collective efforts by many individuals, interest groups, agencies, and jurisdictions. Public leaders must first raise an issue in a way that focuses attention and increases the likelihood that other key individuals and agencies will either be recruited or attracted to address the issue. The second task of public leadership is then to engage people in addressing the problem, convening the diverse set of people, agencies, and interests.

Convening one meeting with one group of individuals is seldom sufficient. Some successful initiatives take years of early-morning breakfasts, late-night meetings, and weekend retreats to move from concern to action. Identifying people to invite "to the table" and then motivating them to join the effort, given competing time pressures, becomes a strategic challenge. Catalysts use their knowledge of the particular issue, knowledge of stakeholders' interests, personal contacts and networks, and personal credibility to convince key stakeholders that participation in the effort is worthy of their involvement. They invest considerable thought and reflection in the beginning of the convening process because the norms and processes established during the first set of meetings have significant and lasting influence over whether people commit their energy and time to addressing an urgent public problem.

There are two distinct approaches to convening critical stakeholders around public issues. The usual approach is to convene around particular solutions, for example, by policy entrepreneurs who champion a particular policy response and develop coalitions around a particular proposed solution or strategy already deemed feasible for addressing the problem (Kingdon, 1984). Mobilizing and coalition-building, political bargaining, trade-offs, and other sorts of compromise tactics are common ways to win support for one's position or solution. The solution-advocacy approach, however, assumes the problem definition as a given. It also tends to divide stakeholders by focusing on parochial interests and preferred solutions rather than on the longer-term results (Chrislip and Larson, 1994).

The second approach is to convene around the problem or issue, rather than around a preferred solution. Here, catalytic leaders do not promote solutions; they promote problems. This is an issue-directed approach where individuals are mobilized around an issue, rather than mobilized around a particular solution. While a catalytic leader is passionate about getting an issue addressed, he or she does not have a strong stake in one particular policy response or predetermined solution. Instead, the leader encourages consideration of a diverse set of strategies. It is a "loose-tight" fit, in which the public leader is tightly focused on the specific issue or outcome desired, but loose about specific strategies.

Collective efforts are successfully mobilized around issues in many ways, but each requires at least initial agreement by key stakeholders. Some approaches are more formal and permanent, such as the North Dakota Consensus Council, which convenes key policymakers around priority issues facing the state. Others are temporary and ad hoc, such as community task forces, action teams, or issue coalitions. Successful efforts are tailored to the issue's unique circumstances and to the broader environment and national context in which the issue is embedded (Bryson, Bromiley, and Jung, 1990; Gray and Hay, 1986). The first question, which typically draws hot debate, is, Who should be invited to the table?

Looking Beyond the Usual Suspects: Who Should Be Invited to the Table?

Although it is often commonly invoked that everyone who wishes to participate must have the opportunity to do so, not all stakeholders participate equally or in the same way (Potupchuk and Polk, 1994). Who is invited to join the effort and who is excluded significantly influences the directions chosen to address the issue and the success of its implementation. In almost all successful cases, a core working group of people is at the table over a long period of time, and other forums and groups tie into the process at various times (Wood and Gray, 1991). Four distinct steps occur when successfully identifying core group members. First, a comprehensive list of all stakeholders is generated. Second, knowledgeholders who can contribute to the problem-solving process are identified. Third, a smaller core working group, coalition, or initiating committee is developed based on such criteria as resources, perspectives, and power. Later, after the core working group is convened and key outcomes or desired results are agreed upon, additional participants are identified to join the problem-solving effort.

The Larger Community of Interests

Identifying specific participants first begins with recognizing all potential stakeholders and knowledgeholders in the issue area. As the definition implies, stakeholders and knowledgeholders are similar in that they hold a stake in or relevant knowledge about the issue. Stakeholders are generally defined as individuals, groups, or organizations with interests in the issue area. As such, they are likely to be affected by either the causes or the consequences of the particular issue. Common questions used to identify potential stakeholders include the following (Bryson and Crosby, 1992; King, 1984):

- Who is affected by the issue?
- Who has an interest in or has expressed an opinion about the issue?
- Who is in a position to exert influence—positively or negatively—on the issue?
- Who ought to care?

Such stakeholder analyses can identify the broad spectrum of individuals and interests that should be considered (see Chapter Seven). In Minnesota's educational reform effort, more than thirty different stakeholder groups were identified (Roberts and King, 1989a). The drawbacks to stakeholder analyses are that they may narrowly focus on the "usual suspects" and that they can overlook two important sets of individuals who add valuable insights and energy to the effort: knowledgeholders and "ripple-effect" stakeholders.

Knowlegeholders

Stakeholder identification is typically based on affected interests, not technical fluency or knowledge. Knowledgeholders, such as academic researchers, think-tank analysts, and institutional planners, hold critical knowledge or technical expertise relevant to the issue, but they may or may not be directly affected by the causes or consequences of the issue. Although sometimes overlapping, both stakeholders and knowledgeholders are critical in developing effective responses to interconnected problems, generating acceptance of specific options, and implementing decisions. Technical analyses can often provide the starting point for group discussions, and knowledgeholders play an important role in defining the scope and the limits of the scientific and technical understanding of the issue.

Four key roles are played by knowledgeholders. First, they assist the discussants to present their concerns and options in more informed ways and with greater technical sophistication. Second, they can level the playing field. In cases where stakeholders are resource poor and where there is an unequal power distribution among group members, technical experts increase access to information. They enable individuals to gain knowledge and insights that help them identify and communicate their interests more clearly (Ozawa, 1991). Third, knowledgeholders can raise new or taboo issues that others may be hesitant to raise publicly. Fourth, and most important, knowledgeholders with more systemic perspectives can stimulate a broader analysis of the interconnected problem. They can suggest novel perspectives that link previously overlooked causes and consequences. They can also offer new information that provides a more coherent picture of an interconnected issue. Such "frame-breaking" and "pattern-making" insights provide powerful catalytic effects.

The strengths of knowledgeholders lie in the application of scientific knowledge to understanding major problems and issues. The interconnectedness of public problems, the often technical narrowness due to specialization by experts, and the interorganizational and political nature of strategy implementation, however, limits knowledgeholder resourcefulness in searching for and selecting alternative options. If technical experts are not following a more systemic perspective, they will view social problems narrowly as technical problems and will naturally recommend technical remedies and correctives. However, interconnected problems, such as homelessness, teenage pregnancy, and economic development, cannot be solved by technical solutions. They require a cross-functional, systemic analysis of interdependent relationships and dynamics among related issues.

Ripple-Effect Stakeholders

As discussed in Chapter One, there are increasing numbers of stakeholders on each interconnected problem and issue. Too often, stakeholder identification considers only the obvious and immediate stakeholders and ignores those impacted by second- and third-order impacts, or ripple effects, of the problem. Although not immediately obvious, ripple-effect stakeholders can be important supporters or antagonists in addressing the issue. One issue provides a striking example of ripple-effect stakeholders and highlights their importance. When asked to list key stakeholders on the issue of global warming, public executives and analysts mention the usual suspects—coastal property owners, farmers, manufacturing industries that produce or use chlorofluorocarbons (CFCs), industries that produce other pollutants such as the auto industry, and air-conditioning manufacturers. Seldom, if ever, is this major ripple-effect stakeholder mentioned: the insurance industry.

In 1980, U.S. meteorological satellites recorded for the first time a growing hole in the ozone above Antarctica, increasing scientists' concerns that CFCs and other chemical emissions were destroying the earth's protective ozone layer. At the same time, the term *greenhouse effect* was coined to describe the global warming resulting from the release of carbon dioxide and other pollutants. Like a greenhouse surrounding the globe, the pollutants let more sunlight in and less heat out, gradually increasing the earth's temperature.

There is broad agreement among scientists that the planet has been warming by, on average, 1 degree over the last century. Although many scientists (as knowledgeholders) have been increasingly concerned about this condition, fewer stakeholders have recognized this as an important issue. The general interest of the population has also fluctuated over the last few years. By 1988, a majority of Americans were familiar with the term *greenhouse effect,* with that year's summer heat wave dramatically increasing Americans' concern. When the weather cooled, however, the number of Americans who considered global warming a threat dropped from the summer high of 77 percent to 53 percent. By 1990 less than one-third of the population was concerned about global warming (Yankelovich, 1991). By the 1990s, the obvious stakeholders were engaged; producers and users of CFCs were slowly responding to increased pressure, and environmental groups were working diligently to raise the public's consciousness on the threat of global warming.

In 1994, however, a new stakeholder joined in the discussion, the insurance industry. Storms, floods, and droughts began hitting populated areas in the United States with greater severity and frequency than predicted. Such natural disasters increased 94 percent over the previous decade, and according to insurance industry analysts, a small increase of 0.9 degrees Fahrenheit could produce a 33 percent increase in hurricane landfalls in the United States, increased severity of storms, an expansion of the hurricane season by 20 days, and a 30 percent annual rise in catastrophic losses. These threats have focused the attention of the insurance industry on global warming, because 50 percent of the U.S. population lives within fifty miles of a coastline. Insurance companies have discovered that they have profound economic stakes in climate change and global warming. They became ripple-effect stakeholders because global warming could, as one executive noted, "bankrupt the industry. . . . The insurance business is first in line to be affected by climate change" (Linden, 1994, p. 79). As a result, the industry has assumed an advocacy role in the global warming debate, and is considering alliances with environmental groups to focus increased attention on climate changes that may be resulting from global warming.

The Right Balance of Stakeholders and Knowledgeholders

Many efforts to address public problems fail because the right people were not included. For example, stakeholders who are excluded can interfere with the implementation of agreed-upon strategies. Later on, they can introduce damaging or conflicting information and visibly question the legitimacy of the group or its decisions. They can also prevent approval by key organizations, agencies, or legislative bodies needed to implement or sustain action (Wood and Gray, 1991). To avoid this, the initial impulse is to involve everyone who wants to participate from the beginning. The inclusion of all stakeholders, however, is seldom practical. A balance must be reached between "getting everyone in on the act and still getting some action." (We are indebted to Harlan Cleveland, who first used this phrase in the 1970s in defining one of the most difficult challenges facing public leaders.) Once the larger community of interests—all potential stakeholders and knowledgeholders—is identified, several iterations can occur to cull the large list down to a more practical size. Consultative forums of various formats are then used as mechanisms to stimulate constructive involvement from those not invited to join the core working group but who still need to be heard.

Individuals Who "Make Things Happen"

A first step is to identify people who can facilitate or ensure implementation of decisions made by the working group. These individuals include public, private, and nonprofit executives who can commit resources—funding, information, or staff—to the implementation of the agreed-upon actions. They are most often individuals who can make on-the-spot decisions to commit to action without having to seek someone's permission first. (This is particularly important in public-private partnerships. See Waddock, 1989.) Facilitators also include individuals who may be active in a broad range of organizations and who can commit portions of their diverse personal network to the effort (Selsky, 1991). Further, when enabling legislation is likely or necessary, successful efforts also include participants who can lobby or mobilize others to lobby and legislators who can champion and defend the initiative in legislative committees and other political arenas (Bryson and Crosby, 1992).

Although *power* is often considered a dirty word in leadership, both organizational and personal power are exercised in addressing any urgent issue. The more systemic the actions that might be needed to get at the root of the matter, the more strength and energy is required. With interconnected public problems, no hierarchically based authority can make command-like decisions. Instead, agencies are "arrayed like beads on a bracelet," with some beads larger and brighter than others and none possessing identical power and influence within the problem area (Laumann and Knoke, 1988).

Assessing stakeholder power is central to the early stages of convening. Reflecting on her efforts to stimulate statewide educational reform, a former Minnesota commissioner of education noted, "You had to find out where the power was and those are the ones you have to court first" (Roberts, 1985, p. 1039). Power is not solely a function of hard resource holdings, such as money, size of staffs, public authority, or information sources. It also emerges from one's connectivity to others—one's central role in relevant networks. Power is generally the ability to influence or block change within an issue domain. Roberts and King (1989b) note that stakeholder power in an interconnected arena can be assessed in four dimensions:

- Access to key decision makers
- Credibility, a history of committed action in the issue area, and good contacts and interpersonal networks
- New, fresh ideas, including background expertise on the issue plus a willingness to consider and champion new alternatives
- Resource control and an ability to dedicate money, time, and people to address the issue

A first pass at identifying who should be invited to the table commonly includes those who have the capacity or power (that is, connections, credibility, openness, and control of resources) to further the implementation of any options by the working group. This includes those who can make things happen and those who can block things from happening. Those with the power to block or thwart implementation must be considered at the beginning stages because, as one public leader warned, "Negative energy can oftentimes be much more powerful than positive energy."

Individuals Who Think Outside the Box

A common error made by public leaders is convening only well-regarded professionals and opinion leaders with recognized interests and power in the issue area. However, effective analysis of interconnected problems also requires the participation of individuals who can see the issue in entirely different contexts. Those with a broader, systemic, and long-term perspective often can initiate what is called "frame-breaking." Indeed, Thomas Kuhn's classic analysis of paradigm shifts (1970) found that major scientific breakthroughs were stimulated by scientists who were not the field's established thinkers, but who were usually either very young or very new to the field.

Such innovators are often new to the issue or to the community and have little commitment to established practice. They are more likely to see connections and options others may have missed or disregarded. In analyzing a collective effort to change Minnesota's educational system, researchers found that involvement of the usual stakeholders for educational reform—teachers and educators—generated enthusiasm for reform through incremental change. In contrast, business leaders and others outside the system promoted more radical innovations and restructuring (Roberts and Bradley, 1991). There is a key role for individuals, typically outsiders, in stimulating innovative, frame-breaking, and system-changing responses to public issues (Grady and Chi, 1994; Gersick, 1989).

Varied Sizes of Successful Working Groups

Most often, a small working group (called a planning group, core group, or initiating committee) consists of a critical mass who emerged from the stakeholder assessment. Unfortunately, there is no magical size. Successful core working groups can vary from six to sixty. Different process designs can accommodate larger or smaller numbers of individuals. Although some public initiatives are open to all interested parties, there are usually multiple levels of participation, and not all critical stakeholders need to participate fully or in the same fashion. Generally, the core working group must be large enough to include those considered critical to implementation, but small enough to think creatively about potential strategies.

Three general guides are important when deciding on the size of the working group (although in practice they are infinitely more complex to balance). First, a diversity of viewpoints and perspectives should reflect the complexity of the issue. Effective working groups include members who do not all think alike and who will not discourage new or different ideas. The more complex and more tightly interconnected the problem is with other issues, the more diverse the perspectives must be. Such diversity generates considerable conflict in defining the issue and in deciding appropriate responses, and requires additional time in dialogue and deliberation. However, when effectively facilitated, conflict leads to increased involvement among participants, a richer discussion, and a wider array of options considered (see Chapter Eight).

Second, working groups should be large enough to include those considered critical to implementation, but small enough to develop agreement. Those who will be responsible for implementation must be included in the process. This includes those who have sufficient power and resources to make things happen as well as those who can block things from happening. It may be better to include too many rather than too few to prevent influential outsiders from seriously challenging the agreements reached. However, as mentioned earlier, not all critical stakeholders need to participate fully or in the same fashion.

Third, design other forms of participation for those not enlisted to the core working group. A dynamic and evolving inclusion process uses tiers or layers of stakeholder and knowledgeholder groups, some with full participation and some with partial participation. Size is best managed by creating a core group connected with multiple working groups, task forces, or planning committees. A core working group generates and requires more intense participation, while additional working groups and task forces can facilitate involvement by other stakeholders and knowledgeholders. Although it requires coordination and additional resources, such a multilevel approach with clear roles and responsibilities is more inclusive and less likely to become "elitist," and it integrates a wider range of interests, experts, and citizens. Inclusion is not driven by a sense of equity or mandate for citizen participation. Rather, it is motivated by the need to connect core participants with sound ideas and unique perspectives that might otherwise be overlooked, and to develop a broader ownership for reaching tangible public outcomes.

Three Rules of Successful Efforts

1. Do not start without considering all the potential stakeholders and knowledgeholders, particularly ripple-effect stakeholders and others beyond the usual group of suspects.
2. Do not invite all stakeholders and knowledgeholders to join the core working group. Those to be considered can make things happen, can block things from happening, and can contribute to making the best decision.
3. Create multiple tiers of participation, such as consultative forums, to generate input from those not participating on the core working group but who still need to be heard.

Unfortunately, there is no one "right way" to structure the multiple levels of full and partial participation in every issue area. The appropriate configuration must be custom-designed for each effort. A common multilevel approach to stakeholder participation, however, includes at least three levels of participation: a small group that acts as a group catalyst or initiating committee; a core working group of diverse stakeholders; and multiple working groups that engage a wider circle of stakeholders and knowledgeholders who are affected by or interested in the issue.

The initial catalyst for convening a working group is typically one person or a few individuals who feel compelled to stimulate action. This smaller group most often includes a few passionate individuals who act as an initiating committee to then mobilize a larger core group. The core working group can range in size from nine to twenty-five members; it represents the diverse set of perspectives necessary to arrive at a high-quality decision; and it includes individuals with implementation power once agreements are reached. The core working group gathers relevant information from a variety of sources, generates and analyzes multiple options, and develops recommendations or reaches agreement on specific directions for action. In addition, they craft appropriate task groups or consultative forums to invite quality input and expand participation.

Task groups ensure that critical perspectives and information are not overlooked, and expand the technical resources for addressing the issue. Task groups can be established around substantive areas, geographical areas, or interest areas. The core working group can use one set of task groups to gather information and identify subissues. It can then create new task groups to generate strategies and action plans for addressing the issue, or it can retain the same working groups throughout the entire process.

Eliciting the Participation of Key Individuals

Public leaders not only must be able to identify a core group of potential participants, but also must have sufficient influence and connections to elicit their participation. Recruiting is essentially an interpersonal process, done one by one. People get recruited into alliances and collective efforts through friends, acquaintances, or individuals who are perceived as credible and trustworthy. Catalysts almost always begin with an existing network—a set of relationships developed and nurtured over years. Trust has been established, and there is a history of interaction and exchanging information. A prior understanding of strengths and resources can jump-start the catalytic process.

Because each new issue requires somewhat different players for success, an existing network is merely the starting point of contact. Public leaders then move out of their comfort zones to engage others who can contribute. Even with existing networks, identifying and motivating participants to join a collective effort can take considerable energy and time, sometimes years (Jones and Siegel, 1993; Olshfski, 1990). Convening becomes even more difficult when no preexisting network can be used as a foundation. People may be suspicious of the convener's agenda. If trust is low or if the convener has no previous track record, convening a working group takes even more time. Catalysts use their knowledge of the problem area, the knowledge of stakeholders' interests and interrelationships, and even personal charm to convince key stakeholders that participation in the effort is worthwhile.

Willingness to respond to recruitment efforts and join in a collective effort often depends on whether or not the stakeholder or knowledgeholder feels he or she has something to gain. Common reasons for unwillingness or inability to join include the potential loss of power or funding, ideological or cultural differences that create uncompromising conflict in core values, and legal barriers for joint action. Closer analysis reveals that willingness to participate is more complex. Individuals and organizations will join in collective efforts when they feel

- An interest or stake in an issue and that the issue is urgent (Logsdon, 1991)
- A sense of interdependence—that they cannot solve this issue alone but must join in a collective effort to address it (Logsdon, 1991)
- That the convener is credible, and the other stakeholders invited to the table belong there (legitimacy of membership) (Gray and Wood, 1991)
- That they have skills or insights to offer (Hinton and others, 1997)
- That the effort is likely to produce desirable results and is worthy of their expertise and energy (Bryson and Crosby, 1992)

Participation can also be induced through forced compliance. Mandel (1984) found that dominant agencies in interorganizational networks can use their formal power and authority to force or induce participation. This could be a legislative mandate to collaborate or a requirement by a funding source. In this type of recruitment, the formal authority uses implicit or explicit references to the control of critical resources to "convince" stakeholders and knowledgeholders to participate. It may not be overtly coercive, but stakeholders and knowledgeholders are aware the formal authority has access to coercive measures, if necessary, to force participation or sufficient mechanisms to reward participation.

Short of forced compliance, the two most critical factors influencing the willingness of an individual to participate in collective efforts are the perceived stakes or interests one has in addressing the issue, and the perceived interdependence with other agencies and groups in effectively addressing the issue. A revealing analysis of several successful public-private collaborative efforts found that an organization or group must realize its interests are achieved by resolving or ameliorating the problem. The organization or group must also believe it has to participate with other organizations and groups for the issue to be effectively resolved or ameliorated. The organization or group must see that its interests cannot be achieved solely through independent action (Wood and Gray, 1991; Logsdon, 1991). In other words, key stakeholders must recognize they have a significant stake in addressing the issue and must believe that participation with other legitimate and resourceful stakeholders is required for any successful action to occur.

Having strong stakes or interests alone does not provide sufficient motivation for an organization to join. It may believe that it can solve the problem independently and that a collaborative, joint effort is not required. For example, a corporation coping with difficulties in recruiting qualified entry-level staff may develop a remedial education program in reading and mathematics, as Motorola did with a $30 million training program (National Alliance of Business, 1989). Individuals or agencies with high stakes but low perceived interdependence will not join a collective or collaborative effort. Motivating them to commit time and resources to join a collective effort requires a heightened sense that the problem can't be solved alone and that it requires a joint, interdependent effort to be addressed successfully.

Similarly, perceived interdependence alone does not provide the necessary motivation. Although the organization may understand that it is tied into a network or web, the issue may not be urgent or salient enough to commit time and resources jointly. Organizations are highly selective in their attention to issues and they attempt to conserve or husband their resources (Laumann and Knoke, 1988). If an issue is not a priority—if the stakes are seen as too small or too ambiguous to warrant participation—then the organization will pay attention to other issues that seem more urgent or critical to its central mission or interests.

The catalytic spark provided by the public leader in convening a working group is often the quality and credibility of his or her relationships. Without adequate credibility, stakeholder and knowledgeholder participation and commitment is unlikely to materialize. Research in convening working groups (Gray and Hay, 1986; Gray, 1989, Pasquero, 1991; Kingdon, 1984) shows that credibility is something that has to be earned in several ways:

- Through perceived expertise combined with political savvy
- Through perceived competence in group facilitation and negotiation generally
- Through an ability to be even-handed and a willingness to consider diverse points of view (but not necessarily be unbiased)
- Through a formal or informal position of authority and influence recognized by potential participants
- Through a reputation, history, or track record of successful collaborative efforts that were clearly not a vehicle for personal gain

For individuals to participate, they also need to feel that the effort is "do-able" and has a potential for success. People will not commit time and energy if the effort seems hopeless or out of their realm of influence. Further, people are more easily engaged when they feel they have something to offer beyond financial resources, such as personal talent, expertise, and skills. An analysis of civic entrepreneurs in several regions and states found that they not only had a sense of the interdependence between the long-term success of their company and the community's vitality (that is, the interconnectedness of the economy and the community), but that they also wanted to contribute their unique skills to "making a difference" (Henton and others, 1997).

Convening the First Meetings

There is no one prescribed set of activities or rigid steps to convene a core working group, although several key elements often lead to successful beginnings. Particularly critical are a safe or neutral space for meetings, especially when the issues are hot, and a credible process for proceeding based on a shared sense of purpose with clear roles and norms. In particularly conflictual areas, it may take several meetings before individuals overcome skepticism or mistrust and feel comfortable committing to a collective effort. They want to believe that the process is focused, not driven by hidden agendas, and is relatively open. Thus, catalysts pay close attention to first meetings and invest considerable time and energy in the initial process of convening.

Safe Space for Informal Exploration

Successful efforts across the country have discovered the importance of investing in beginnings. A common thread in these successful first meetings is that they are convened in a safe space—a neutral location—and that it is understood there is no commitment in first attending. The North Dakota Consensus Council explicitly designed its facilities to provide a safe space that encourages informal exploration and enables groups "to meet comfortably to explore ideas in a neutral, friendly, yet businesslike, environment" (Jones and Siegel, 1993). A major problem with all working groups of diverse stakeholders is getting them to trust each other. Successful initiatives recognize this dilemma and provide opportunities in a neutral way for informal exploring of interests, perspectives, and backgrounds while avoiding paralyzing "lock-ins" at the beginning of the process (Chrislip and Larson, 1994).

First Meetings of the Applegate Partnership

The Applegate River watershed encompasses nearly 500,000 acres of forested land in southern Oregon. It became the site for the establishment of a nationally recognized model for developing community-based responses to the timber conflict gnawing at the economy of the Northwest. The Applegate Partnership began in 1992 over a cup of coffee between an environmentalist and a member of the logging industry. Together they decided to engage a larger group of community citizens in addressing a potentially explosive confrontation between these two opposing stakeholder groups. Nearly fifty guests representing a range of people and affiliations were invited to an evening barbecue. During that first meeting, individuals were asked specifically not to talk about their job, position, or affiliation. Instead, they were asked to share something personal about their background, their pastimes in the communities, and their experiences in the forest. The loggers talked about their love for the woods and for fishing and hunting. Environmentalists spoke of their concern for maintaining the traditions and culture of their towns in this rural area. The first meetings between these very divided stakeholders avoided speeches and debates and focused on what they valued about their forest. They explored each other's hopes and fears for the Applegate watershed and the communities nested in it. Sharing their experiences and concerns during the barbecue helped to begin breaking down long-held stereotypes of each other. Many participants realized that they shared common goals for the forest.

At the end of the first meeting, a smaller group agreed to meet again to discuss common concerns. They planned to explore potential ways to preserve the ecology of the watershed's forest while allowing sufficient timber harvest to maintain economic viability of the communities in the region. The group of fifty was distilled to a group of eighteen, which included individuals from a wide variety of backgrounds and interests. A month later, an even smaller group began meeting every other week and became the Board of the Applegate Partnership (Buffum, 1993).

Legitimate Process for Proceeding

Participant commitment hinges on the belief that the process is legitimate, is not dominated by a particular stakeholder or group, and will lead to desirable results. Particularly with public-private efforts, participants desire a disciplined process that is fair, minimally political, and outcome-driven (Henton and others, 1997.) The three most common concerns during initial meetings revolve around purpose, procedures, and timelines. As participants struggle with these issues in first meetings, a more structured process usually evolves for the working group to explore and analyze potential strategies. (For more detail, see Chapter Five.)

Clear Purpose

During the first meetings, there will naturally be differing perceptions of the issue and different assumptions and interests at work. There is typically concern about the group's relation to other groups, agencies, and initiatives around this particular public problem. If the group's purpose remains vague during first meetings, or its activities appear to duplicate the purpose of any member organization, individuals may be unwilling to participate and may even attempt to subvert or sabotage the efforts of the core working group. Successful working groups must have a unique purpose and a sphere of activities that differentiate it from other groups, agencies, and institutions. The sphere of activities can overlap but should not be identical to that of related agencies. This unique quality starts to create an important psychological boundary required for successful joint action by multiple organizations. It establishes a defined niche for the group that can more easily generate the support (or acquiescence) of established authorities or powers (Hood, Logsdon, and Thompson, 1993; Chrislip and Larson, 1994).

Ground Rules and Norms

Typically, groups will want to dive into their work with little thought about ground rules. Expectations about acceptable behavior are imported by the individual members, and only when something dramatic occurs does the group examine and collectively establish core norms to guide member behavior (Gersick, 1989). With effective working groups, procedural ground rules and behavioral norms are established during first meetings, setting clear guidelines about how the group will handle issues, conflicts, and decision making. In particularly difficult areas, it is also essential to discuss and agree how the rules will be revised and how guidelines will be enforced.

Procedural ground rules are the written and understood operating procedures that help create a fair, safe, and legitimate process (Carpenter and Kennedy, 1988). They often cover such procedures as

- Decision-making process (Will voting be by consensus or by majority?)
- Representation (Do individuals represent their respective agencies or are they free agents?)
- Proxies (Can members send substitutes if a meeting cannot be attended?)
- Relationship of the core working group to other external agencies
- Logistics such as minutes and record keeping

In collective efforts that have strong inherent value conflicts, or which have a large web of affected and interested stakeholders, additional time is spent in the first meetings considering additional procedural guidelines, such as What is the appropriate use of an outside facilitator or mediator? and Who is responsible for paying for the services? How will new members to the core working group be selected and invited? What is the structure and process of participation for additional working groups so as to involve the larger circle of stakeholders and knowledgeholders? How will confidentiality of the meetings be maintained? What is the relationship to the media?

One of the more difficult ground rules to address is how new members are to be selected and invited to join. It is very common that once the working group agrees on a common purpose or outcome, participants realize that certain stakeholders or knowledgeholders may have been overlooked and need to be involved. The core working group will need to agree on who is invited to join the core working group, and how others can be involved who are not asked to join but whose input might be relevant and helpful.

Equally important in establishing a safe and legitimate process is the identification of behavioral norms shared by group members. Norms are unwritten or implied rules guiding individual behavior in groups (like those governing behavior in elevators) and exert a powerful influence on the group process. Unless norms are explicitly articulated in the first meetings, the ones that naturally emerge early in the group formation tend to set the tone and culture of the group throughout its existence. Norms common to successful efforts revolve around four areas:

1. How to respond effectively to (or sometimes stimulate) differing perspectives, values, and other sources of conflict
2. How to ensure equal airtime in group discussions (and how to prevent one or more from monopolizing airtime)
3. How to stimulate continued mutual learning among group members
4. How to build in social time, such as lunch breaks, dinners together, and facilities tours, to nurture and sustain personal relationships during the process

Clear Roles

In addition to having explicit guidelines and norms, an effective work group establishes relatively clear functional roles. Role clarity is important for several reasons. Cross-boundary work groups, interagency task forces, and other multiparty groups lack the formal authority that would designate leadership in an hierarchical organization. This leadership ambiguity can be problematic in interorganizational collaboration because group members are typically leaders in their agencies. Without sufficient discussions during first meetings, people will naturally operate on different assumptions about their roles and those of others.

Role clarity requires an understanding about who or what each group member represents. Do individuals represent themselves or represent their group, association, agency, or institution and its particular point of view? Even when individuals do not sit as formal representatives of an organization, some feel they are carrying the weight of representation. They may tend to behave toward others in terms of their corresponding group membership or feel constrained by the viewpoints and policy orientations of their associations (Hood, Logsdon, and Thompson, 1993; Roberts and Bradley, 1991).

A credible process also requires a clear understanding of the role of staff assistance. Staff support may strike some as mundane or obvious, but the presence of sufficient staffing assistance and organizational support dramatically fosters a working group's ability to explore strategies for action (Hackman, 1990). In all interorganizational and intersectoral working groups, and particularly in lay citizen task forces, participants must have easy access to research reports and experts, data, forecasts, trend analyses, and research to invent, generate, and select appropriate strategies for addressing the public problem.

Appropriate Sequence of Activities

Joint problem solving by diverse and interdependent stakeholders obviously takes more time than decisions on simpler issues. Unfortunately, participants face time pressures, external deadlines, and other demanding commitments. During initial meetings, views naturally differ over the possible sequencing of activities, tasks, and related time frames, and there is usually a tendency to jump to solutions. Groups feel driven to rush, meet multiple deadlines, search for solutions, and seek agreement quickly to get visible results. They adjust their rate of work based on time constraints (Gersick, 1989).

Legislative, regulatory, or other types of deadlines compel groups to compress time, limit discussion, and generate solutions without spending sufficient effort to understand and define the issue.

During first meetings, catalysts thus seek agreements on the sequencing of various tasks (but not necessarily on the exact scheduling). A custom-tailored sequence of activities fits the parameters facing a group's unique circumstances, timelines, and authority. It is guided by externally imposed dates, such as legislative timelines, funding cycles, and other expected events. Successful groups, however, ensure they spend more time in problem identification and redefinition than on searching for solutions (Bryson, Bromiley, and Jung, 1990). What matters most is whether or not the group has first spent enough time identifying and defining the problem that needs to be addressed. Throughout first meetings, as more information is revealed, the problem is further refined and redefined. This sequence slows a working group's natural tendency to move too prematurely toward adopting one particular solution.

Public Leadership Summary

Engaging People in the Effort

- Identify the full spectrum of stakeholders and knowledge-holders.
- Enlist core working group members and design multiple levels of participation to ensure a broader reach.
- Convene the first meetings and invest in beginnings.

Once the problem has been elevated to a priority status, the second task of public leadership is to convene the diverse set of stakeholders, knowledgeholders, and decision makers needed to initiate and sustain action. Public leaders bring people together—different factions with often diverse perspectives and sensitivities—to focus their collective attention. Various mobilizing strategies are used, but committing one's time and energy is based significantly on having high stakes and an awareness of the interdependence required in addressing the issue. Key questions asked by catalysts include

- Who are the stakeholders, knowledgeholders, and other resources?
- Who can make things happen in this issue area? Who can block action?
- Who are appropriate newcomers or outsiders with unique perspectives?
- What is an appropriate critical mass to initiate action?
- Who should be invited to participate in the effort to address the issue?
- How can core participants, once identified, be motivated to join the collective effort?
- What other forms and levels of participation could generate quality ideas?
- How can first meetings be convened to create a safe space and legitimate process for problem solving?

Stimulating human effort in pursuit of common goals is an essential leadership task, and public leaders provide an important catalytic role by eliciting the participation and commitment of diverse and interdependent people to address a troubling situation. Merely convening a meeting, however, is not enough to stimulate concerted action. Successful efforts require sufficient investment of time and attention to planning the first meetings, to creating a safe space to informally explore interests, and to offering a legitimate process for diverse and independent stakeholders to engage each other in deliberative discussions. Such beginnings help build trust and a shared perspective—essential components for success. As the process unfolds, catalysts engage the working group in a more intense and reiterative process of problem defining and problem solving. In practice, they facilitate, negotiate, and mediate a pinball-like process of defining the issue, identifying shared outcomes, and developing multiple strategies to achieve the outcomes.

Chapter Five

Creating Strategies
Stimulating Multiple Strategies and Options for Action

We realized that we needed multiple strategies, by multiple agencies, all aiming toward the same outcome.

Public leaders convene diverse stakeholders and then help to convert and transform their concerns for the issue into viable strategies for action. They create, stimulate, and facilitate common directions out of disparate energies. This task is a critical dimension of public leadership. It involves providing a catalyst to a group of diverse stakeholders to develop multiple strategies to achieve specific outcomes.

Group processes cannot be controlled or tightly managed among diverse stakeholders. Working groups develop unique styles, rhythms, and performance guidelines. However, catalysts provide leadership in two unique ways. First, they help create conditions that increase the likelihood that the working group will successfully forge agreement and commitment to specific strategies and actions. Second, they help fashion a custom-tailored strategy development process to fit the parameters facing the working group's unique circumstances, timelines, and authority. Selective interventions by catalysts in these two areas significantly help interdependent stakeholders to work together in stimulating and productive ways.

Essential Conditions of Effective Working Groups

In the corporate world, creative and productive working groups are characterized by a preoccupation with the organizational task, intellectual intensity and exchange, emotional intensity and commitment, and dissolution once the work is finished. (Such groups are called "hot-groups" by Leavitt and Lipman-Blumen, 1995.) Such energetic working groups targeting interconnected public problems are less common, but are increasingly receiving attention. Analyses of recent public-private partnerships and cross-sectoral alliances, international collaborative projects, collaborative community alliances, and consensus-based planning initiatives reveal four elements or conditions that provide the essential foundation for successfully forging agreements on strategies and actions.

- A core of committed and motivated group members, with sufficient skills and knowledge, who do not relinquish their organizational autonomy or institutional independence
- A unifying purpose based on agreement on desired outcomes that identifies the desired results, or end-outcomes, the group hopes to achieve
- A deliberative form of interaction with agreed-upon norms that enhances mutual learning and conflict resolution, stimulates shared leadership, builds trust, and is facilitated by both personal and electronic linkages
- A structured, credible process of strategy development that is custom-tailored to the context and situation and that allots sufficient time to problem defining and redefining

(Research that highlights these four features includes groundbreaking and award-winning analyses on successful cross-sectoral alliances and public-private partnerships, by Hood, Logsdon, and Thompson, 1993, and Roberts and Bradley, 1991; on fifty-eight cases of community change projects, by Bryson, Bromiley, and Jung, 1990; on successfully sustained international collaborative projects, by Cleveland, 1993; on innovative cross-boundary and cross-functional corporate teams, by Lipnack and Stamps, 1993; on state and regional civic entrepreneurs stimulating innovative economic development strategies, by Henton and others, 1997; on five consensus-based models applicable to transportation planning, by DuPraw and Potupchuk, 1993; on twenty-seven diverse teams, including customer service teams, performing groups, and task forces, by Hackman, 1990.)

Core of Committed and Motivated Group Members

As noted earlier, there is no magical number of core participants. Although larger groups generate more alternative options per member, the potential for agreement declines. Large groups are thus preferable in the early phases of exploring and generating options, but smaller groups are best in the later phases of selecting options and making choices (Nutt, 1989).

Getting the right size is less important than getting the right mix. Working groups require a mix of members with adequate task-relevant and interpersonal skills, each contributing specific capabilities—perspectives, interests, skills, and resources—to address the issue in innovative, sustained ways. Successful working groups have a core of committed members with adequate skills and knowledge to contribute to a strategy development process. The commitment and motivation of the multiple participants are essential ingredients to sustain the group through its deliberations, particularly if group members have little experience in working together collaboratively.

Although participants may come together for joint problem solving, sustained commitment and motivation requires that they retain their individual independence and autonomy. Collaborative groups seeking interdependent solutions do not require members to relinquish independent decision-making power. Individual members retain their independence even when they work toward common or shared interests. In successful international and cross-border initiatives, such as developing the global weather satellite system, combining resources, imagination, and technology for joint problem solving required working group members to pool their actions, not give up independence (Cleveland, 1993).

Unified Purpose Based on Agreement on Desired Outcomes

Effective working groups develop a clear understanding of their purpose and objectives. In ineffective groups, the lack of goal clarity is a major reason for failure. Agreement on purpose happens in two ways. First, the group agrees on a tangible product that will be produced at the end of their efforts. End-products most often take the form of written reports and recommendations for specific projects, programs, or policies. In some cases, the product is a negotiated agreement that commits stakeholders to specific actions. For example, the Louisiana Department of Environmental Quality's action plan, *Leap to 2000* (1991), documents specific agreements on responsibilities for enhancing the natural environment of the state. Often the end products are action plans that identify commitments of time and resources, responsibilities for implementation, and measurable benchmarks for monitoring and evaluation.

The second type of agreement focuses on the end-outcome. The end-outcome describes the ultimate outcome or result that individuals are attempting to achieve. For instance, public-private partnerships benefit from developing a process discipline oriented to producing results. They identify desired results and outcomes early in first meetings, and continuously revisit and refine the outcomes during their deliberations. The most effective end-outcomes are highly motivating and are seen as worthwhile, but they are not overly general visions. Reducing child abuse or teenage pregnancy are clear outcomes that can mobilize diverse agencies and stakeholders. The mere goal of creating jobs, on the other hand, is often too vague to rally diverse, and often competing, agencies.

End-Outcome as Magnet for Collaboration

Individuals typically start with passionate discussion of the problem and their often competing views on how to resolve it. Without a common purpose or shared outcome, the group will not coalesce and may even disintegrate. Agreement on end-outcomes is essential when diverse stakeholders try to accomplish something together that they could not achieve alone. As former state legislator and chair of Oregon's Multnomah County Board of Commissioners Beverly Stein emphasized, the agreed-upon outcome becomes "the magnet for collaboration" in diverse policy groups, serving as a point of reference that sparks energy and creates a focus that holds individuals' attention. Outcomes serve as the starting point to begin the group's deliberations. They provide the unifying purpose—its guiding Northern Star—to help navigate the working group through a chaotic and conflict-ridden process of strategy development that can otherwise overwhelm and discourage key participants. (See Chapter Seven for details on defining outcomes.) Outcomes focus attention toward a future desired state. Working backward, participants develop energy, enthusiasm, optimism, and high commitment (Weisbord, 1992).

Nonhierarchical Guidance Mechanism

In nonhierarchical groups, the desired outcome replaces the traditional glue of hierarchy. Rather than a formal leader or hierarchical authority asserting control, outcomes drive the group, focusing and orienting its actions. Agreement on end-outcomes provides a powerful nonhierarchical "guidance mechanism" for making ongoing course corrections during the strategy development process. It is not an agreement on a set of underlying values or a common ideology, but rather an agreement on a common future state of affairs.

Early agreement on desired outcomes provides an underlying stability when the deliberations get turbulent, heated, and emotional. It creates a buoy to which the participants can repeatedly return to reorient discussions when confronted with deeply held value conflicts. The existence of a superordinate goal or outcome has long been recognized as an important element in resolving conflict. Thus, agreeing on outcomes during first meetings provides an important foundation to assist working groups during the inevitable storms of personality conflicts, value differences, and politics.

Getting initial agreement on outcomes also reduces the potential for early group derailment due to eruption of solution wars and turf battles. Typically, participants come with predetermined solutions to meet underlying interests, and therefore want to jump to the identification of solutions. Initially focusing on outcomes helps avoid debating preconceived solutions. Competition among alternative proposed strategies for action is natural and expected; however, agreeing on the desired outcome provides a focus and direction for information gathering, a broader solution generation, and a measure by which various strategies can be compared and selected.

Caution Against Ambiguous Group Visions

Analysis of successful cross-functional teams and interorganizational task forces clearly highlights that the more boundaries that need to be crossed in any collaborative effort, the greater the need to agree on specific desired outcomes or tangible results (Lipnack and Stamps, 1993). This contradicts earlier organizational leadership orthodoxies that suggested that a unique, inspiring vision "as vague as a dream" is sufficient to stimulate successful collective action toward interconnected public problems. Visions can often be inspiring, but without specific end-outcomes, they do not provide sufficient "pull" or focus to stimulate a diverse, nonhierarchical group to move in the same direction. Because visions are often too vague, various stakeholders project their interpretation, thus creating no more than a collective "Rorschach test" where everyone sees his or her interests as primary and others' as secondary. With broad, vague visions, stakeholders can justify almost any strategy or option as relevant to reaching the general vision. From the local level of reducing juvenile crime to the global arena of eradication of infectious diseases, agreement on desired end-outcomes is essential for successful group deliberations and concerted action on interconnected problems.

Unfortunately, clarifying end-outcomes tugs against a tendency in the public sector to achieve early consensus by developing lofty visions and ambiguous goals. Competing interests are clumped into a broad vision that includes everyone's personal or agency agenda. One example occurred with a small group of state legislators who had convened to consider improvements in the state's juvenile system. In the first meeting, they quickly expanded the group's focus to capture each of their personal issues. The purpose broadened to include reform of the state's criminal justice system (including adult corrections); issues of social justice, particularly racial and ethnic inequities in incarceration rates; and increased funding for human services reform. Although juvenile crime is interconnected with these critical issues, the broad purpose resulted in diffused attention, arguments over the root causes of the problem, divisiveness, and early dissatisfaction of the process among group members. After several meetings, each one attracting fewer and fewer participants, the group refocused its attention on an agreed-upon outcome, reducing juvenile crime, particularly in the state's metropolitan areas. Consensus on the desired outcome allowed for a more diverse and wide-ranging discussion of the multiple causes of the problem and multiple policy options.

Deliberative Form of Interaction That Enhances Mutual Learning

Effective working groups develop and nurture a deliberative process of mutual learning about the issue and alternative policy and programmatic responses. Mutual learning is characterized by shared leadership during various phases, personal and electronic communication links, and a spiral of rising trust. Catalysts help design and initiate the early establishment of a deliberative interaction process because interaction patterns created early in the group set lasting precedents. If not attended to in the first meetings, recurring interactional patterns emerge that are heavily influenced by expectations and by the dynamics established before the group convened (Gersick, 1988).

Process of Mutual Learning

Mutual learning is not necessarily a sequential process. It is more like a pinball game than an orderly progression. Ideas are clarified and modified on an ongoing basis, and progress is marked not by perfection of consensus, but by the refinement of the discussions. Discussions are designed to assure that group members learn about each other's perspectives, underlying interests, and unarticulated assumptions. It is not merely a permissive atmosphere that tolerates thinking out loud. It is an active spirit of inquiry where new information and insights are sought and shared, initial assumptions are questioned, competing ideas discussed, differences explored and addressed, and multiple options considered to achieve agreed-upon outcomes (Gersick, 1988; Innes, 1992; Weisbord, 1992). Catalysts provide a spark for mutual learning by avoiding commitment to preconceived solutions and by clarifying and summarizing shared insights at key points in discussions (see Chapter Eight for more details).

The success of the North Dakota Consensus Council is based on a nonattributive environment where policymakers could "play with preliminary ideas without being embarrassed publicly and test ideas in nonpolarized forums" (Jones and Siegel, 1993, p. 54). Mutual learning is enhanced through self-critical reflection that seeks to improve the process. Time is taken to evaluate and reexamine where the group is going, how the process is unfolding, and how far the group has progressed. The norms, structure, and process are adjusted to reflect the group's evolving relationships (Roberts and Bradley, 1991). If this self-reflection is not structured into the process from the beginning, individuals will discuss their concerns about the interactive process during a break or after meetings, instead of raising their concerns in the group. If specific times and norms are not established at the beginning for self-critical reflection, a group will naturally take a step back around the midpoint of its lifespan and adjust its pace of work based on a more private or internalized assessment of the group's task accomplishment (Gersick, 1988.)

Mutual learning relies on the group's ability to address differing perspectives, interests, and values. Conflict is a natural part of multiparty, collaborative attempts to address public problems. In cross-sectoral working groups such as local public-private sector efforts, strongly held stereotypes of government and business tend to create conflicts that inhibit productive interaction (Waddock, 1989). Conflicts in community collaboration among multiple public and nonprofit agencies are also common when the chronic or unstable resource shortages provoke interagency competition. Within these natural tensions, a balance must always be worked out. On the one hand, a lack of conflict may indicate low involvement or commitment by group members. On the other hand, excessive conflict can be destructive, creating vicious circles of negative emotions, posturing, and personal attacks. A balance must be created where members work constructively on their differences and use their different perspectives and interests to invent new strategies and options. (For more details, see Chapter Eight).

Shared Leadership

Leadership diversity and fluidity is an essential feature of successful working groups. The leadership function shifts and is shared by several participants. Individuals come to the fore depending on the task at hand, inspiration, or problem facing the group. At different times, individuals step forward to argue for a need, enlist support, resolve conflict, or obtain resources, and then they step out of that lead role. This is particularly important in cross-functional teams (Lipnack and Stamps, 1993) and in public-private collaborations, because most or all of the members are already leaders to some degree in their home organizations (Hood, Logsdon, and

Thompson, 1993). Working group members take responsibility for leadership at different times for different tasks, thus allowing relevant expertise and skills to be applied during the process. In this fashion, group leadership is maximized. It is a "leader-full" process rather than a "leader-less" one.

Personal and Electronic Communication Linkages

Lipnack and Stamps (1993) found that the key ingredient in cross-boundary networks for shared leadership is ongoing communication and information sharing among members. In temporary working groups and ad hoc task forces, relationships are similarly critical. If people have no easy way to connect with each other, necessary interpersonal connections will not crystallize. Again, there needs to be a balance. Too many meetings can produce overload, and communication is time-consuming. Therefore, effective and efficient interaction processes are crucial. The amount and quality of discussion among group members are critical to success.

In successful groups, there is space, time, and support for personal relationships and physical communication systems. Regular meetings and telephone messaging may be sufficient for members in small groups to stay connected. In larger, more dispersed groups, such as a statewide effort to reduce teenage pregnancy, modern information and communication technologies are essential to maintain adequate links and connections. Tools like local area networks, e-mail, and distance conferencing efficiently link individuals despite distance and time and regardless of organizational boundaries. Nevertheless, human contact is still required. One member of a networked team emphatically stated, "You can't have a virtual conversation unless you also have real conversations" (Stewart, 1994, p. 56). Face-to-face contact facilitates relationship building and nurtures group member trust.

Spiral of Rising Trust

Trust is the underlying foundation for cooperative, collaborative, and collective efforts. Building and maintaining interpersonal trust is vital. Trust allows working group members to stay focused on outcomes. The absence of trust easily diverts the energy of the working group onto other, often more personal issues. Trust encourages less-guarded communication and less discomfort at confronting disagreements, and it promotes more effective use of group members' resourcefulness.

Because of the natural differences in interests and values and the dispersion of power and authority in a group, development of trust is particularly challenging. Trust is built by making and keeping promises and agreements, and by being open and sensitive to other group members' needs, values, and interests. Unfortunately, interpersonal trust is fragile. It develops slowly and can easily be destroyed (Slovic, 1993). Past relationships and collaborations among group members may have resulted in low trust levels. This must be dealt with early in the process. In multiparty working groups targeting public problems, full trust may never be achieved and, once achieved, may be temporary. Successful groups, therefore, foster an interactive process characterized by a spiral of rising trust.

Loosely Structured Yet Credible Process

Successful working groups establish a strategy development process, agreed to by participants, that provides a structure for the group's deliberations (Roberts and Bradley, 1991). There is no perfect process. Generally, it must be flexible enough to accommodate unforeseen developments, yet structured enough for the participants to have confidence that positive results will occur. A credible process can be established during the first meetings by developing commitment to a few basic procedural norms and guidelines, relatively clear roles within the group, and a structured strategy development process that allots sufficient time for problem definition (see Chapter Four).

Beyond an early focus on problem definition, specific process sequences are difficult to describe. No single model of collaboration or collective action exists. There is no exact order of decision-making steps or set of sequential stages in selecting strategies for addressing interconnected problems (Wood and Gray, 1991; Gersick, 1989; Mintzberg, Raisinghani, and Teoret, 1976.) Forging agreement on strategies and actions among diverse stakeholders seldom follows an undisturbed progression through a series of rational, concrete steps.

With interconnected problems, strategy development is seldom as tidy as earlier group development theories (and many consultants) suggested. The most common model prescribed by consultants suggests that all groups go through a five-step sequence of forming, storming, norming, performing, and adjourning; and that a group cannot progress to stage four without first going through stages one, two, and three (Tuckman and Jensen, 1977).

However, more recent research on task forces and working groups confirms what most experience indicates: the process is messy, dynamic, immensely complex, and chaotic. Even the more passionate, highly focused working groups face interferences, feedback loops, and dead ends. They are unable and sometimes unwilling to follow a rigidly structured decision-making process. It is most often a disjointed, messy process characterized by competing interests and perspectives, oversimplified images of the problem and its solutions, and a continuous open-endedness.

Although each group is unique and the process is organic, effective strategy development processes essentially include three core routines:

Essential Tasks in the Strategy Development Process

1. Identify outcomes: focus and refocus the direction of the group's analysis by identifying the end-outcomes and desired results.
2. Explore multiple options: gain shared insights on core problems and their interconnections, and explore multiple options and strategies to reach the outcome.
3. Identify and agree on multiple strategies: develop criteria and assess, select, and commit to multiple strategies, such as a strategic portfolio, to reach the outcome.

In practice, the process moves in feedback and "feed-forward" loops, but each returns to higher levels of detail, understanding, and commitment (Harwood Group, 1993a). It is not important to do the tasks in a certain order. What counts is that they are performed. Poor strategy development occurs when any one of these core tasks is treated superficially or is totally skipped (Nutt, 1989; Fischoff, 1983; Mintzberg, Raisinghani, and Teoret, 1976).

Identifying Desired Results and Outcomes: Establishing Directions for Action

The original issue or problem that attracted critical stakeholders is commonly too general to stimulate initial in-depth exploration and analysis. "The hardest part," one group member explained, "is agreeing on what the problem is. Usually there are far more parts to it than people realize." Disagreements about the definition of the problem are central to all intense debates on strategies and policy options. Stakeholders see their interests and solutions directly linked to a specific policy definition. They naturally define the problem in a way that protects their turf, advances their interests and stakes, or reflects the way in which they collect and analyze information (Milward, 1982; Fischoff, 1983, 1985).

When individuals come together to solve problems, their efforts are hampered unless they can agree on a common definition or formulation of the problem. With no agreement, it is extremely unlikely the group can choose the best courses of action. Focusing on outcomes, rather than problems or services, noticeably increases the quantity and quality of the strategies and options generated by the working group (Volkema, 1986). It directs the analysis away from preconceived solutions and instead focuses the group on the results they want to achieve and on multiple strategies for achieving them.

Problem Defined as Desired Outcome or Result

In most instances, individuals begin by advocating for a particular solution to the problem. Early advocacy, however, oversimplifies the issue and easily divides the group (Chrislip and Larson, 1994). Effective working groups postpone solution generation and first spend time defining the problem, translating it from an issue to a desired outcome. The Annie E. Casey Foundation provides an excellent example with its "New Futures Program," initially designed as a response to an alarming number of kids dropping out of school, becoming teen parents, and leading unproductive lives. To provide a more potent, catalytic influence on five targeted cities, the foundation identified three key outcomes on which to focus multiyear initiatives:

1. Improve school achievement, particularly decreasing the dropout rate and increasing the middle school and high school graduation rates.
2. Reduce the incidence of teen pregnancy and adolescent parenthood.
3. Reduce youth unemployment and inactivity after high school.

The foundation understood that youth problems are intertwined and believed that success in these three outcomes would also affect other important issues, such as substance abuse and juvenile delinquency rates. Federal and state government agencies are similarly learning how to target outcomes and benchmarks as the focus of strategic management processes in addressing public problems (U.S. Government Accounting Office, 1994).

Outcomes are not problems or services. Outcomes describe results, impacts, or consequences of action. Stakeholders who have strong passions about particular services or strategies may struggle to think about outcomes. Identifying and defining outcomes require the analytical capability to separate the problem from the desired results, to separate needed services from desired results, and to avoid using needed inputs as the desired outcome. (See Chapter Seven for details on how to identify and define outcomes.) However, even individuals with no prior experience with an outcome orientation to problem solving can produce an initial strategic analysis, based on outcomes, within three to six hours of work.

Outcomes provide a useful framework within which working group members can concentrate their thinking and construct an initial exploration of the interconnected problem. This framework allows them to shift their attention from immediate, preconceived solutions and services to a concern for long-term impacts and desired results. It essentially shifts the group's focus from problem solving to one of searching for effective strategies (Radford, 1990). Focusing on outcomes provides a point of reference that guides the mutual learning process of data gathering and solution generation, and thus provides a magnet for collaborative analysis and development of a wider array of options.

Focusing on outcomes also opens up a broader range of strategies and options, stimulates and sustains the option generation phase, and reduces the potential for prematurely fixating on one solution. When individuals begin to discuss what the problem really is, they initially define the issue in terms of something that is lacking, such as not enough federal funding, or insufficient level of services. By formulating the problem in terms of desired results, the number of different alternative strategies and action ideas generated by a working group increases by 20 percent to 40 percent

(Volkema, 1983). This increase in option generation occurs for several reasons.

- It slows the tendency for working groups to jump to solutions.
- It better targets the information gathering, decreasing the tendency for more selective searches for technical information based on an individual's preferred options.
- It allows for analysis of multiple, alternative strategies, targeting multiple causes and individuals' multiple interests.
- It leads to objective criteria for making choices, providing a common measure for comparing and evaluating alternative options.

Quality of "Ongoingness" Required

A clear and succinct formulation of the issue rarely exists before the working group begins. Even when the group starts with a relatively clear problem definition, the initially targeted end-outcomes are refined as the group's understanding of the issue grows. Catalysts assist the working group to review, refresh, and refine its desired outcomes as deliberations unfold. The initial outcome is often discovered to be a symptom of a larger problem and needs to be expanded or modified. The Arizona Strategic Planning for Economic Development (ASPED) working group redefined its economic development target after reviewing the best practices across the country. The group originally targeted job creation as its outcome, with industrial attraction as its main strategy. It later changed its focus to creating quality jobs and raising per capita income. The targeted strategies also changed, shifting to public-private investments in the economic foundations that could sustain high-value-added industry clusters (Henton and others, 1997).

Sometimes working groups "unbundle" the initial outcome into several targeted outcomes, such as specific subpopulations or geographical regions of high need or importance. As the group gathers and organizes information and explores various options, intermediate outcome targets emerge. One example is a regional private industry council that convened a working group to figure out how to educate and train a more competitive workforce. During the first meetings, discussions quickly centered around such inputs as capturing more federal training funds, increasing the number of clients enrolled in training programs, reducing employee-client ratios, and increasing the percentage of disabled served. However, potential options and strategies were constrained by this narrow set of preconceived solutions. Each participant had a solution that he or she considered a top priority. Consequently, it was impossible to develop a common purpose or strategic intent.

The convener then turned the group's discussion to consider the results they wanted to achieve and identified two outcomes group members had implicitly been seeking: reducing unemployment among dislocated workers and removing people from welfare rolls. With further discussion, the group agreed on a common outcome to guide their deliberations, "increasing self-sufficiency and sustained financial independence for dislocated workers and other unemployed adults." This targeted outcome developed a shared sense of strategic intent and common focus in the working group, and the deliberations expanded to include a larger array of important intermediate outcomes, such as increasing the percentage of displaced workers who were reemployed within twenty-four months and earning at least 90 percent of previous income, and decreasing the length of time of unemployment for dislocated timber workers, a critical target group in the region. From this list of intermediate results, the working group moved to consider new, innovative strategies targeted at intermediate outcomes.

Membership of Working Group Reassessed

Once an outcome has been identified, public leaders often reexamine whether additional stakeholders need to be invited to the table. As the group's end-outcomes are clarified and refined, the group may decide to add participants who were not included in the initial core working group but may now be particularly relevant (see Chapter Four for criteria for selection). If the working group's size is already too large, additional consultative forums can be designed for gaining input and participation from emergent stakeholders and knowledgeholders without adding new members to the core working group. Regardless of the response taken by the group to enlarge deliberations, once it has found common desired outcomes, reassessing who is at the table ensures that key perspectives and ideas are not overlooked.

Exploring Multiple Strategies: A Reiterative Process of Gaining Shared Insights and Generating Options

Members of successful working groups develop a shared understanding of the issue—particularly its multiple causes and interconnections—by first agreeing on desired outcomes, then by considering multiple strategies to reach the outcome. They seek to develop shared insights, not necessarily in-depth analyses. Catalysts encourage individuals to reveal, review, and assess relevant information. Again, the process is not mechanical or sequential (that is, following the steps of gathering data, surfacing all possible alternatives, evaluating each alternative, and selecting the best options). The process is more fluid and organic, even when a well-designed and sequential process is established in the group's first meetings. There is a constant "backing and forthing" between gathering information and analyzing options. A catalyst's challenge is to transform the discussion from a mere exchange of personal perspectives—or worse, a forum to narrowly argue for one's personal or political interests—to a process of mutual learning and joint analysis. This process doesn't merely tolerate differences and conflicts, but uses them to develop a portfolio of strategic actions.

Insights, Not Just Information, Needed

Insight occurs when confusion recedes. Insight is a new or clearer way of seeing the problem and its multiple causes. In addition, insight formation is not merely fact gathering, but also involves "feeling gathering." Understanding how people feel about an issue is often as important as discussing what they think is causing the problem. Working through difficult interconnected issues, such as teenage pregnancy reduction or economic development, often forces working group members to reveal and discuss their deeper values (Yankelovich, 1992). Effective insight formation engages individuals both intellectually and emotionally. Through this deliberative process, group members pool knowledge, reveal interests, develop a shared perspective of the issue, identify information gaps, and redefine the problem based on shared insights.

Gathering information from working group members requires an openness to analytic exchange, a willingness to consider different ideas and feelings, and sufficient time to work through ambiguities and conflicts. Although conflict is not eliminated, a climate is created that views different perspectives as opportunities for learning more about the specific issue. When group members have strong opposing perceptions, they try to discover underlying interests and assumptions. With strong hidden agendas, however, individuals will tend to make certain claims of truth or expressions of fact that are, in reality, merely disguised personal preferences.

Personal Insights Revealed Through Stories and Anecdotes

Developing shared insights involves not just data and technical information, but also relevant interests, stories, and anecdotes. As mentioned earlier, people's primary sources of information on public problems are typically what they hear from their neighbors, discuss with folks at the office, and see in the news. As a result, a person's initial way of understanding a problem is not often guided by analysis or expert judgment, but by what is observed and discussed among friends. Stories, rather than data, often drive problem identification and solution generation by citizens and elected officials. For instance, an examination of policymaking in city government found that city managers gather information by exchanging and analyzing data, while elected city officials rely on personal anecdotes and stories in their policy deliberations (Nalbandian, 1994).

People are bombarded daily with bits of facts, figures, and media headlines. Although the media plays a leading role in raising awareness about an issue, friends and neighbors are more influential when an individual explains a public problem and evaluates potential solutions. A person typically interprets the issue through a story or anecdote that reflects his or her personal experiences or that of a trusted friend. People rely on friends' stories and anecdotes more often than data or official reports for a variety of reasons. The information received from officials can be considered slanted, partial, and "not the whole truth" (Harwood

Group, 1993a). More important, individuals give much more weight to information that is vivid and readily available than to information that is distant, detached, and removed from their personal lives. Engaging, dramatic case studies capture attention more readily, are more readily stored in memory, and remain longer in our thoughts. For example, stories and anecdotes set out in boxes in news magazines, such as *Time,* have high reader appeal and are more often read than the accompanying news article (Nutt, 1989).

Many who are motivated to join a working group do so because of personal stories or anecdotes about the issue. Such stories oversimplify the issue and reveal a single cause, and a single point of leverage to address it (Stone, 1989). Teenage pregnancy, according to some, is due merely to poor parenting. Others believe it is simply the lack of adequate sex education. Each explanation is usually followed by a story of a young girl or family that reveals and confirms the person's belief about the problem's cause. Therefore, it is very important to raise and discuss personal stories because they reveal the individual's mental model of what the problem is and why it is important. Individuals also tell stories that reveal their underlying interests, issues, and preferred options.

Underlying Interests Among Group Members

Personal stories and anecdotes can reveal many underlying issues of working group members and can lay the groundwork for finding out which issues are most important to them and why. The stories not only help members understand other points of view, but they begin to illuminate underlying interests. Individuals tend to get involved due to self-interest. However, self-interest is not necessarily defined as self-centeredness. Interests are the specific needs, concerns, or desired outcomes that an individual considers important. For example, a member of the Newark Collaboration Group noted that "not only were we zeroing in on our own agendas, we were also looking at other people's input and their particular agendas" (Chrislip and Larson, 1994, p. 134). Strategies that generate sustained action toward addressing a public problem are based on meeting multiple interests, not on hard-held positions (Carpenter and Kennedy, 1988). Effective working groups help members articulate their underlying concerns and interests.

Most of the effective ways to identify underlying interests are based on principle-based negotiation, which separates people from the problem and focuses on interests, not positions (see Chapter Eight). Interests are uncovered by looking closely behind the preferred solutions and by asking, What is the outcome or result you desire? Catalysts assist in uncovering interests and help make connections between the individual's revealed interests and those of other working group members. As interests are revealed over several meetings, catalysts help illuminate which interests are shared, which are different but not in conflict, and which are in direct opposition. Most often, identifying interests reveals that there is much less direct conflict than initially assumed. The group can then redirect its energies toward generating multiple options for pursuing the desired outcome. After the first few meetings of the Applegate Partnership, the members found that "we had agreement on about 80 percent of the issues we were facing. The remaining 20 percent were significant, yes, but the 80 percent common ground gave us something to stand on while we debated the rest" (Buffum, 1993).

Specialized Knowledge Shared

On personal problems, individuals easily seek advice from specialists. With an injury or illness, one quickly seeks information and advice from the medical community. Yet with public problems such as crime, teenage pregnancy, school failure, or economic development, most people pay little attention to what science already knows. Instead they pursue solutions based on personal opinion. Specialized, technical, and scientific information are essential in exploring interconnected problems and generating options. Increasing members' technical competency occurs through obtaining the best credible evidence available, such as through briefings, field trips, and soliciting reports. Key questions include: What scientific or technical evidence exists that could help us understand this issue better? What are the multiple causes of the problems? and What alternative options does the evidence suggest to achieve our outcome?

Outside experts and knowledgeholders can help bring working group members to a level of technical competency by developing language less laden with generalities and rhetoric. Without a common factual foundation shared by all members, the chances of poorly conceived action strategies are very high (Ozawa, 1991). Constructing a common technical understanding of the issue allows participants to debate values and preferences explicitly. Political conflict isn't necessarily reduced, but the technical knowledge increases the clarity of the discussions and often lowers the debate from a screaming pitch to a more audible discussion level. Disagreements and disputes based on a common technical understanding can elevate the level of analysis and help participants state their concerns more clearly. Expert knowledge can also help working groups broaden the list of alternatives toward achieving their desired results and develop a clearer distinction among the alternatives. Knowledgeholders are especially critical in pointing out blind spots.

The use of technical and scientific analyses requires several cautions. First, there are legitimate scientific disagreements and disputes among technical experts, particularly in public problems revolving around the environment and natural resources (Ozawa, 1991). Second, people cannot readily detect omissions in the evidence from technical experts (Fischoff, 1985). They may be at a loss when trying to make sense out of seemingly contradictory technical or scientific evidence. Data can be difficult to evaluate, particularly when information is provided in fragments of facts and figures. The difference between "good" science and flawed science may be obscure.

In seeking technical advice, metaphors and scenarios are as essential as facts and logic. Information in the most technical areas, such as the economy, is often better communicated through analogies, metaphors, and scenarios. Many economists use metaphors and stories as core parts of their theories to explain economic dynamics, for example, the "invisible hand" of the marketplace. Metaphors and analogies can vividly portray a strategic focus. David Frohnmayer, former Oregon attorney general, once argued that "the long-time solution to our crime problem lies in addressing crime at its roots, not in constantly trimming off dying and diseased branches." The chief strategic planner for Shell Oil found that the most effective way to communicate pertinent data on strategic trends to executive managers was through the creation of economic stories and scenarios that vividly portrayed trends and possible options.

Individual Mental Models Revealed and Discussed

Most public problems are characterized by incomplete, ambiguous, and contradictory data and by multiple causes, constraints, and interconnections. Individuals manage this complexity by developing a simplified "mental model" of the issue. Once created, a mental model becomes internalized and is used automatically, almost unconsciously, by the individual. Although coherent, it captures only a few of the causes and relationships among multiple causes. It is based on personal knowledge developed through conversation, stories, and anecdotes with friends more than through the reading of research reports or published analyses by technical experts. The mental model becomes an unconscious lens that influences how an issue is defined, and serves as a reference point for analyzing what would or would not work in addressing the problem (Newell and Simon, 1972).

Although mental models are often implicit and internalized, they can be revealed, discussed, and analyzed in group settings. Forging agreements on action strategies requires the partial merging of individual mental models into a common framework (Bryson and Finn, 1995). A shared map of the issue and its many causes and interconnections allows group members to conceptualize and communicate effectively about the issue. Oregon's economic development working group, for example, crafted the "cycle of prosperity," a framework that guided discussions and analysis (Oregon Progress Board, 1989). In Arizona, a shared mental map called a "vital cycle" guided the ASPED working group in its strategic thinking about state economic development initiatives (Henton and others, 1997).

A shared framework is crafted by capturing and integrating the various mental models while simultaneously valuing each individual's perspective. The purpose is not to change someone's internalized mental model of the issue. Indeed, trying to change someone's mental model is seldom successful and can produce high levels of resistance. Rather, the aim is to reveal individual assumptions and insights, clarify the perceived relationships and linkages among variables, and begin to develop a larger shared perspective that encompasses as much of each person's mental model as possible. Catalysts attempt to secure enough agreement on a shared perspective that each working group member is committed to expending energy on generating multiple strategies and action options (Eden, 1990).

Visual Incorporation of Individual Mental Models

The simplest way to capture mental models is to elicit verbal explanations that reveal assumed causalities. For example, when asked to identify the cause of violence in the schools, one person may say, "It is because of the increased gang activity in our neighborhoods." It's easy to say, "the reason why there is 'X' is because of 'Y' and 'Z.'" "Verbal descriptions reveal internalized models: how a person thinks a situation works, why something has happened, what its causes are, and what some potential solutions are.

To move from an individual mental model to a shared model, it is critical to shift from verbal explanations to a visual representation that can capture and integrate various mental models. It is easy to generate visual listings of common factors influencing a particular issue. For example, factors that cause teenage pregnancy or unusually low child-immunization rates can be compiled in a list. In joint analysis, the list of factors can be sorted using simple graphic facilitation techniques. An affinity diagram identifies areas of common ground and common themes among individuals' ideas. Word-and-arrow diagrams go a step further, showing a sequence of events or causal relationships by listing and labeling key ideas, concepts, or variables, and then identifying linkages. More dynamic graphic mapping techniques illuminate systemic connections and leverage points where participants believe that targeted action can assist in achieving the end-outcome. Graphic mapping is well-suited to public-problem areas and has been used with such issues as foster care, homelessness, and public health (see Chapter Seven for specific examples).

Many types of visual mapping techniques are increasingly used in analyzing issues, including causal-loop diagrams, feedback diagrams, policy-structure diagrams, and system diagrams. Soft systems technology uses graphical mapping methods, such as concepts, diagrams, and "friendly" algebra, to capture and structure group knowledge of an issue (Checkland, 1989). An emerging set of collaborative technologies electronically supports individuals in sharing and combining mental models and assumptions. Networked computer software facilitates simultaneous collecting and organizing of ideas and assumptions among many individuals at computer stations. More complex computer-mapping models use mathematical equations to "unbundle the problem" graphically. They describe perceived causes and effects, particularly highlighting strengths of influence, time delays, long-term impacts, and ripple effects (Richardson, 1991; Martin, 1993.)

Software for modeling public problems enables working groups to translate combined mental maps into computer-simulation models. They can then test the impacts of various interventions and strategies. Systems-dynamics models generate a more complex shared mental map by using modeling symbols such as stocks, flows, and converters, and using algebraic equations that indicate strength of connections and causal interdependencies. Assumptions about interconnections, intensity of interaction, causal relationships, and time intervals are modeled through computational equations and then run as simulations. This encourages working group members to think about causal linkages that generate feedback loops and that maintain the problem in its existing condition. Computer-generated simulations are powerful catalysts for systemic analysis. They allow group members to test assumptions and alternatives, focus attention on critical interrelationships among issues, and create opportunities for the working group to experiment with various alternatives before reaching agreement (Richardson, 1991).

Catalytic Impact of Articulating Mental Models

Graphically showing the group's collective mental model can be a powerful catalyst for gaining shared insights. First, bringing individual views together within a common visual format can jump-start a group discussion of the various facets of the issue. It stimulates productive dialogue by allowing individuals to reveal safely their interpretations of the problem and its causes. It creates a safe, nondefensive mechanism for people to make their internal views explicit and more easily communicated to others. One community leader said, "We don't have to agree, but we do have to share." Once revealed visually, the graphic model provides enough cognitive distance to allow members to reflect, analyze, and modify their internal mental models. It can reveal blind spots and internal inconsistencies that are hidden until the mental model is captured in some graphical format. It also reduces the potential for "group-think" and other group dysfunctions by clarifying, often vividly, the points of disagreement among members.

Graphic models activate and capture a working group's knowledge and open up action possibilities. When individuals reveal their internalized mental models and attempt to develop a shared model, the models may not change, but they are expanded. Group members can better understand the system or systems in which the issue is embedded. In addition, the models reveal system complexities and alternative strategies—leverage points—that have influence far beyond what could have been predicted at the outset. Group members' thinking shifts fundamentally from simple cause-and-effect relationships to a more complex understanding of interconnected problems.

Graphing mental models and cognitive maps helps people to see assumed connections among issues and enhances an individual's ability to grasp multiple causes and connections as interpreted by working group members. A one-page mental map constructed by a working group, for example, typically includes twenty-five to forty interrelated ideas, variables, and subissues and takes about nine minutes to understand. In textual form, the interrelationships of the issue takes two to three pages of narrative to describe and about fifty minutes for an individual to comprehend (Bryson, 1996). Graphic techniques that focus on ideas and connections rather than on facts and numbers effectively illuminate alternative strategic options for addressing interconnected problems and significantly open up action possibilities (Vennix and Gubbels, 1992).

Core Issues Clarified and Redefined

When individual stakeholders meet to solve a public problem, they have different notions of what the problem is, and that definition evolves during the analysis process. In case after case, participants learn to approach the initial problem in new ways through gathering and organizing information about how to achieve that outcome. Every interconnected problem is redefined once analysis is under way. Not everything of importance can be known prior to exploring the issue.

As people absorb more data, see more connections, and stretch their perspectives, they understand the issue better and can clarify several core problems central to the issue. Insights are gained through an iterative process of problem definition and redefinition resulting from the exchange of information, feelings, and interests and from the mapping of causal linkages. Participants see the problem from various manifestations, perspectives, and representations, and a new definition of the situation is formulated. This redefinition process is critical because the amount of effort spent seeking solutions matters little if the group is attending to the wrong problem (Bryson and Crosby, 1992).

The information-gathering process typically leads to three types of reformulations. First, the problem is bigger and more complex than initially conceptualized. It has far more parts than people first realized; there are several interrelated core problems, not just one. For example, a 120–member industry stakeholder group analyzed economic development strategies for Oregon. It found that economic growth was not merely a function of industrial attraction, but was highly interdependent with adequate workforce quality and skills, high quality of life, sufficient infrastructure support (including roads and telecommunications), and an international frame of mind (Oregon Progress Board, 1989).

Second, the problem is often different than initially defined. Complaints from neighborhood residents and business owners about street prostitution was initially blamed on the lack of sufficient law enforcement patrols. Further analysis revealed that most of the prostitutes were minors arriving in the community as runaways with no money, no social support, and no access to needed services (Kettner, Daley, and Nichols, 1985).

Third, polarities tend to dissolve and are replaced by a deeper sense of complexity. Issues that generate great emotional debate are often based on a false picture of competing orientations that involve contrasting alternatives, such as spotted owls versus timber jobs or ocean habitats versus offshore drilling. After a diagnosis process like systems modeling, the "either-or" framework is replaced by a more complex picture of multiple causes, linkages, and intervention points. One participant in a community forum to develop a strategic map for neighborhood economic development noted, "It hasn't changed my views, but issues aren't so black and white anymore."

Generating Multiple Options and Strategies

The most difficult catalytic act is to refrain from jumping to popular quick fixes and to maintain pressure on the working group to identify more sustainable strategies and enduring solutions (Senge, 1990; Heifetz, 1995). When generating options to address public problems, effective strategy development requires group members to consider diverse stakeholder interests and shifting alliances, to juggle a multitude of facts and interconnections among issues, and to analyze first- and second-order consequences of potential responses. Unfortunately, the process seldom goes this way naturally. Symptomatic quick fixes are quickly suggested, and stakeholders are hastily judged as allies or enemies. Individuals prematurely commit to a single option or idea, and potential consequences are described in vague quantifiers, such as "likely" or "not worth worrying about" (Fischoff, 1985).

Without strong process leadership, groups too often fail to use structured analytical techniques. Instead, they rely on a few rules of thumb to generate a small number of potential options, from which they select only one (Fischoff, 1985; Nutt, 1989). In making tough choices, individuals have a natural tendency to choose from an *impoverished option bag*. Cognitive research in problem solving shows that individuals usually generate only about 30 percent of the total number of potential options on simple problems, and that, on average, individuals miss about 70 percent to 80 percent of the potential high-quality alternatives (Pitz, Sachs, and Heerboth, 1980; Gettys and others, 1987).

To resist the tendency to narrowly search for options, catalytic leaders must encourage and stimulate a more systematic search and analysis process, without necessarily advocating or pressuring for a particular strategy. Catalysts stimulate a search for multiple action options, and they encourage members to consider alternative perspectives. This is a fluid, messy process rather than a linear one. Many ideas are generated, analyzed, and eliminated simultaneously. Catalysts help working groups during this fluid process in two specific ways: by separating the process of inventing options from the process of evaluating options, and by avoiding both grand solutions and single, narrow-gauge initiatives.

Experience in difficult conflict situations, locally and globally, clearly highlights the importance of separating option invention from option evaluation. Critical judgment inhibits imagination and creative thinking. Thus, the creative act of thinking up possible strategies for reaching the outcome must be separated from the act of evaluating and selecting core strategies (Fisher and Ury, 1981). Postponing evaluation by the working group is one way to help broaden the number of options considered.

Effective strategies are multifaceted, but not necessarily comprehensive. With interconnected problems, public policies tend to create unanticipated consequences, which are not always positive. Grand strategies and large solutions can lead to additional problems, generating uncontrollable and unpalatable ripple effects. The effects can extend unpredictably far into the future, cross jurisdictional boundaries, and interfere with other policies and programs. The consequences of grand strategies are more "numerous, varied, and indirect, and thereby more difficult to predict," and they create outcomes that deviate from the intended (Wildavsky, 1979, p. 64). Further, working groups are seldom willing to commit to just one strategy. A grand strategy can appear overwhelming, too difficult to implement, or too politically tilted, making members reluctant to invest valuable time and resources.

To avoid a grand solution, the natural response is to design a narrow-gauge, single strategy to which everyone can agree and that is targeted to a specific part of the problem or issue. Unfortunately, interconnected problems occur for multiple reasons, and the multiple causes are interrelated. Attempts to solve such problems with a narrow-gauge action will be overcome by the multiple cross-currents of the interconnected system in which they are embedded. Offering accessible birth control alone is insufficient to reduce teenage pregnancy. Providing cheap, accessible industrial land may have only a minor impact on the local economy in generating high-quality jobs. Achieving any important public outcome requires using multiple levers for change.

Strategic Portfolio of Multiple, Reinforcing Strategies

Interconnected problems require multiple strategies rather than one comprehensive solution to achieve sustained improvement. Committed and long-lasting movement toward an outcome requires mutually reinforcing and complementary actions from a variety of stakeholders and citizens. The "New Futures" project in Dayton, Ohio, for example, targeted interconnected, school-related problems with multiple actions. It attempted to reduce school dropouts, improve school performance, and reduce teenage pregnancy. The portfolio of strategies included changes in schools, such as increasing teacher pay and purchasing new instructional computers; student coaching and counseling; individual case management to develop success plans; and youth centers in each targeted school (Agranoff, 1991). Reducing the number of homeless in a community also requires multiple strategies implemented by a variety of independent agencies: emergency provisions such as shelter and clothing, transition assistance such as employment services, mental health and medical services, and stabilization assistance to acquire permanent housing (Luke, 1986b).

Strategies are interwoven but not necessarily comprehensive or centrally coordinated. Integrated and centrally coordinated strategies may at first appear ideal. However, sufficient agreement seldom emerges on integrated policy responses. Therefore, the commitment required to sustain long-term action is less likely to develop. Smaller, multiple, and complementary strategies are particularly effective when major systemic change is attempted; large, comprehensive, centrally controlled strategies invoke deep resistance and often challenge deep political values (Weick, 1984).

A portfolio of reinforcing strategies can be inclusive of various interests, and is more amenable to group support. Individuals' preferences for specific strategies, once formed, seldom change. Therefore, convincing a working group member to value his or her chosen strategy over another is seldom, if ever, successful. Although individuals' perspectives don't change, their perspectives can expand to integrate related strategies that may not be their first choice. A method to reinforce the ties between the strategies can be crafted.

Strategic actions take hold and momentum is maintained when multiple, concrete actions are taken throughout the system. If one initiative fails to make a dent, then other strategies can sustain momentum. Momentum slows when there is too much dependence on one grand strategy. The metaphor of a wheel characterizes this because a "wheel with many spokes won't go off-kilter if one spoke falls out" (Roberts, 1985, p. 1034).

The challenge is to craft the right combination of multiple, sometimes competing, options. Multiple strategies are typically generated by searching for existing ideas, proposals, programs, and strategies that can readily, or with modification, be applied; and by designing custom-made strategies to reach the end-outcome. Designing and inventing multiple options, however, require more intensive efforts at creative thinking.

Inventing and Crafting New Strategies

Designing new strategies is like a potter sculpting clay—experimenting, molding, and shaping multiple strategies that ultimately form a coherent whole. Increasingly, three general approaches can craft a portfolio of strategies: targeting high-leverage points, targeting common interests, and a combination of both.

First, identify high-leverage points. Even though interconnected problems have multiple links and causes, the causal links are seldom equal in strength. Certain "strategic levers" have higher impacts than others on achieving the outcome. Yet an individual's proposal of high-leverage strategies and policy levers emerge from his or her internal mental model. Mental maps reveal where individuals think the most important links are. When analyzed by the group in a systemic way, such as in strategic option and modeling workshops, high-impact leverage points can be suggested that may have more impact in achieving the desired outcome (Eden, 1990; Eden and Huxham, 1986; Vennix and Gubbels, 1992; Richardson, Andersen, Maxwell, and Stewart, 1994). A relatively shared mental model acts as a powerful catalyst for working groups to identify and select multiple strategies and leverage points to achieve a policy outcome. Whether a working group uses a complex, computer-aided model of stocks and flows or a more simple strategic map with hand-drawn arrows showing perceptions of cause and effect, the purpose is to identify high-leverage policy options and strategies to generate a catalytic or cascading effect to help reach the outcome.

Second, consider multiple perspectives and interests. Individuals often think about options only in terms of their perspective.

To generate sufficient commitment to implementing the strategic portfolio, successful working groups invent options to incorporate multiple interests. Considering multiple perspectives helps individuals move past thinking they need "persuasion over" independent actors to realize they should join with interdependent individuals. Successful strategies are those in which individual stakeholders feel their personal and organizational interests will be met. Strategies based on common or similar interests will generate sufficient commitment to ensure implementation. Even when interests are not common or similar, they may be complementary and noncompeting. When interests are in conflict, stakeholders can trade or barter things that are valued differently, "trading less important items for more important ones" (Susskind and Cruikshank, 1987). Multiple and diverging interests can be accommodated within a broad portfolio of interrelated strategies and can provide the building blocks for actions to which an increasing number of members can support and commit.

In crafting custom-tailored options, two distinct approaches can be utilized simultaneously: focusing on multiple perspectives and interests, and identifying high-leverage system changes. In New York, state policymakers and advisors participated in a series of systems-modeling workshops to develop legislative options that addressed the impending threat of insolvency of malpractice insurance carriers due to a dramatic growth in settlement awards in the state. Professionals guided participants in group process and systems modeling to reveal, evaluate, and refine their mental maps of the malpractice insurance system. Key leverage points were then identified. Next, six constituencies were identified, and the participants generated more than forty criteria those stakeholder groups would likely use to evaluate policy options. The increasingly sophisticated systems model helped participants to generate high-level policy options and evaluate them against stakeholder interests. The result was a policy portfolio that included twenty-nine specific strategies to prevent the state's insurance insolvency. These strategies were grouped in four areas: ways to decrease malpractice, strategies to spread costs of the system across a wider base, changes in the tort system, and procedural changes (Vennix, Andersen, Richardson, and Rohrbagh, 1992).

Gaining Commitment on Multiple Strategies

Evaluation and selection of strategies is often considered to be the last step in the process. More often, gaining commitment is an ongoing process. Working group members progressively broaden and deepen their exploration of alternatives, simultaneously screening, inventing, combining, and synthesizing acceptable strategies to which they commit. Although textbooks suggest that evaluating and choosing preferred strategies are separate and sequential tasks, in practice they are inextricably intertwined and often occur simultaneously. In addition, seldom is the process purely analytical. Selecting strategies always contains elements of personality, emotions, bargaining, and power politics. Commitment requires both emotional and intellectual resolution. Strategic decision making in working groups of diverse stakeholders is a social and political process, not just an analytical process. The selection of strategies will be strongly influenced by the interests and goals of those involved.

Agreement on multiple strategies is essential because concerted action on interconnected problems requires specific commitments to action and usually commitments of resources. Strategies are courses of action that commit people, funds, and time to achieve the agreed-upon outcome. In efforts where collaboration is the norm, or where consensus by a work group is a prerequisite for moving forward, public leaders seek agreement on a portfolio of strategies based on some criteria (see the Appendix for a discussion of general criteria).

Silicon Valley engaged fourteen different working groups and produced forty-three economic development initiatives in its strategy development process. Several criteria were established to create a fair and disciplined process for selecting priorities and minimizing political favoritism. Guided by explicit criteria, the core group selected fourteen initiatives by a Darwinian process in which "some initiatives were championed, some combined with others to create a critical mass of support, and most withered away for lack of commitment to actions or an inability to articulate the purposes and outcomes of their proposed effort" (Henton and others, 1997, p. 135).

Once sufficient commitment exists, group attention turns to discussions of outsiders' expectations and to the preparing, editing, and packaging of written materials. The working group must seek and secure authorization in general or specific terms if individual members do not have the authority to commit crucial actors and agencies to the courses of action. Seeking permission or authorization is critical to success. Catalysts often spiral back and use mobilizing strategies to develop sponsors and champions, and build networks and coalitions to support the portfolio of strategies (Bryson and Crosby, 1992).

In other initiatives less amenable to community-wide consensus, such as reducing teen pregnancies, multiple strategies emerge when separate groups adopt "self-organizing" initiatives that fit their unique interests and resource base. Tillamook County's dramatic 75 percent reduction in teenage pregnancies over five years used this approach to gain individual commitment by multiple stakeholders. The community agreed on the outcome but differed about the best strategies. Multiple, smaller, self-initiated programs emerged that were not controlled by a single agency or coordinated by a core working group. The YMCA started new recreation programs for at-risk girls, school districts restructured their sex education curricula, churches stressed abstinence in their youth programs, and the health department focused on easy access to birth control. A community leader stated, "One agency approached it from one angle, another from another, but they were all aiming for the same result" (Luke and Neville, 1996). When diverse agencies can agree on the same outcome, they can then pursue actions that best fit their mission without being centrally coordinated.

Encouraging self-organizing efforts allows agencies, groups, and individuals to participate in ways they know best and care about most. Less time and resources are lost on fighting about who is in charge, and conflict on which strategy to commit to is eliminated. Self-organizing groups add energy and can be stimulated without requiring or forcing collaboration or commitment to others' actions. A range of complementary actions are generated that stakeholders can accept, whether it is concerted action resulting from multiple, separate initiatives or more collaborative action forged through consensus among diverse agencies.

Public Leadership Summary

Build and Nurture an Effective Working Group

- A core of committed and motivated group members
- A unifying purpose targeting outcomes and results
- A deliberative group process that enhances mutual learning
- A structured, credible process that allots time for problem defining and redefining.

Promote and Facilitate Strategy Development

- Identify outcomes.
- Gain shared insights and explore multiple options.
- Identify and commit to multiple strategies.

After convening stakeholders, public leaders help convert and transform their concerns and interests into viable action strategies to which they can commit energy and resources. They facilitate agreement on specific strategies, projects, and initiatives intended to achieve the desired results. They also seek common interests and mediate among conflicting interests. Although no single model guides collective strategy development among diverse stakeholders, effective working groups commonly have four essential elements or conditions. Effective public leaders become process champions, helping participants to work in constructive ways by building and nurturing four essential foundations: a core of committed and motivated group members with sufficient skills and knowledge and who do not relinquish their organizational autonomy or institutional independence in joining the action team; a unifying purpose based on agreement on desired outcomes that identifies the desired result; an interactive group process with agreed-upon norms that enhances mutual learning and conflict resolution, stimulates shared leadership, and builds trust; and a structured, credible process of strategy development, both decision making and action planning, custom-tailored to the context and situation and that allots sufficient time to problem defining and redefining.

The goal of a custom-designed strategy development process is to develop shared insights, not in-depth analyses, on which a set of multiple, interrelated strategies can be based. A catalytic leader attempts to prevent a working group's natural tendency to move prematurely toward a particular solution. To do this, the group undertakes three core tasks or routines: it identifies outcomes by focusing and refocusing the direction of the group's analysis on the end-outcomes and the results desired in addressing the issue; it promotes shared insights on core problems and their interconnections and explores multiple options and strategies to reach the outcome; and it analyzes and agrees on a set of strategies by developing criteria and assessing, selecting, and committing to multiple strategies to reach the outcome.

Poor decision making occurs when any one of these core tasks is skipped or treated superficially. During the working group's "backing and forthing" of strategy development, public leaders play an important catalytic role. They help participants articulate and work through the interconnected problem by surfacing both shared assumptions and sources of disagreement, raising awkward or "too-obvious questions," and challenging participant's current thinking. Key questions guiding their leadership interventions include

- What do we hope will be the outcomes or results of the strategy or actions?
- Where is there conflict? Is it on the ultimate goals and outcomes, or is it on the strategies and means to reach the goal? What are the underlying interests driving the conflict?
- What are the underlying assumptions or mental models shaping how this public problem is approached or perceived?
- What are the multiple strategies that can be included in a strategic portfolio on which the working group can agree?

Chapter Six

Sustaining Action
Implementing Strategies and Maintaining Momentum

Getting things done is just as important as figuring out what needs to be done.

A firm foundation for successful implementation is established by convening stakeholders and stimulating multiple strategies. However, sufficient energy, focus, and support are needed to implement and sustain action. Public leadership provides the spark to initiate both collective action and the energy to sustain it.

Implementation is more complex and difficult than commonly assumed. The often-overlooked challenge of public leadership is not necessarily the adoption or approval of policy options, but sustained implementation. It will encounter roadblocks, resistance, and interferences; no single person or agency can implement the strategies alone. Implementation creates unique leadership challenges to sustain action beyond the initial burst of energy following the development of strategies by key stakeholders. It is easy for momentum to fade: people lose interest, attention is caught by other urgent public problems, budgets tighten, and energy dwindles. In multiagency efforts with international development initiatives, more than half of the projects fail to be sustained (Brinkerhoff and Goldsmith, 1992). Thus, the task of getting things done is as important as figuring out what needs to be done.

Implementing Strategies Successfully: What Works and What Doesn't Work

Successful implementation strategies vary from community to community and from issue to issue. After thirty years of implementing significant changes in large organizational systems, experts still disagree on how strategic changes are best implemented, that is, whether there is a logical sequence to implementing change, or even whether large-scale change can be planned at all (Mohrman and Associates, 1989). More than two decades of research on implementation of public policy reveals more than three hundred key variables with no single theory or simple model on which to rely (Matland, 1995; O'Toole, 1995).

Indicators of Successful Implementation

A few common themes appear in efforts that successfully sustain momentum, however. Efforts commonly start with the adoption of an action plan, which includes "action detailing" to clarify initial commitments and to chart specific action steps. Action plans that reveal first steps can serve as important symbols that increase the legitimacy of the actions. But action plans alone are not sufficient to stimulate and sustain action (Weick, 1984; Kanter, 1983). Planning in too much detail can paralyze or reduce flexibility to respond to emergent opportunities. Successful implementation requires enough stakeholder commitment and constituent support to take the actions called for in the multiple strategies. It also requires sufficient financial and human resources allocated over the long term, and sustained cooperative behavior among multiple agencies and individuals (Nutt and Backoff, 1995; O'Toole, 1995).

A pivotal question is whether successful implementation is defined by fidelity to the initial action plan or by the achievement of specific outcomes. The fidelity approach measures success by the careful implementation of the initial action steps. With this approach, if all action steps are successfully carried out, then the implementation is deemed successful.

More effective approaches to define success measure progress toward the agreed-upon outcome or desired results, regardless of the precision of the action plan implementation. Reaching outcomes should not always be the sole criterion. Four indicators best measure successful implementation:

- Shows progress toward outcomes agreed to by the group
- Maintains or enhances relationships among key stakeholders
- Stimulates policy learning
- Achieves personal goals of group members

Progress Toward Outcome

Successful implementation is often measured by the degree to which the agreed-upon outcome is realized. Outcomes, not activities, are targeted. Therefore, the ultimate measure for success is how much progress has been made toward achieving the outcome. Public leaders who maintain momentum over the long term typically view implementation not as a short-term fix but as a continuous, ongoing process that can take years to achieve the desired results. The process of implementation is best understood as long-term and continuous, a learning process rather than a blueprint, whereby individuals adjust strategies incrementally as new information and feedback emerges and as unforeseen organizational and political constraints become clearer (Luke, Ventriss, Reed, and Reed, 1988).

Relationships Among Key Stakeholders

Mobilizing and sustaining action requires the capacity to maintain viable relationships with others in the implementation network. Successful implementation preserves and expands existing relationships and creates and nurtures new ones. Positive interpersonal connections and information sharing are fundamental to carrying out commitments, reducing uncertainty in implementation, building trust, and managing inevitable conflicts. If relationships are damaged during implementation, action becomes more difficult to sustain. Because individuals will likely seek assistance from others in future initiatives, maintaining positive relationships with other members will thus encourage their involvement in future efforts.

Policy Learning

With interconnected problems, there is limited knowledge about the exact cause-and-effect relationships that can predict successful strategies and interventions. Strategies and policy options are best seen as long-term experiments. The problems are so complex that general approaches to resolving problems may involve substantial allocations of public and private resources, which carry no guarantee of success. Implemented strategies can have significant delayed effects and indirect and hidden costs. Experience during implementation can illuminate the depth, complexity, and interaction of public problems, revealing more potent strategies and actions. Because implementation is a continuous process, policy learning is critical for achieving a long-term outcome.

Personal Goals of Group Members

Successful implementation can be evaluated by the degree to which members' personal goals are met. The personal satisfaction of key stakeholders is vital to sustained action over the long run and significantly adds to the "staying power" of a group's actions. Even though they are related and may overlap, personal outcomes should be distinguished from larger group outcomes and should be assessed independently (Hood, Logsdon, and Thompson, 1993).

Common Barriers to Implementation

Implementing and sustaining action faces unique challenges and requires interorganizational responses among many individuals, agencies, jurisdictions, and sectors. Research and experience from cross-functional teams and project implementation by public-private partnerships reveal five common barriers to implementation that need to be addressed:

- Turf barriers
- Communication and language barriers
- Lack of enabling structures and norms
- Leadership limited to one champion
- Excessive pressure for immediate results

Turf Barriers

Stimulating and sustaining action on public problems is a collective process, as well as an individual one. It requires interaction across traditional boundaries and territory. Implementation can arouse an individual's fear of loss or threaten a group's domain, resulting in turf battles for resources, power, information, and legitimacy. Group lines can get sharply drawn, and value differences can be accentuated. Agencies even reward individuals when they protect their turf, such as when they withhold their area of expertise or limit access to information or resources (Hutt, Walker, and Frankwick, 1995; Hood, Logsdon, and Thompson, 1993).

Communication and Language Barriers

Even if turf barriers are nonexistent, different language and interpretations by diverse stakeholders can impede communication. Successful implementation requires communication across boundaries, with diverse actors contributing special knowledge and competence to the implementation process. Unsuccessful implementation can often be traced to limited or narrow communication channels. These are characterized by one-way communication, the exclusion of key stakeholders in ongoing activities, and the withholding of critical or emerging information (Coe, 1990). Particularly in public-private partnerships, stereotypes create fundamentally different understandings and perceptions that result in communication distortion and miscommunication during implementation. Communication will never be perfect or undistorted, but networks or channels are necessary for sharing information and managing conflicts.

Lack of Enabling Mechanisms

While the desired result or outcome provides the magnet for multiple agencies, an action vehicle or institutional mechanism is often lacking to manage interdependencies on an ongoing basis. In large corporate initiatives, the failure of strategies often has more to do with the lack of an institutionalizing mechanism than with inherent problems in the strategies or policies pursued (Kanter, 1983). With interconnected public problems, the dilemma is the same. To institutionalize new policies or strategies, stable, valued, and recurring patterns of interorganizational cooperative behavior must be created, rooted, and highly esteemed (Brinkerhoff and Goldsmith, 1992; Ring and Van de Ven, 1994). Interorganizational cooperative behavior cannot occur without enabling structures. These become vital when the composition of the group is expected to change, such as after public elections.

Limited Leadership

Staying power is not the product of one strong personality with a commitment for getting things done. On the one hand, one individual seldom can sustain a group's energy for the duration of implementation. On the other hand, implementation is not a "leader-less" process where no one steps forward. As stated earlier, successful implementation is a "leader-full" process with multiple champions and many participants sharing leadership at various times.

Pressure for Immediate Results

Excessive demand for immediate results forces attention away from developing and institutionalizing the cooperative behavior essential for addressing public problems. Short time frames and pressure to show immediate results make it difficult to move beyond a quick-fix mentality. Public leaders may feel forced to attend to fast-paced implementation schedules. They may overlook the development and funding for the sustained operation of their chosen strategies, which undermines the potential for sustained long-term action (Korten, 1980).

Sustaining Action During Implementation of Strategies

Although public leaders can get involved in the details of implementation, they pay closer attention to these broad-scale barriers and focus less on the smaller steps of action planning (Kotter, 1991). Effective public leaders act as catalysts to sustain action by engaging in a unique set of political, institutional, and interpersonal strategies to reduce or remove barriers.

Commitment and Support from Key Decision Makers

To stimulate and sustain action, leaders build commitment and garner support from key decision makers and implementers. They develop broad legitimacy and acceptance, and encourage independent agencies and jurisdictions to allocate scarce resources. These strategies are essentially political, because they mobilize attention and allocate resources among competing priorities. Interorganizational political dynamics, rather than rational action planning, strongly influence implementation.

Multiple Champions

Assigning responsibilities within an action plan does not guarantee implementation or sustainability. Implementation champions—much like product champions in the corporate world—are critical to stimulating broad interest, acceptance, and support for the actions being implemented (Bryson and Crosby, 1992). Champions have a tenacity or passion to work through unexpected roadblocks, conflicting interests, and unanticipated crises. Champions broaden awareness and expand acceptance, asserting and persuading that the policy is necessary, vital, and workable. Analyses of implementation efforts to develop a "wellness" or "pro-family" approach to children and family services reveal several common characteristics of effective champions (Melaville, Blank, and Asayesh, 1993). Similarly, analysis of organizational innovations highlights the importance of champions addressing natural barriers and resistance (Kanter, 1983). In particular,

- They are not impartial, but are emotionally committed to advocating for a set of strategies.
- They are strategically opportunistic and flexible, taking advantage of unexpected events to further stimulate and sustain implementation.
- They use data and information to stimulate more action, rather than just to accumulate information for measuring progress.
- They advocate the new strategy or policy, repeating their message as often and in as many ways as possible.

Public leaders also identify and nurture executive champions, who are critical when agency resources must be committed over a long period. Executive champions are those who make decisions on organizational commitments and have authority to dedicate organizational resources—dollars, information, and people (Kanter, 1983). They not only demonstrate commitment toward a strategy or policy, but they also apply resources. They use power not for private gain but to stimulate organizational action toward a larger public outcome.

Constituent Support and Advocacy Coalitions

Even with active implementation champions, unless the new policy is viewed as legitimate and supported by a broad set of key decision

makers, power holders, and advocacy coalitions, significant movement will not occur. Especially with extreme strategies, respected
and credible policy leaders with substantial political capital are necessary to support a major change and to confront a vast array of
entrenched interests (Crosby, 1995; Kanter, 1983). The commitment
of other public leaders and elected officials is the resource that may
be in shortest supply, particularly with major reform efforts and large
strategic initiatives (Bryson and Crosby, 1992). Such power sources
do not have to be actively involved as champions, but through their
visible support they add legitimacy and credibility.

Identifying and targeting high-priority power holders requires
strategic analysis. First, specific parties are identified who might
influence the success of implementation and might determine the
needed resources. Second, plans are devised that garner the necessary resources and build support among power holders. Then
tactics for capitalizing on supporters and managing nonsupport-
ers are developed (Nutt and Backoff, 1992, 1995; Bryson and
Crosby, 1992; Matland, 1995).

Without the support of power holders, implementation is likely
to falter. However, action cannot be sustained solely on the shoul-
ders of powerful elites. Success depends on a broader base of support with other stakeholder groups and networks—multiple
coalitions and alliances that form constituencies to support and sustain the new policy or strategy. Public leaders align existing coalitions around the proposed strategy, or they create new coalitions
and constituent groups to champion implementation. Developing
and mobilizing a constituency is particularly critical in strategies
requiring the passage of legislation or regulations (Bryson and
Crosby, 1992). Without an effective constituency, it is much easier
for others to assemble opposition to block implementation. Constituent groups and advocacy coalitions lend force to implementation champions and amplify the legitimation process.

Constituency support is vital, but not just any support will work.
The proposed strategies must have the support of key advocacy
coalitions to ensure continued implementation after the initial
burst of energy. Advocacy coalitions are groups of policy advocates
that share the same sets of policy beliefs, problem perceptions, and
preferred solutions. Although there is no limit to the number of
advocacy coalitions within a particular policy area, the number is

often small, ranging from two to four important coalitions in any one policy area (Sabatier, 1988, 1991).

Commitment of Resources

Unless changes occur in how public and private dollars are spent, it is unlikely that action can be sustained over time. The commitment of resources is the acid test for joint action to address public problems. The mobilization of new resources can make a significant difference. Even when sufficient resources exist, they often must be reconfigured or reallocated in appropriate directions.

The challenge goes beyond securing "seed" funding. Continuity of funding, or the availability of adequate and permanent resources, is equally important. New policies or strategies are more easily sustained when they have a legitimate and permanent place in agencies' budgets and in the resource allocation process. Public leaders ensure that strategies and necessary resources are integrated or incorporated into their institutional plans and budgets, with a permanent flow of adequate resources earmarked to keep joint, interagency efforts up and running. In successful strategies, a predictable level of funding allows implementers to make longer-term plans and to consider strategic priorities beyond day-to-day survival. Particularly in public sector initiatives, unless support is authorized to extend beyond an elected official's term of office, strategies reliant on funding from governmental support can easily suffer following election cycles.

Obviously, implementation can fail if sufficient human, technical, and financial resources are not committed. Nevertheless, discussions of resource allocation and reallocation are often avoided or approached with great hesitation by the working group or implementation network. In an era of budget austerity in public and private sectors, and a reduced confidence in the ability of government to solve problems, funding for implementing new strategies is extremely limited. There is always competition for scarce resources. The topic of mobilizing and reallocating resources often meets serious resistance or even antagonistic reactions because it is seen as threatening. Existing programs or functions could be eliminated, or entirely new institutional structures might need to be created to stimulate and sustain action. An analysis of strategies to reduce homelessness in Los Angeles found that the competition for scarce funding by nonprofit providers was so fierce it became predatory (Rocha, 1995).

Interorganizational Enabling Mechanisms for Collective Action

Although implementation of public programs has historically been accomplished through the efforts of a single agency or organization, addressing current public problems requires sustained attention and efforts by multiple independent agencies, networks, and systems that transcend the operation of a single organization (O'Toole, 1995). To sustain implementation, interorganizational relationships must be developed that enable cooperative action toward common outcomes. Yet multiorganizational efforts face unique and difficult challenges, for example, diverse and multiple interests and perspectives, continuous multilateral bargaining and negotiation, and the lack of a central authority or hierarchical controls. Nevertheless, sustained action on interconnected problems requires connections with other agencies.

Interorganizational enabling mechanisms bring key implementers together in ways that facilitate and orchestrate concerted action among multiple and independent agencies. These mechanisms vary from formal agreements to interorganizational networks to newly designed institutions. Without a formal or informal enabling mechanism, individuals cannot easily maintain forward momentum. Conflicts are too easily left unresolved and nagging uncertainties stall action. Information systems, norms of cooperation, sets of working rules, forums for communication, and institutional incentives are also needed for collective action. Strategies will remain only great ideas and good intentions until concretized in actual institutional structures, processes, interactions, and resources.

Since the 1970s, considerable research and experience have revealed several key themes in developing multiagency action vehicles.

- Interorganizational arrangements develop and grow in a cyclical fashion, based on levels of trust.
- There is no "one best way" to structure interorganizational arrangements.
- Rapid information sharing and feedback energizes the network.

Cyclical Nature of Interorganizational Arrangements

Implementation of action strategies takes place in a network that is constantly changing, forming, reforming, and occasionally dissolving. Joint ventures and agreements are negotiated, monitored, and renegotiated. Interorganizational networks are continuously shaped and restructured by network members' actions. Contractual agreements, networks, self-forming groups, and joint ventures follow a cyclical, repetitive process of negotiation of joint expectations, commitment to specific action or behavior, and execution of commitments (Ring and Van de Ven, 1994).

Interorganizational agreements, networks, and self-organizing groups begin in small ways, initially requiring little reliance on trust and involving little risk. They evolve in a gradual, incremental process over time as trust increases (Waddock, 1989). Interorganizational cooperation relies on trust and perceived equity rather than on monitoring and controlling capabilities. Trust is the result of repeated past interactions. Interorganization cooperative behavior grows and builds on previous successful exchanges between agencies where the cooperation was perceived as efficient and equitable to the members (Ring and Van de Ven, 1994).

As the interorganizational partnership evolves, and as small successes lead to increased levels of trust, "purpose reformulation" occurs that can lead to a broadening of the network's agenda. When stakeholders first come to the table, they are hooked by an issue or problem seen as urgent and salient, and by strategies that are "do-able" (see Chapter Four). During implementation, action is sustained as network members are continually "rehooked." Interest is maintained when the agenda expands to include new, related issues and strategies. A spiraling pattern expands to broader purposes and contracts inward as efficiencies are seen to decline or if trust is broken. Sustained action is thus a process, rather than an end state.

Variety of Structural Options

Implementation research shows that there is no "one best way" to structure interorganizational arrangements, even for implementation of easy strategies. Groups must examine a variety of structural options. Inventiveness is crucial in aligning existing organizations into new cooperative networks and in creating new and more sustainable arrangements (O'Toole, 1995; Myrtle and Wilbur, 1994).

There are several ways to bind and sustain cooperative networks during implementation. Informal agreements emerge when agency executives or stakeholders meet on a regular basis, such as at weekly breakfasts, to compare notes, to monitor progress of individual actions, and to keep abreast of challenges and opportunities facing the achievement of the agreed-upon outcomes. More formal types of agreements include interagency memoranda of understanding (MOUs), in which several agencies agree to specified goals and principles, working independently but cooperatively for a common purpose. An example in California is the MOU developed by federal and state natural resource agencies (such as the U.S. Fish and Wildlife Service and the California Natural Resources Agency) to protect particularly vulnerable ecosystems, watersheds, and habitat areas while simultaneously maintaining the economic viability of a region (State of California, 1991).

Joint power agreements and joint ventures commit individual organizations to specific resource contributions and responsibilities. One of the most publicized is the *Boston Compact,* an education-business partnership established in 1982. It grew from the sponsorship of a small-scale summer work program for high school youth to include adult literacy programs and a housing development partnership (Waddock, 1989). An example in the area of economic development is *Joint Venture: Silicon Valley.* This broad-based consortium of local businesses, local government agencies, and educational institutions formed in 1992 to address common industrial, infrastructure, and regional problems (Saxenian, 1994; Henton and others, 1997).

Interorganizational networks realign and focus existing organizations and agencies. They involve more frequent and intense interaction. The networks sport such labels as strategic alliances, collaborative alliances, consortiums, federations, and service systems. Generally they are self-regulating and seek to orchestrate distinctive competencies and diverse resources, harnessing the collective strength of different autonomous groups and independent agencies toward a common outcome.

The common element in network structures is that they are not mandated or driven by an external authority. Rather, they are self-organized due to common interests and the desire to create and nurture an exchange relationship among a myriad of public and private agencies. Organizations do not give up their independence in networks, but commit to recurring types of cooperative behavior. In addition to a sense of interdependence that causes them to join in interagency efforts, there is also a perception that there are specific benefits to be derived for each partner. "Individuals and organizations do not become involved in [such] partnerships completely out of altruistic motivations. An essential element of partnerships derives from each organization gaining some benefit from the interaction" (Waddock, 1989, p. 96). Mature networks often have a strategic center, for example, a lead agency or an interunit coordinator who provides a central link to coordinate the network of affiliated organizations (Fleisher, 1991; Lorenzoni and Baden-Fuller, 1995). The strategic network center has several unique features, such as

- Developing the core skills and competencies of network members to enhance their effectiveness
- Nurturing an atmosphere of trust and reciprocity
- Transferring new ideas to partners by borrowing, developing, and transferring innovations to network members, thus enhancing the learning process with network members
- Creating and sustaining a sense of common purpose among members

A new institutional structure and organization may be required if extensive or systemic changes are necessary in the existing institutions. In many ways, current organizations are institutionalized structures to deal with old problems. Creating effective interorganizational networks often demands that existing organizations reorganize, restructure, or retool for new tasks or functions, thus altering existing rules, procedures, and personnel. Because of the difficulty in establishing new routines, it is often more politically feasible to create new organizations (Crosby, 1995).

The formation of self-organizing groups is another type of action vehicle. Self-organizing groups are often overlooked because of traditional assumptions that to be efficient, all efforts must be integrated or somehow centrally coordinated. In policy areas with intense value conflict, organizations may pursue self-designed strategies and initiatives separate from an existing network of partners or larger, integrated institutions.

For self-organizing groups to be effective, members of the network must commit to an agreed-upon outcome. In Tillamook County's effort to reduce teenage pregnancy, a group of Fundamentalist Christian activists self-organized and pursued an independent set of strategies toward abstinence because of deep value differences with other community stakeholder groups. Although separate and independent, their strategies targeted the same outcome: the reduction of teen pregnancies. Action can be sustained collectively, if not collaboratively, as long as self-organizing groups remain committed to achieve a common outcome and avoid excessive formalization and control.

Creating a new bureaucracy, adding layers to existing systems, or consolidating interconnected networks does not necessarily enhance interorganizational coordination or provide cost savings (Jennings, 1994; Korten, 1980). An analysis of community-based systems of care for the elderly found that rather than build a new bureaucratic organization, a more effective approach is to create joint ventures or strategic alliances between organizations within the "aging" network (Myrtle and Wilbur, 1994).

If the interorganizational relationship is to last beyond the tenure of current network members, informal commitments and understandings must be formalized to create sustainable action routines. However, excessive formalization of interorganizational implementation can lead to conflict and distrust among network members, creating barriers to sustaining action over the long run (Ring and Van de Ven, 1992). Agencies strive to maintain their autonomy and unique identity as the web of interdependencies grows. Rather than creating interorganizational arrangements that are centralized, tightly coupled, or consolidated, successful strategies involve organizations, networks, and systems that are loosely coupled and connected by rapid information sharing through communication linkages (Myrtle and Wilbur, 1994).

Rapid Information Sharing and Feedback

Successful implementation requires information and feedback to assess whether the new policy or action strategies are being implemented as expected, and whether the results are the ones intended. Important information is often passed on in meetings, in hallways, and during social events. However, sustained implementation requires a more consistent and dependable means of collecting and sharing information. Although less tangible than an institutional structure, a feedback system is essential for enabling and sustaining implementation, linking together key stakeholders and implementers to facilitate the rapid sharing and feedback of information.

Rapid and Continuous Feedback

Feedback acts as a catalyst to sustain action. Momentum cannot be sustained if accomplishments are not revealed and celebrated. Visible successes and small wins build momentum by maintaining focus on the desired outcomes, building confidence among implementers and stakeholders, and drawing attention to new directions for action.

Creating a system to produce and rapidly disseminate information requires two core elements: an outcome-based monitoring system and a communication network or web that links key implementers. The purpose is to sustain action by building trust and keeping everyone focused on the ultimate purpose of the strategies. Rapidly shared information during implementation increases understanding of practical difficulties and pitfalls and facilitates midcourse corrections and ongoing adjustments. The more accurate and immediate the feedback, the more potency it has in providing a continuing source of energy in sustaining action.

Measuring and reporting how well a strategy is working or not working energizes individuals and sustains their attention and energy. Effective information and data-collection processes often target two specific questions: Are strategies being implemented according to the accepted plans? and Are we getting the results we intended?

Monitoring the progress of strategy implementation provides performance information that can stimulate and facilitate *adaptive learning*. Adaptive learning includes evaluations and assessments conducted during the implementation process that provide important insights necessary for midcourse adjustments. This common form of monitoring, called "formative evaluation," generates evaluative information during the formative stages of implementation and attempts to measure whether planned activities are occurring as intended. Monitoring the implementation process requires agreement on process measures that indicate whether the interorganizational network or web is doing what it agreed to do and what adjustments are necessary to manage the implementation process better. Much of the progress monitoring can occur with routine data collection and informal measures.

Measuring and obtaining information on outcomes and results stimulates *policy learning* that seeks to evaluate the effectiveness of a specific strategy, or set of strategies, in reaching intended outcomes. Measurement is not limited to the completion of an activity or the delivery of a service. Measuring outcomes helps focus on whether there has been measurable change in the public problem being targeted. Information systems that focus on outcomes and keep track of results allow the interorganizational network to reset priorities and modify strategies as they learn what works and what doesn't (see Table 6.1).

Government and nonprofit agencies have less experience measuring outcomes than measuring activities. Recent trends, however, enhance the ease by which outcome-based information systems can be created. There is a national movement to create "benchmarks," "milestones," and other measurable outcomes in federal, state, and local governments. These focus attention on results rather than merely on program activities (Campbell and others, 1994). Many government agencies are starting to demand outcome information from coalitions and service providers, often as a precondition to awarding service contracts. The expanded use of computers and

Table 6.1. Information for Learning.

Key Monitoring Question	Type of Measure	Type of Learning
Are strategies being implemented according to accepted plans?	Process measures	Adaptive learning and strategy adjustment
Are we getting the results we intended?	Outcomes or results measures	Policy learning

the implosion of computer technologies have put powerful computers onto the laps of public, private, and nonprofit executives,
greatly increasing the accessibility of data and analyses previously
available only to "data junkies." Information on results is more easily obtainable, and outcome-based information gathering and feedback is becoming an integral part in addressing public problems.

Outcome-Based Information and Feedback System

Catalysts ensure that an outcome-based information and feedback
system is established for maintaining focus over time. Unfortunately, many confuse the counting of program activities with the
measuring of results. Counting the number of clients served, grants
received, or funds spent are indicators of work activity. Although
they may be important to individual government or nonprofit managers, they show very little about the impacts of those activities. To
sustain implementation, relevant outcome indicators or benchmarks for the desired results must first be selected. Data and information on the selected benchmarks can then be gathered and
analyzed, and the results can be fed back to the interorganizational
network and to stakeholder groups, funding sources, and the
media. These four components—defining outcomes, selecting
benchmarks, measuring impacts, and reporting results—provide
the information infrastructure necessary to sustain collaborative
interorganizational action. Development of such an "info-structure" is guided by four questions:

1. What results or ultimate outcomes are the strategies attempting to achieve?
2. Which intermediate outcomes or benchmarks can and should
   be measured?
3. Who in the interorganizational network will be responsible for
   collecting the data?
4. Who should use the information; when and how will it be helpful for sustaining action?

An outcome feedback system does not provide in-depth evaluations of specific program activities, nor does it provide definitive
information on the extent to which the strategies caused the results
indicated by the outcomes. Outcomes and benchmarks do not

provide evaluative information on why one strategy is working or isn't. As one community leader noted, outcomes "give us the score, but they don't tell us why we're winning." Designing and establishing an outcome-based information system has a very significant catalytic impact. More in-depth program evaluations are also critical to assessing the constraints and challenges of successful implementation, but they are a function of program management rather than public leadership. The unique role of public leadership is to identify the outcomes of collective action and ensure the establishment of an outcome-driven feedback system.

Method to Identify and Select Benchmarks

Measuring and reporting progress requires outcome indicators, or benchmarks, that cover the desired results of a strategic portfolio, represent reasonable consensus among key implementers, and provide reasonably valid data that can be efficiently obtained.

Experience at the national, state, and local levels during the 1990s illuminates several detailed guidelines for identifying and selecting outcome indicators or benchmarks by interorganizational networks and partnerships (Hatry, 1993; Hatry, Liner, and Rossman, 1995).

• Benchmark measures should reflect results (reductions in teen pregnancy), not activities (the amount of money spent on teen pregnancy programs). Benchmarks are more telling indicators of achievement than services provided or funds expended to achieve outcomes.

• Multiple benchmarks should be sought for monitoring implementation and tracking progress toward each outcome. Following several town hearings, a community-wide survey, and an analysis of the research literature, community coalitions organized in urban areas to reduce alcohol, tobacco, and other drug abuse typically choose up to fifteen outcome indicators, while rural coalitions are likely to use fewer measures (Copple and others, 1993). Synthesizing outcomes into a single measure is seldom adequate and will be more misleading than informative (Hatry, Liner, and Rossman, 1995).

• Consider the multiple perspectives of various customer and stakeholder groups in selecting benchmark measures. The set of benchmarks or indicators should be carefully selected with awareness of the multiple constituencies involved. Involving relevant policy and citizen advisory committees, holding interviews, and convening focus groups with key officials and clients can enhance the acceptance of key outcome indicators (Henry and Dickey, 1993).

• Benchmark measures should be reasonably easy to gather. It is vital to generate and report outcome data within available financial and personnel resources. When the outcome-based information process is viewed as onerous, cumbersome, or too expensive to maintain by network members, the system will probably not be used to provide quick and timely feedback on progress. Collecting outcome data should keep demands on staff time to a minimum. If possible, use an existing interorganizational arrangement or enlist a subgroup to aid in gathering analyzing and data (Bloomquist and Ostrom, 1985).

• Benchmark measures should be reliable over long periods of time. Data should be collected over a sufficiently long period of time; thus, measures should be reasonably easy to gather and analyze at yearly intervals. Complex multiagency strategies may take months or years to show any impact, and premature assessments can generate flawed information about what is working and not working. Measurements should be reasonably stable over time for progress and trends to be captured. (This requires that frequent changes to the outcome indicators be avoided. Improvements in the identification and measurement of indicators will occur, and modifications to the indicators will be made, but a relatively fixed set of outcomes should be used.)

• Benchmark measures should come from credible sources, whether primary (official record or commissioned research surveys) or secondary (published research by others) and be comparable with other jurisdictions. Comparisons provide important information and feedback on successes.

• Benchmark measures should be understandable and useful to a nontechnical audience. Gathering outcome data alone will not sustain attention without dissemination to key stakeholders and implementers. Outcomes should be understandable and useful to lay audiences. Reports should not be designed for the scientific, technical audience, but should instead serve as progress reports for key stakeholders and implementers.

Communication Network

The gathering of information, particularly on outcomes and contextual factors, is central to sustaining the implementation of multiple strategies by multiple organizations. Particularly in addressing public problems, when each partner's resources are scarce and individual competencies so essential to success, an information system requires the generation of new outcome-based information. It also becomes a communication process that links the interorganizational network through rapid information sharing and feedback, and facilitates discussion about emerging implementation issues, potential joint responses, and implementation successes.

Analysis of successful cross-functional teams and corporate alliances reveals important insights for networks addressing public problems. Most important, dissemination of large amounts of quality information facilitates a more rapid response to threats and opportunities during implementation. Information between partners in effective corporate alliances flows relatively easily (Lorenzoni and Baden-Fuller, 1995). In joint ventures and business alliances that fail, critical information is guarded, overly filtered, and slow. An analysis of the implementation of several public-private partnerships in Colorado revealed that communication linking network partners was a central element in successful implementation of joint initiatives (Coe, 1990). Extensive networking and supportive communication occurred formally and informally among individuals and emphasized attention to common interests, highlighted accomplishments, and acknowledged partners' contributions.

Tangible results can be demonstrated through an outcome-based information system and disseminated through the communication network. Small, measurable successes at the outset build individual confidence levels, attract others to join the effort, and deter opposition. If the interorganizational network fails to get successes or measurable progress, members may be unwilling to invest future energy, political capital, and time. Recognizing achievements gives network members renewed energy and enthusiasm. In addition, it increases credibility and generates ongoing support from key members outside the group. Successes in a particular problem should also be communicated to citizens and the media.

Failure to show progress can lower the sense of "do-ability," resulting in the issue fading from public view and falling from its prominent status on the policy agenda. Demonstrating results to policymakers and key stakeholders is critical to sustaining action in interorganizational networks.

Role of Network Facilitators

Implementing multiple strategies by multiple organizations is extraordinarily difficult, and no one person or agency alone can stimulate and sustain action. An interorganizational action vehicle and an outcome-based information system are not sufficient to manage the multiple interconnections. A skillful network facilitator or multilateral broker is crucial for sustaining interdependent action toward agreed-upon outcomes (Matland, 1995; O'Toole, 1995; Jennings, 1994; Waddock, 1989). Interorganizational network brokers or facilitators are catalysts with a unique vantage point to stimulate an ongoing process of action, reflection, and spiraling back.

They manage the web in three unique ways. First, they connect common interests and mediate diverse interests among key implementers, highlight closely aligned interests, help network members connect and weave together shared interests, and manage the natural conflicts that emerge. As implementation unfolds and the agenda broadens, they help build additional agreements. Second, network facilitators encourage the development of trust. They do this, for example, by developing appropriate norms that enhance predictability and trust across a network and reduce the level of ambiguity and uncertainty in implementation. Third, they maintain focus on desired outcomes. They highlight small successes, maintain a commitment to learning and adaptation, and spiral back to earlier phases while always keeping the ultimate outcome in mind.

Ultimately, effective implementation is an ongoing process of negotiation of roles, commitment, and execution among diverse, interdependent agencies and individuals. Sustainability is a process, not an end-state. Maintaining momentum requires ongoing expenditures of time, energy, and resources. Institutionalizing a new policy, strategy, or set of strategies is less important than establishing an ongoing process of focusing on the outcome, acting, reflecting on results, and acting again.

Relationships Built on Trust

Implementation networks do not last long without something strong going for them. Historically, it was assumed that what was needed was a person with a strong personality whose commitment and energy pushed implementation. Individuals with strong personalities or strong egos, however, too frequently create more resistance than action in interconnected webs (View and Amos, 1994). The real strength of multiorganizational implementation networks lies in the supportive relationships and strong bonds of trust among partners in the network. Due to the ongoing nature of implementing interorganizational strategies, relationship building is fundamental to sustaining action. Next to having sufficient resources, the key to building "staying capacity" of an implementation network rests on the development of supportive relationships (Ring and Van deVen, 1994; View and Amos, 1994).

Cooperative interorganizational networks fundamentally rely on trust among network members. The network grows or contracts as the level of trust increases or declines. Interpersonal trust is based on confidence in the predictability of another's actions and in another's moral integrity or goodwill. Confidence stems from the cumulative impact of repeated past interactions. The greater the trust, the greater the ease in negotiating, reaching agreements, and implementing the set of strategies (Ring and Van de Ven, 1994). With this trust goes the willingness to share credit for successes. One community activist stated, "You can accomplish most anything if you are willing to give credit rather than take it." Developing and nurturing trust requires catalysts to embody a strength of character rather than a forceful, strong personality. (This subtle but important distinction is discussed in Chapter Nine.)

Value of Small Successes

Outcomes are most often achieved through a series of smaller achievements, including anticipated planned steps, unpredictable strategic opportunities, and unanticipated policy windows. Although one or a few small wins initially seem unimportant, a series of small wins fitting the larger mosaic of the strategic action can lead to the desired outcomes and results. With small-scale action, there is less conflict and resistance, and ambiguities are reduced to acceptable levels. Feedback is more immediate and can guide timely strategy adjustment and policy learning.

In addressing public problems, grand strategies and comprehensive action plans are often self-defeating. They create higher levels of arousal and resistance, which results in higher levels of implementation failure. People lose faith in the strategy and reduce their activities and efforts. Momentum is lost and interest shifts to other issues. Starting with smaller, more limited actions toward the desired outcome generates immediate, though smaller, results (Weick, 1984). These results can leverage more resources, raise levels of enthusiasm and commitment, and sustain additional activities (Brinkerhoff and Goldsmith, 1992). In addition, the implementation network gains experience and builds trust by solving smaller, and perhaps easier, problems first.

Commitment to Learning

People naturally strive to learn when they are engaged in an effort considered worthy of their fullest commitment (Senge, 1990). Catalysts tap into this natural tendency. When resources are scarce and problems are interconnected, sustaining implementation requires continuous adjustment, reflection, and learning.

To a large degree, all strategies for interconnected problems are working experiments rather than the final solution. Maintaining an experimental approach to implementation enhances the policy-learning potential. It allows groups to compare the results of alternate strategies and to learn which have stronger potential for reaching the desired results. *Adaptive learning* seeks to improve and better understand the practical difficulties in implementation, but does not seek to change the core strategies themselves. Policy learning involves the discovery that strategy A is less effective than strategy B in achieving a certain outcome. It reveals additional points of leverage in the interconnected system to achieve the desired results. The implementation challenge in addressing interconnected problems, however, is not to execute agreed-upon strategies efficiently, nor merely to replace ineffective strategies with more effective strategies. The long-term challenge is to increase the understanding of the depth, complexity, and interdependencies of public problems. Policy learning aims at better understanding how problems are interrelated.

Importance of Spiraling Back

Implementation networks often repeat earlier public leadership tasks, such as raising the issue with key stakeholders, convening additional meetings as new people are engaged, clarifying and refocusing on desired outcomes, and developing agreements on new or revised strategies. Spiraling back does not indicate that the implementation network is failing to make progress. Rather, it is a sign of success, a natural process essential for interorganizational networks to move forward with energy and sustained commitment (Melaville, Blank, and Asayesh, 1993). As new information is generated, unanticipated political events unfold, or new stakeholders emerge, network members are forced to spiral back to integrate, broaden, or adjust. Spiraling back requires network facilitators to expect and seek continuous learning and adjustment.

Public Leadership Summary

Building Commitment and Political Support

- Find multiple champions and prime movers.
- Develop support from power holders.
- Build constituent support and advocacy coalitions.
- Mobilize and allocate resources.

Institutionalizing Cooperative Behavior

- Create enabling mechanisms and action vehicles.
- Support self-organizing groups as they focus on the outcome.
- Develop an outcome-based information system.

Becoming a Network Facilitator

- Maintain focus on desired outcomes.
- Develop and nurture relationships built on trust.
- Seek small wins and strategic opportunities.
- Maintain a commitment to learning.
- Spiral back to earlier catalytic tasks to build commitment.

Solving public problems requires sustained attention and effort by numerous and diverse individuals and agencies in an interconnected implementation network. These joint efforts can be hard to sustain. Trust can be broken, attention is caught by another urgent public problem, and energy turns elsewhere. Strategy implementation is more complex and difficult than typically assumed. In many cases, the real challenge of public leadership is not in adopting or approving a strategy, but in ensuring its implementation.

Addressing interconnected public problems most commonly occurs in multiagency or network settings. It creates unique leadership challenges to sustain cooperative behavior beyond the initial burst of energy following agreements by working group members. Key leadership questions include

- What is the appropriate institutional structure or action vehicle to sustain attention, action, and feedback?
- How can the effort be kept outcome-oriented, not structure-oriented?
- How can we rapidly share data and information on progress, both internally and externally?
- How can the social network be maintained to facilitate implementation?
- Are there existing institutional barriers that need to be eliminated?

First, energy is needed to sustain movement toward achieving an outcome, while also providing feedback that stimulates policy learning and adjusting. This catalytic energy is created through agreement on a shared outcome, resource targeting and allocation, support and commitment from key power holders, and broader support from constituent groups. Second, a form of cohesion or "glue" holds the key implementers together throughout implementation, yet does so without controlling or coercing the participants. Cohesion can be developed through formal and informal networks, partnerships, formal agreements, and the establishment of new organizations. The development of professional relationships builds an increasing spiral of trust. In addition, the information infrastructure creates a necessary basis of cohesion that can hold together a critical mass of key stakeholders and sustain the effort over the long run.

Part Three

The Foundational Skills for Catalytic Leaders

For public leadership to effectively address interconnected public problems, individuals must step forward and act as catalysts. With a diverse group of individuals, they must forge sustainable agreements on action strategies, set into motion multiple strategies, and sustain momentum over time. Such catalytic leadership requires a set of analytical skills and interpersonal competencies and is characterized by a common set of attitudes, traits, and habits.

The three chapters in Part Three elaborate on the crucial analytical and interpersonal skills that cut across the four public leadership tasks. These skills are learned through experience and trial and error. The core set of analytical skills involves thinking strategically, while the core group of interpersonal skills clusters around an individual's ability to facilitate and mediate within working groups and networks. A strong character, rather than a strong personality, provides the foundation for the core skills.

Chapter Seven, "Thinking and Acting Strategically," emphasizes that to address interconnected problems, strategic analysis is required. This type of analysis raises an issue to public attention, identifies common and conflicting interests of key stakeholders, and illuminates linkages and interconnections. Strategic thinking involves framing and reframing issues and their strategic responses, identifying and defining end outcomes or desired results, assessing stakeholder interests to discover common and complementary interests, and thinking systemically to reveal interconnections and strategic leverage points. Catalytic leaders must think strategically and they must encourage and nurture key stakeholders to do so, too. Failure to engage in strategic thinking commonly prevents working groups from making significant progress on some of our most pressing public problems. A wide variety of analytical techniques and tools are discussed that have proven successful in stimulating work group members and other key stakeholders to engage in strategic thinking.

Public leaders must also be catalysts for their productive working group, assisting it in reaching durable and sustainable agreements on strategies aimed at a particular outcome. Chapter Eight, "Facilitating Productive Working Groups," focuses on the interpersonal skills necessary for facilitating a productive working group or network. Public leaders use a repertoire of process skills to understand the multiple points of view and stakes in the particular issue, to draw clarity out of poorly stated positions, and to synthesize statements and actively integrate varied interests. Encouraging and stimulating a productive working group process with diverse stakeholders, with varying and often opposing views, requires a strong set of facilitation, negotiation, and mediation skills. These process skills essentially involve four distinct challenges: generating fresh ideas and new insights, coping with conflict, getting a group unstuck and moving forward, and forging agreements.

Such public leadership is more than a set of analytical skills and interpersonal competencies. Chapter Nine, "Leading from Personal Passion and Strength of Character," outlines the underlying character of successful catalysts in an interconnected world. Character is the spirit and intent of one's leadership actions to make a difference. Character undergirds and infuses energy into the specific tasks and skills discussed in earlier chapters and is characterized by a common set of attitudes, traits, and habits. Rather than having a strong personality, successful catalysts exhibit strength of character. This trait establishes their credibility to convene diverse groups, builds confidence to facilitate and mediate difficult agreements, and develops a long-term perspective to focus and refocus attention when faced with minor defeats. Character lies behind one's conduct and encompasses the "inner" side: one's will, dispositions, and inclinations. What distinguishes catalytic leadership is the strength of character based on three key habits: a passion for results, a sense of connectedness and relatedness, and exemplary personal integrity.

Chapter Seven

Thinking and Acting Strategically

When you bury your head in the sand, it leaves one part of your anatomy exposed.

Analysis is an important skill in public leadership, yet too often it's overlooked. Some consider analysis too hardheaded, too detached, too detail-oriented, and too academic to lead to effective action. Nevertheless, with interconnected problems, strategic analysis is required, analysis that raises an issue to public attention, that identifies common and conflicting interests of key stakeholders, and that illuminates promising strategies for action. Indeed, it is the failure to engage in such strategic thinking that prevents us from making much progress on our most pressing public problems.

Defining Strategic Thinking

The common exhortation to "Think strategically!" is heard in both public and corporate circles. But what exactly is strategic thinking for interconnected problems? It is more than just systemic thinking. It is more than just creative or divergent thinking. Strategic thinking involves four distinct sets of analytical skills:

1. Framing and reframing issues and their strategic responses
2. Identifying and defining end-outcomes or desired results
3. Assessing stakeholder interests to discover common and complementary interests
4. Systemic thinking to reveal interconnections and strategic leverage points

Several common obstacles, both cognitive and emotional, deter analysis and constrain strategic thinking. Unfortunately, many of these barriers are so difficult to overcome that strategic thinking has even been described as "an unnatural act for most humans."

Failure to Analyze

Without another's prodding questions or the appearance of an unusual anomaly, people often fail to take the time to analyze. People naturally rely on personal judgment and often neglect to use structured analytical techniques (Nutt, 1989). First, people have a universal passion to simplify things, particularly complex or emotionally charged issues. Second, when confronted with making strategic choices among competing alternatives, individuals rely on traditional or habitual ways of thinking, often persisting with old approaches to problems, even if an approach had not been necessarily successful. These persistent ways of thinking about an issue are based on one's mental model, an internalized image that simplifies and shapes how one views the issue and what one believes will work.

Third, people are often overconfident and think they know more than they actually do. They underestimate gaps in their knowledge and have difficulty detecting inconsistencies in their thinking and internalized beliefs. When they feel they are missing important information, they look for guidance and advice from those close to them, relying on what they hear from coworkers, neighbors, and other trusted friends. Thus, it is not surprising that advice and insight on key issues emerge in the form of anecdotes (Isenberg, 1984; Fischoff, 1983; Nutt, 1989).

These very common intellectual habits inhibit individuals' tendency to analyze problems in much depth. Complicating matters are three barriers to strategic thinking, the form of analysis needed for interconnected problems.

Prefrontal Lobe: The Brain's Center for Strategic Thinking

Strategic thinking occurs in the prefrontal lobe of the frontal cortex, which is the center for human planning and essential to the brain's strategic thinking functions. It mentally represents possible future events, attaches significance to them, and devises actions and strategies to respond to, or influence, the events. People with impaired frontal lobes have great difficulty engaging in coherent goal-directed activity, particularly when this activity extends into the future (Ingvar, 1985; Luria, 1980).

The prefrontal lobe creates mental representations of objects in their absence and anticipates ripple effects and probable outcomes. These activities are inherent in strategic thinking: identifying what issues or trends need attention, detecting obscure interconnections and systemic relationships, imagining long-term outcomes to be achieved, and planning an appropriate sequence of actions. An important challenge for catalysts is to create situations in which individuals' prefrontal lobes are engaged, such as by using cause-and-effect diagrams and strategic mapping.

Psychological Biases and Preferences

In addition to cognitive barriers, there are formidable psychological barriers to thinking strategically. Individuals have certain personality biases and preferences that increase or decrease interest in strategic thinking. For example, some individuals have preferences for divergent thinking, an open-ended, *what-if* thinking style. Divergent thinkers make unusual connections among events, patterns of behavior, and underlying systemic relationships. Other people prefer a more detailed and pragmatic cognitive style that focuses on *what is.*

Although many psychological instruments attempt to measure these different cognitive biases, the Myers Briggs Type Indicator (MBTI) most easily reveals such preferences. (See Nutt, 1989, for a detailed discussion of personality types and their impacts on decision-making styles.) In the MBTI, convergent thinkers typically score high as "sensing" types. Estimated to be about 65 percent of the general U.S. population, sensing types prefer details and tangible, measurable short-term objectives and milestones. They think of the immediate impacts. Analysis that excites sensing types focuses on detailed numbers and immediate action steps, and excludes *what-if* options and longer-term strategies.

"Intuitive" types on the MBTI prefer the big picture. They identify long-term trends and their connections to current or proposed actions and larger systems issues. Intuitive types are more comfortable with strategic thinking: developing potential scenarios, anticipating trends, assessing potential stakeholder responses, and predicting possible consequences and ripple effects. Sensing types are much more hesitant. They prefer not to waste time in "stupid, fruitless brainstorming meetings." Catalysts stimulate sensing types to see longer-term scenarios and make actions and potential consequences tangible and salient. They also assist intuitive types to understand the need to focus on certain details.

Denial and Resistance to Strategic Thinking

Emotional barriers often create feelings of denial and resistance, which can further constrain and limit strategic thinking. Individuals go through stages of denial. They feel anger, express blame, and become withdrawn when faced with crises or new and different challenges. In declining local economies, such as those found in rural agricultural communities of the Midwest or timber-dependent communities of the Northwest, local residents confront the stages of death and dying typically encountered by individuals who first learn they have a terminal disease (Luke, Ventriss, Reed, and Reed, 1988). Faced with a declining or dying economy, community members first deny the reality of the situation, saying, "These are difficult times, no doubt, but things will work themselves out."

Once past denial, anger and blame set in and finger-pointing begins. When people blame economic decline on the President's embargo, or increased teenage pregnancy rates on society's decaying moral fiber, it is unlikely they will undertake strategic analyses toward the problem. Withdrawal, the next attitudinal phase, is characterized by individuals becoming passive observers rather than active decision makers. Pessimism creates a sense that "nobody can get this mess straightened out." Research on organizational transitions shows that corporations confronting new or different markets similarly proceed through denial and resistance (Bridges, 1988).

It is very natural to experience these attitudinal phases when confronting difficult-to-solve interconnected problems. However, until a critical mass of individuals reach the stage of acceptance and perceive a situation as real and urgent, little or no strategic thinking occurs, because people simply see no need for it. At the acceptance stage, individuals realize that long-term strategic actions are needed rather than blame or quick fixes. Public leaders are challenged to stimulate individuals and working groups to move past denial, anger, and blame to acceptance, so that strategic thinking and analysis can illuminate public problems that need to be attacked and identify potentially successful action strategies.

Framing Issues Strategically

Public leaders not only illuminate and define emerging problems and issues, but they also interpret and explain them (Bryson and Crosby, 1992). Public problems are not simply the objective facts of a particular situation; rather, they are matters of personal interpretation and negotiation (Rochefort and Cobb, 1994). For instance, an eight-ounce glass containing four ounces of water could be seen as half full or half empty. Although both perceptions are true, each conveys a different impression. Each description colors the situation differently and suggests a different assessment of the problem and alternate courses of action.

Every social problem can be defined or framed in a variety of ways. There are usually powerful tensions among the multiple, often conflicting definitions of problems and their solutions. Strategic responses are socially constructed and negotiated (see Chapter Five). As a result, there is seldom a natural consensus on whether a problem exists, and if so, what it is and how to respond to it effectively. The choice of an issue definition has far less to do with data and scientific analysis than with values, mental models, and personal experience. For example, some link teenage pregnancy to poor sex education or the lack of available birth control. Others see it as a problem of insufficient parenting by the teen's parents or poor moral development.

The process of issue definition is at the center of public leadership. How a public problem is defined or framed affects how quickly it will rise to the policy agenda, how it structures the debates on alternative action strategies, and how it influences which strategies are considered useful or irrelevant. Once the problem definition has crystallized, it can remain as a long-term fixture in the deliberations. In a few cases the definition can undergo revision, which reframes the original problem. Reframing strategies broaden or change the definition of the issue in ways that focus attention, expand support, capture multiple interests, and sustain attention during implementation. Public leaders act as catalysts when they interpret problems by defining, framing, and reframing them strategically in ways that focus attention, stimulate an urgency for action, and provide a framework for the debates on action strategies (Rochefort and Cobb, 1994.)

Catalyst's Role in Framing and Reframing

Catalysts lend great sensitivity to how a condition, problem, or issue is initially framed because it influences whether or not individuals will feel the problem is urgent and worthy of attention or merely one of a myriad of other problems that people talk about and the media report on. Initial problem framing has several other important impacts:

- It influences how fast the problem gets recognized and reaches the public agenda.
- It influences who sees this condition as compelling or urgent and who does not.
- It influences who will be naturally drawn to discussions on the issue, ultimately widening or narrowing who will join in the efforts to address the issue.
- It guides how one sees his or her interest in the issue.
- It shapes and directs the generation of options for action.

When people are first confronted with a complex issue, with no previous way of framing or defining it, individuals are more malleable and suggestible in how they come to see the issue. People are strongly influenced by how the issue is first formulated. Later analysis of an issue is directly shaped by how the issue was initially framed. Further, once a situation or issue is conceived as problematic and framed in a particular fashion, one's subsequent thoughts on that problem typically wander in directions closely related to the earlier framing (Fischoff, 1983).

Reframing involves breaking existing perspectives or old patterns of viewing a problem and articulating a new definition or interpretation (Bryson and Crosby, 1992). If an issue has already surfaced onto the strategic agenda and has sunk to a lesser level of visibility and support, strategic reframing can heighten interest and arouse emotional concern. Reframing can make a public problem more vivid and urgent, generating new or increased attention. Reframing also occurs when conflict seems intractable and expanding the problem definition is needed to sustain action. In addition, reframing is popular when a particular strategy needs to be described more succinctly to facilitate implementation.

Catalytic Strategies for Framing and Reframing

- Clarify and simplify an issue, defining a problem in terms that citizens can easily understand and support.
- Increase a felt sense of urgency and salience to the problem.
- Expand the issue to broaden support for action.
- Capture strategic intent in order to facilitate and sustain implementation of the action strategies.

Examples of Framing and Reframing

Framing and reframing can often be a complex, analytical endeavor. Several common techniques are used to frame and reframe issues. One important technique is to clarify and simplify an issue by eliminating obscure terminology and by defining a problem in terms that citizens can easily understand and support. To reach public and policy agendas, problematic conditions are simplified to make them more understandable. Drawing attention to the increasing air pollution problems in Central California, for example, the regional Council of Governments decided to avoid technical jargon. Instead of defining the issue as PM10 readings (particulate matter less than 10 microns in diameter) that far exceed healthy limits, the issue was framed by highlighting that "this air pollution is like you and your children smoking a half-pack of cigarettes a day." This approach not only avoided technical jargon, but attempted to increase a felt sense of urgency and salience to the problem by comparing it to children smoking cigarettes.

A more vivid example comes from public health. The Love Canal problem in Niagara Falls, N.Y., was initially framed as an environmental issue of contaminated soil. After reframing it as a horrifying public health issue—one that produced deformed babies—the New York metropolitan press picked up the story and, within days, the issue gained national visibility and notoriety.

Another common strategy is to define the issue in general terms that encompass several elements. This technique can expand the issue to broaden support for action. By expanding the definition to include larger groups of people, an issue can be revived or resurfaced. In Tillamook, Oregon, part of the community's success in reducing teen pregnancies can be attributed to reframing the issue. Early in the community debates, the goal was defined as reducing teen birthrates among adolescent girls. During the discussions, the issue was redefined: the goal became the reduction of teen pregnancies, not teen births. This may appear as too subtle a difference to matter. However, the goal of reducing teen births could be accomplished by increasing the number of abortions by teens, which church leaders did not want to promote. Reframing the problem to focus on teen pregnancies implied the goal of reducing both births and abortions. This made the issue more palatable to conservative citizens who wished to participate. Targeting "teen pregnancies" instead of "teen births" expanded the issue to include a broader set of interests in reducing abortions and promoting abstinence (Luke and Neville, 1996). Expanding the issue definition essentially captures mutual or complementary interests.

A national example is the reframing of welfare reform efforts. Initially framed by conservatives as an initiative to remove people from welfare rolls, it did not have the necessary support of a wide range of groups. During the late 1980s and early 1990s, a general consensus formed based on a new framing of the issue: to increase self-sufficiency and sustain financial independence. With this reframing, several different complementary interests were captured: using education and training strategies to help welfare recipients become self-sufficient, and increasing personal responsibility of recipients while strengthening the family (Reischauer, 1987). Issues can be framed to find areas of mutual or complementary interest, despite serious value differences among stakeholders. The key is to craft a frame within which key stakeholders or constituents can identify their interests, without focusing on sacrosanct values or preexisting positions.

Once strategies have been selected, groups can frame action strategies by succinctly capturing strategic intent to facilitate and sustain implementation. In the Central California air pollution example, the regional effort was labeled "Project Clean Air." Its goal was captured in the slogan "Let's see the mountains!" referring to reducing the level of pollution that covered the valley basin and obscured the view of the nearby Sierra mountain range.

Proposed strategies are also amenable to creative framing and reframing. Action strategies can be defined in terms of specific activities to provide a more tangible or vivid description of strategic intent. For example, to help focus tourism strategies in local economic development, several communities frame their strategies as "ecotourism," in which visitors are attracted to a region to experience a natural environment. Other communities tout "heritage travel," in which visitors learn about the area's rich cultural history. One strategy targeting the reduction of teenage pregnancies was framed as "parent talk," a support group for parents to talk with each other about how to engage their sons and daughters in discussions about abstinence pregnancy prevention.

Individuals can use strategic framing to focus attention among diverse stakeholders. They can also use it as a ploy to define a problem to fit their preferred solutions, to narrow debate, and to limit consideration of certain strategies. Building relationships and inspiring trust, however, are fundamental to catalytic leadership. Selectively casting something in a certain way to gain personal or political advantage can lead to suspicion and to a downward spiral of distrust and loss of confidence. This fine line between influence and manipulation must be guided by one's personal values and sense of integrity (see Chapter Nine).

Communicating Data Strategically

Although often overlooked as an important strategic tool, how data are communicated or framed has significant impacts. To communicate an issue as an urgent need, groups often frame data to evoke concern and drive people out of their comfort zones. Publicly discussed issues compete for attention and energy. To mobilize attention in this competitive context, data must be understandable and meaningful to the general public and interesting to the media.

Data can be framed by three general communication strategies (see Table 7.1). Regardless of which approach is used, the issue must appear concrete and clear to policymakers, key stakeholders, the media, and the general public. In addition, credibility and trust in the sources of information are the most important elements in strategically communicating data.

Absolute Numbers, Frequencies, or Percentages

Using absolute numbers to highlight an issue generally has the least impact among the three communication strategies. For example, in 1991, there were 38,317 shooting deaths (an absolute number) in the United States. What is left unsaid is that in 1991 there were more traffic fatalities (43,536) than shooting deaths (38,317). Many advocate groups use a variation by showing how often a particular event or behavior occurs. For example, the Children's Defense Fund notes that every nine seconds, a child drops out of school; every 25 seconds, a baby is born to an unmarried teen mother; and every two hours, a child is killed by a firearm. Using a frequency of occurrence approach may be eye-opening, but it provides little insight into whether the problem is getting worse and is therefore more urgent than other critical problems facing public leaders.

Another approach is to use a percent of a total population or number of occurrences. This approach also lacks potency. For example, it is not clear if a 9.0 percent dropout rate is good or bad without a reference point. Without a reference point, it is difficult to interpret the seriousness or urgency of a condition or issue. Reference points are critical to communicate important trends or conditions strategically. They can be derived by comparisons with past performance or by comparisons with other jurisdictions. Absolute figures—numbers, percentages, or frequencies—have less salience than using comparative data and have less impact than highlighting worsening conditions or troubling comparisons.

Worsening Conditions

Comparing current data with past data illuminates trends and highlights situations that are worsening or growing beyond acceptable levels. For example, deaths by firearms in the United States soared by 60 percent from 1968 to 1991. This percentage of increases amplifies the changes in absolute numbers. When

Table 7.1. Communicating Information Strategically.

	Techniques	Description
Using Data to Convey Information	Absolute Numbers, Frequencies, or Percentages	Include using absolute numbers to highlight an issue, a frequency of occurrence, or a percentage of some total population or number of occurrences. Sometimes these data may be eye-opening, but provide no comparisons to assess if the problem is getting worse or better.
	Worsening Conditions	Current data are compared with past data to highlight situations that are worsening or growing beyond what is acceptable. Describe an issue in relative terms, not absolute terms.
	Troubling Comparisons	Compare current situation with other jurisdictions, issues, or populations. Provide revealing comparisons that can suggest urgency.
Using More Vivid Methods to Convey Information	A Story or Narrative Analysis	Stories engage emotions and make an issue more real by way of a personal example. Using stories to support and stimulate strategic thinking challenges individuals to recall actual event, in ways that are vivid and personal, and that may also be backed up with details and data.
	Metaphors and Analogies	Metaphors frame an issue by providing a succinct label, such as the "homeless," that directs attention to one aspect of a problem. Analogies describe the issue's similarities to something else, such as "welfare has become more like a 'hammock' than a 'safety net.'"
	Scenarios	Scenarios are a set of stories about the future—logically constructed, internally consistent, and data-driven—and they provide plausible frameworks for strategically analyzing the future consequences of decision options. Good scenarios do not result in a more accurate picture of the future, but in more strategic analysis prior to decisions.

described in relative rather than absolute terms, it provides a broader perspective from which to assess its urgency.

Troubling Comparisons

Comparing the current situation with other jurisdictions, issues, or populations provides insights that can also stress urgency. A common strategy is to compare one jurisdiction with a similar jurisdiction on a particular condition. For example, in 1994, there were 58 million Americans uninsured for health care. This absolute figure provides no comparative perspective that frames the issue as urgent. But when compared with other industrial countries, the situation becomes more staggering: the United States is near the bottom in health care coverage to its citizens (thirteenth out of fourteen Western industrial nations). Comparing and contrasting by subpopulations also highlights a condition so that it can more easily become an urgent problem (for instance, comparing teenage pregnancy rates between rural and urban counties, or between different ethnic populations). A variant on this approach was used by pediatricians in Oregon. Urging for more child immunizations, they would make statements such as, "In our state, 98 percent of all cattle have their appropriate immunizations, but only 52 percent of our children have received the recommended levels of immunizations."

Stories, Metaphors, and Scenarios

More information is not always better. When bombarded daily with bits of facts and figures, people make sense out of the array of data through stories or anecdotes that reflect personal experiences. People rely on personal stories and anecdotes more often than on data. We reason from prior experience and make decisions by abstracting essential themes from our past.

Stories are an ancient way of organizing knowledge. In working through an issue, rather than relying on experts or institutions, people naturally turn to personal experience and to the experiences of coworkers, neighbors, and trusted friends. The information received from officials is often considered slanted and partial or not the whole truth. National survey data show that Americans place confidence in other people like themselves, rather than in the media, government, or business (Harwood Group, 1993a; National Civic League, 1994). Second, vivid case studies versus dry or pallid data capture attention more readily, are more readily stored in memory, and remain in our thoughts longer. Personal anecdotes, case studies, and hands-on demonstrations are often more persuasive than tables, charts, and statistics. Cognitive psychologists clearly tell us why: the mind is driven by pattern recognition and is less suited for computation.

As a result, people do not naturally seek out all the necessary information. They often rely on stories and anecdotes to make sense of an issue and to identify and select potential strategies. Stories, rather than data, often drive problem identification and solution generation by citizens and elected officials. Analysis of local policymaking found that city managers gather information by exchanging and applying their knowledge to the problem, whereas the elected officials use anecdotes and stories in their public policy arguments (Nalbandian, 1994). What is needed to stimulate strategic thinking is not just data and technical information, but also stories and anecdotes to illuminate the issue, its multiple causes, and its potential solutions.

Stories and Narrative Analysis

Using stories to support and stimulate strategic thinking will challenge public leaders to recall events vividly and personally. If necessary, the stories can be backed up with details and data. Upton Sinclair's *The Jungle* (1906), a narrative description of the unsanitary conditions in Chicago's stockyards, was a personal and anecdotal analysis that initiated major policy reform. Marjory Douglas's *The Everglades: River of Grass,* initially published in 1947, was so striking that it fueled generations of strategic thinking. The book's impact resulted in the expansion of the Everglades State Park and the creation of the Big Cypress National Preserve. It also was a catalyst in the analysis that created Florida's 1972 growth management law, and the law's successors in the 1980s and 1990s (Popper and Popper, 1996).

Catalysts use current and past stories to stretch the consciousness of the audience by bringing new attention to a certain aspect, or by giving it a fresh twist. Some create fresh stories not known to the working group, narratives that include parts of other members' stories woven like strings on a bead. (See Gardner, 1995, for a summary of how innovative leaders use stories.) For someone who intends to stimulate strategic thinking, a good story or narrative analysis has several qualities that make it potent or stimulating (Taylor and Novelli, 1991).

A good story is vivid; it is told in sensory language to aid retention. Some of history's most famous figures create a full sensory experience through their speeches and stories. Sensory language uses verbal predicates that create visual, auditory, and kinesthetic images to help listeners see, hear, and feel an experience (Swanson, 1986). If the story is about a real person and has a strong sense of time and place, credibility is increased. If a story is evocative and believable, it is likely to be recalled, repeated, and commented on, thus magnifying its effect. A good story can provide a sense of causal relationships. Instead of being a complex picture of the situation, it cuts through the clutter and confusion of interrelated problems and their multiple causes to reveal a few factors worth thinking about.

Metaphors and Analogies

Metaphors and analogies describe an issue's likeness to something else. Using metaphors to frame an issue provides a succinct label or a way of thinking about a problem, such as "the homeless," "the feminization of poverty," or "the graying of America." Metaphors crystallize thinking, focus attention, and stimulate discussion. Information in such complex areas as the economy are most easily communicated through metaphors. Technological advances in manufacturing industries allowed many firms to expand production while reducing the number of workers. Economists labeled this complex phenomenon by using a metaphor, calling it the "decoupling" of labor from productivity. When frustration increased with the U.S. welfare system, many argued that the "safety net" had become a "hammock." Metaphors and analogies can provide bold images that stimulate people to think in new and different ways, either to advocate for a solution or to think strategically. However, overused metaphors lose their richness and become tiresome clichés.

Future Scenarios

Scenarios increase understanding of present trends and illuminate potential responses. Scenarios are a set of stories about the future— logically constructed, internally consistent, and data driven. An individual uses scenarios by telling stories in coherent, structured, and consistent ways based on the expertise of people in a company, industry, or policy domain. In corporate planning, scenarios provide frameworks for strategically analyzing the future consequences of decision options. In the public sector, scenarios are used to stimulate options for improving strategic choices.

A person begins by constructing two or three scenario plots. These are plausible alternative scenarios, not necessarily best-case, worst-case, and most-likely scenarios. One community, for example, created three scenarios to stimulate strategic analysis around growth management, including high-growth, slow-growth, and no-growth scenarios. The test of a good scenario is not whether it accurately portrays the future, but whether it enables a group to consider possible conditions, interconnections, and options (Lindbloom, 1990). Once two or three scenarios are fleshed out and woven into a narrative, the group analyzes possible implications and key leverage points. Ultimately, good scenarios do not always result in a more accurate picture of the future, but in more strategic analysis prior to decisions. They help individuals to expand their thinking and to question implicit assumptions.

Despite scenarios' story-like features, developing and using scenarios to stimulate strategic thinking follows rather systematic phases (Schwartz, 1991):

1. Select a policy or outcome area for the focus of scenario development, such as growth management.
2. Identify and analyze the social, economic, political, and technological driving forces.
3. Identify and analyze the existing givens or inevitable elements.
4. Identify and analyze the critical uncertainties.
5. Elaborate two to four plausible scenarios that could occur as a result of the preceding phases.
6. With each scenario, analyze and identify implications for decisions on action strategies.

Defining Strategic Intentions as Outcomes or Desired Results

Strategic thinking is enhanced when diverse stakeholders first focus on outcomes and end-results. In many cases, individuals learn to see old problems in new ways through gathering and organizing information about how to achieve an outcome. Available empirical research clearly shows that by formulating the problem or issue in terms of desired results, the number of different strategies and alternatives for action generated by a working group will increase by 20 percent to 40 percent (Volkema, 1983; Eden and Radford, 1990).

Focusing attention on the desired results requires a shift in thinking. When members begin to discuss what the problem really is, they initially define or frame the issue in terms of something that is lacking (such as not enough federal funding, or insufficient level of services). This approach essentially shifts the group's focus from problem solving to searching for effective strategies. This requires a level of comfort to ask continually, What is the outcome we are trying to achieve?

In early stages of multiparty problem solving, outcomes and results are often confused with problems or services. Outcomes describe the results or consequences of action, not the *why* (rationale) or the *how* (specific strategies). Outcomes can be described as the impacts of programs and policies on individual citizens and clients, such as the self-sufficiency of low-income families or the independence of senior and disabled citizens, or as impacts on larger geographical areas, such as the environmental quality of an estuary, the teen pregnancy rate for a county, or the vitality of a state's economy.

Catalytic Strategies for Identifying Outcomes

- Separate the desired results from the problem.
- Separate the desired results from proposed services.
- Avoid defining desired results as increases in inputs.
- Separate end-outcomes from intermediate outcomes.

Desired Results in Relation to the Problem and Proposed Services

It's important to separate desired results from the problem and proposed services. To catalyze attention, problems are often stated initially as an unwanted condition or trend, such as a dramatic increase in juvenile crime. Centering attention on the problem is appropriate for stimulating awareness and mobilizing key stake-holders. After a working group has convened, however, a problem orientation can cause defensiveness, generate blaming, stifle creativity, and drain off valuable energy. Turf battles and solution wars can erupt when members begin prematurely proposing competing solutions and services. Outcomes are the results of activities and services for individuals, communities, states, or the nation. A service such as increasing police patrols is an organizational or interagency response to a need or problem. Premature focus on needed services narrows discussion early in the process and prevents a broad examination of multiple strategies, especially strategies and options that are not direct services, such as passing a curfew ordinance. Outcomes, on the other hand, are more generally stated as the hoped-for result, such as reduced juvenile violence (see Table 7.2.).

Desired Results in Relation to Increased Inputs

Working groups should avoid defining desired results as increases in inputs or other service measures. For instance, some participants may identify the problem as the need to increase the budget of the Department of Juvenile Services by at least 40 percent. Others may state that the community needs to double the number of cops in the neighborhoods. Defining the problem as a lack

Table 7.2. Desired Results in Relation to Perceived Problem and Proposed Services.

Perceived Problem	Services	Desired Results
Increasing numbers of gang members committing property crimes	Increasing police patrols in targeted neighborhoods	Reducing juvenile crimes committed by gang members
Kids not ready for emerging global economy	Increasing school requirements	Improved literacy and numeracy rates
Polluted estuary	Increasing environmental enforcement	Improved water quality

of funding narrows the quantity and quality of solutions considered. If the underlying problem of urban decay is stated as not enough federal dollars, then thinking about restoring urban health will focus narrowly on how to attract more external federal funding. Public leaders need to focus the discussion on desired results by asking, What services would be provided if more urban funding were successfully captured? and then, more important, What would the impacts be on the urban neighborhoods and the population if these services were provided? Once working groups identify desired outcomes, multiple strategies can be generated. An analysis of a public health program targeting healthy babies, for example, reveals several distinct inputs, activities, or services and outcomes (see Figure 7.1).

No matter how accurate or pressing, statements such as "we need more public health nurses" or "we must increase the number of home visits" are translated into outcome statements such as "we have to reduce the low-birth-weight rate among babies in this region." Constantly asking, What results will this get? directs attention to desired outcomes that implicitly inform the need for services. Then the working group can strategically work backward to develop a broader array of potential services and strategies that might be successful in reaching that outcome.

Relationship Between End-Outcomes and Intermediate Outcomes

Consensus or agreement is more easily developed on the more general levels of end-outcomes. As the process unfolds, outcomes move from the more general to the more specific. End-outcomes are refined by identifying several intermediate outcomes that provide a clearer focus and strategic intent for the group. For example, an estuary protection effort by local governments, businesses, and boaters in Tampa Bay initially targeted an outcome as "improving water and sediment quality in the bay." Over several meetings, the "bay quality outcome" was refined to include several intermediate outcomes, such as "the reduction of discharges into the water and soil," which led to developing a set of more targeted pollution reduction strategies (Hatry, Liner, and Rossman, 1995). Other intermediate outcomes generated additional sets of strategies, all

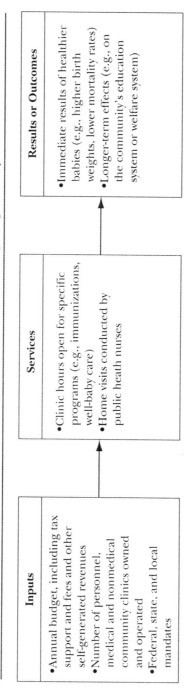

Figure 7.1. Analysis of a Public Health Program Targeting Healthy Babies.

Inputs

- Annual budget, including tax support and fees and other self-generated revenues
- Number of personnel, medical and nonmedical community clinics owned and operated
- Federal, state, and local mandates

Services

- Clinic hours open for specific programs (e.g., immunizations, well-baby care)
- Home visits conducted by public health nurses

Results or Outcomes

- Immediate results of healthier babies (e.g., higher birth weights, lower mortality rates)
- Longer-term effects (e.g., on the community's education system or welfare system)

designed to achieve the general outcome of improving the water and sediment quality of the bay (see Figure 7.2).

Stakeholder Analysis: Identifying Stakeholders and Their Interests

Successful problem solving requires engaging a diverse set of stakeholders and their multiple interests. Stakeholder analysis is most critical when convening a working group to address a public problem and in identifying common and shared interests to forge agreements on strategies. A continuous and reiterative stakeholder assessment process, however, is also important for developing advocacy coalition strategies and institutional networks that enhance strategy implementation (see Chapter Six). Strategic thinking thus involves two different levels of stakeholder analyses: stakeholders must first be identified through a stakeholder mapping process, and their diverse interests must be defined, understood, and updated as situations change.

Stakeholder Identification

Stakeholders are individuals, groups, and organizations with interests in the issue area. They hold a stake in either changing the issue or maintaining the status quo. Stakeholders also include individuals, groups, or organizations affected by the causes or consequences of the particular issue (Bryson and Crosby, 1992).

A stakeholder map graphically represents important stakeholder groups in the policy system, the smaller policy community, and the decision network. A good stakeholder map can easily have more than twenty specific stakeholder groups. An effort to reform education in Minnesota, for example, included more than thirty distinct stakeholder groups, which were eventually grouped by the state education commissioner into nine clusters (Roberts and King, 1989b). A stakeholder mapping process conducted by a regional private industry council targeting the improvement of workforce quality categorized groups into four clusters: those needing their service; agencies controlling their funding; agencies needing funding; and other constituents (see Figure 7.3.)

Figure 7.2. Estuary Protection Outcomes.

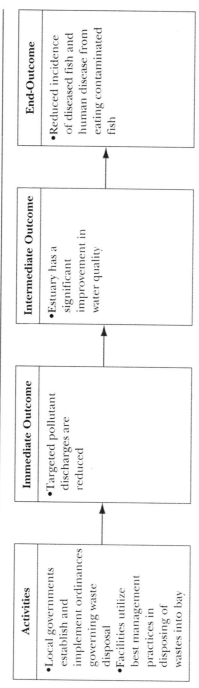

Source: Adapted from Hatry, Liner, and Rossman, 1995.

Sustained action on important public problems requires leaders to involve not only the obvious and well-known stakeholders, but to go beyond the usual suspects (see Chapter Four). In a rush to convene groups and to hurry agreements, two important groups or sets of individuals are often overlooked. Knowledgeholders, particularly those with comprehensive, systemic perspectives, are critically important. In addition, ripple-effect stakeholders can add focus, attention, and energy to strategic efforts (see Chapter Four). With interconnected problems, the ripples affect a wider audience and expand to include people and organizations that one may never even see or meet. Ripple-effect stakeholders are affected by the second- or third-order consequences of an issue. As a result, there are no easily discernible boundaries that limit the number of stakeholders who have direct and indirect interests.

Stakeholders' Goals and Interests

Identifying stakeholders alone is not sufficient for thinking strategically. Determining each stakeholder's goals, concerns, or stakes can reveal strategic options ripe for consideration. Catalysts don't merely imagine others' interests. Stakeholders, once engaged in the effort, often reveal their interests either explicitly or implicitly, through stories and anecdotes. Successful catalysts look for underlying interests to forge agreements on strategies that satisfy the multiple interests of stakeholders. It is critical to recognize and work with the underlying concerns, desires, or fears that motivate an individual or agency to participate. However, it is sometimes necessary to take the analysis a step further and examine the underlying values of the stakeholders. Agreement on underlying values is not necessary for building agreement on viable options, yet understanding core values significantly helps in identifying underlying interests (Fisher and Brown, 1988).

Strategic thinking requires the capacity to recognize the basic needs and interests of key stakeholders, revealing areas of shared, complementary, and conflicting interests. Shared or mutual interests emerge when something is commonly valued by stakeholders and where working group members share an interest in a particular goal, outcome, or strategy. Complementary interests occur when differing interests or goals exist but are not in direct opposition. When priorities among stakeholders differ, specific trade-offs can

Figure 7.3. A Stakeholder Map:
The Southern Willamette Private Industry Council.

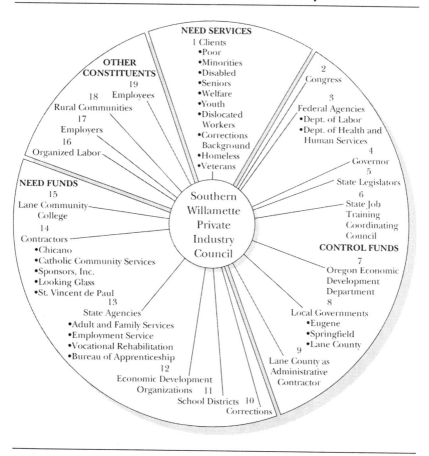

Source: The Southern Willamette Private Industry Council, 1991.

be made, and each stakeholder feels a sense of joint gain even though her or his goals may not be the same. Contradictory interests are defined as interests and goals of equivalent priority or value that are diametrically opposed. Contradictory or conflicting interests require further digging to see if there are any underlying outcomes and goals that can provide deeper agreement. Short of that, external objective criteria must be identified to determine potential areas for negotiating agreement (see Chapter Eight).

Questions that begin to reveal underlying interests of stakeholders include the following (Bryson and Crosby, 1992):

- What are each stakeholder's goals and concerns related to the problem area?
- How well does the status quo meet each stakeholder's goals or satisfy her or his concerns?
- What criteria will each stakeholder use in deciding to come to the table?
- What criteria will each stakeholder use in evaluating proposed strategies?

Once a working group has convened and multiple strategies have been identified, further stakeholder analysis helps to guide a public leader's efforts to sustain implementation. Although stakeholders cannot truly be directed or controlled, relationships must be managed to sustain action during implementation. Some actions are necessary to capitalize on supporters, while others help to neutralize resisters or opponents (Nutt and Backoff, 1992). Questions that stimulate strategic thinking around stakeholder relations during implementation include

- Given stakeholders' interests, what coalitions are likely to form around the issue?
- What actions are needed to deal effectively with each stakeholder and emerging coalitions?
- How can each stakeholder influence the agreement-building process?
- What is needed from each stakeholder to implement agreed-upon action strategies?

Systems Thinking: Seeing Interconnections and Linkages to Identify Strategic Leverage Points

There is often no absence of information or data regarding an issue being addressed. However, cause-and-effect relationships may be ambiguous. Persistent public problems confronting public leaders are caused by a web of relationships tightly interconnected with other public problems. For every problem, there is a constellation of other core problems. Unemployment, alcoholism, and drug abuse can easily lead to domestic violence and child abuse. Child abuse and neglect can later lead to increased potential for teen pregnancy, which then increases levels of unemployment and welfare. Poverty is linked to other social and economic problems as both a cause and an effect.

There are no optimal solutions, quick fixes, or easy remedies. Individuals must learn to deal with more variables, unknowns, nuances, and interactions than can usually be handled at one time. Rather than seeking one comprehensive solution, a portfolio of strategies is crafted—multiple strategies by multiple stakeholders targeting multiple leverage points.

Systems thinking is an increasingly used language and set of visual tools for communicating about and seeing multiple connections and interrelationships. Although the term "systems thinking" has no consistent definition, it generally involves the capacity to see the whole as well as its parts, to see multiple rather than single causes and effects (Forrester, 1992). Working groups need time to develop insights into these interrelationships. Systems thinking tools are critical to stimulate discussions in an analytical and reflective manner (see Table 7.3 for summary of tools).

Systems thinking in groups relies on a set of visual tools and systems diagrams that help clarify complex issues by clearly and concisely identifying core elements of a problem, and by drawing out the perceived interrelationships and assumed causal links. These links and connections are not equal in strength, however. Sophisticated visual tools such as structural diagrams and computer simulations can suggest which system elements might have the most leverage power. Systems thinking helps detect and clarify interrelationships, assesses the importance and potency of these relationships, and helps reveal high-leverage interventions.

Visually Mapping Causes and Effects

The most simple approach to stimulate systems thinking is to brainstorm how an issue is interrelated with other issues. Impact network analysis provides a graphical presentation of potential ripple effects

Table 7.3. Tools to Stimulate Systems Thinking.

	Tools	Description
Brainstorming for Causes and Effects	Impact Network Analysis	This technique provides a graphical presentation of potential "ripple effects" of an issue or action strategy. It is generated by brainstorming the possible impacts that might follow from an issue going unaddressed, or the multiple impacts that might result from implementing a particular strategy.
	Simple Cause-Effect Diagram	A brainstorming method of identifying both the causes and consequences of some condition or problem. Starting with a short statement of the issue in the middle, individuals develop a map of primary, secondary, and tertiary causes on the left, and first-, second-, and third-order consequences on the right (see Bryson and Crosby, 1992).
Diagraming Interconnected Relationships	Cognitive Mapping	Also called "strategy-mapping" (Bryson and Finn, 1995), cognitive mapping is a facilitative device to develop a shared view of an issue's key elements, their interconnections, and their perceived causes and effects, thus revealing potential strategic options (Eden, 1989).
	Causal Loop Diagram and Systems Archetypes	Graphically portrays causal linkages between a few key variables, with reinforcing and balancing loops that keep a condition stable over time. Causal loop diagrams that represent common patterns over time are considered "system archetypes," such as "shifting the burden" and "fixes that fail (see Senge, 1990).

Modeling Structures and Systems Dynamics	Conceptual Model	Captures the more complex relationships between multiple variables in a particular policy or problem area, showing perceptions of how each variable affects other variables, in multiple interconnected loops, over time (see Vennix and Gubbels, 1992).
	Policy Structure Model	A more detailed conceptual model that also indicates the perceived strength and direction of several interrelated variables, for example, "stock and flow" diagrams that show levels, rates, and accumulations (see Richardson, 1991; Morecraft, 1992).
	Computer-Aided Simulation	Graphically diagrams the relationships identified as significant, and then generates a computer model using mathematical equations. Various strategic options can be tested through multiple computer simulations to assess potential impacts and resulting changes within the target system (see Richardson, 1991).

of an issue or action strategy. It is generated by brainstorming the possible impacts that might follow from an issue going unaddressed, or the multiple impacts that might result from implementing a particular strategy. A detailed cognitive map or causal diagram reveals individual perceptions of the various causes of a condition or problem. Individual interviews regarding the causes of teenage pregnancy in Tillamook County, Oregon, for example, revealed multiple causes (see Figure 7.4). Although such a diagram of causes and effects is difficult to confirm in an empirical, scientific manner, it does represent agreement by key stakeholders and stimulates their strategic thinking about an interconnected public problem.

Diagramming Interconnected Relationships

A third and increasingly popular approach to representing dynamic relationships graphically is the use of causal loop diagrams, which use simple loops to portray the relationships among policy variables. The *Oregon Benchmarks*, for example, is based on a policy model that ties together several elements in a circular cause-and-effect system called the "circle of prosperity" (see Figure 7.5).

A more complicated influence diagram or conceptual model suggests interconnections between multiple variables to explain a dramatic increase in foster care caseload in New York during the 1980s (see Figure 7.6). This concept model was used by key decision makers as a basis for developing a more complex computer simulation model that was then used to test various strategic options to reduce the costs and caseloads of foster care.

Graphical diagrams provide a visual, simplified way to surface individual assumptions about key variables, to portray causal linkages among multiple factors, and to illustrate interdependencies and implications. Simple word-and-arrow diagrams are often too general to develop computer simulations, but they are effective in communicating system insights that can be a foundation for a more detailed analysis. When greater precision is sought, computer-based models translate a working group's pen-and-pencil diagrams into simulations that can be tested, refined, and used to illuminate high-leverage points.

A first step in developing computer-based models is to build a structural map or concept model (such as the one in Figure 7.6).

Figure 7.4. Cognitive Map of Teenage Pregnancies in Tillamook County, Oregon.

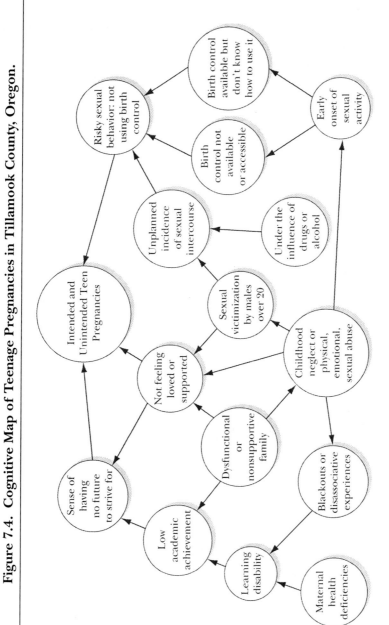

Source: Luke and Neville, 1996.

Such models take several days to develop collaboratively and test with key stakeholders and require the assistance of systems modelers and trained facilitators. Computer-aided simulations are more easily developed with commercial software such as *ithink* or *STELLA*. They graphically diagram significant relationships and generate a computer model using mathematical equations. Through multiple computer simulations, various strategic options are tested to assess potential impacts and resulting changes within the target system. Although high levels of technical proficiency are needed to create and run computer simulations, very little advanced training is required to use them once they are developed (Richardson, 1991).

Benefits and Cautions

Systems thinking is critical for effectively addressing interconnected public problems. Systems thinking tools can have important catalytic impacts. From simple cause-and-effect diagramming techniques to more sophisticated and expensive computer-modeling processes, systems thinking tools allow individuals and working groups to reveal and reflect on internal mental models and to grapple with the complexities of interconnected public problems. Systems thinking tools not only change the way working groups discuss interconnected and complex issues, but they also expand how individuals think about a particular problem or issue.

There are several virtues of using systems thinking tools in addressing public problems. First, the tools can help people recognize and analyze connections and interrelationships between and among variables that initially appear too complex and incomprehensible. Visual diagrams enhance a working group's ability to understand an issue and its multiple causes and connections. Diagrams achieve this in a much more efficient manner than a typical text format. A strategic map, for example, is a one-page graphical representation of a proposed portfolio of strategies, including visual links that show interrelationships between proposed strategies. Such diagrams can distill the essence of a problem into a visual format that adds precision, can be easily remembered, and yet is rich in implications and insight (Richardson, 1991).

**Figure 7.5. A Simple Causal Loop Diagram:
The Oregon Progress Board's "Circle of Prosperity."**

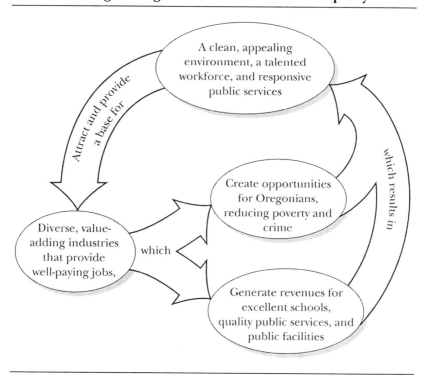

Source: Oregon Progress Board, 1989.

Systems tools have the potential to change or expand individuals' internalized mental models. They closely fit what we know about how humans process information: people simplify complex issues into single constructs and then into mental models of simplified cause-effect relationships. Graphical diagrams and conceptual models elicit these underlying beliefs of cause-effect relationships, and when input into a computer model, they provide valuable insights on alternative strategies and their trade-offs. Even without developing a computer simulation to test various alternative strategies, the simple act of developing a shared conceptual model of an issue or a strategy map of potential action strategies can stretch people's ability to think strategically.

Figure 7.6. Concept Model for Foster Care Caseloads in New York.

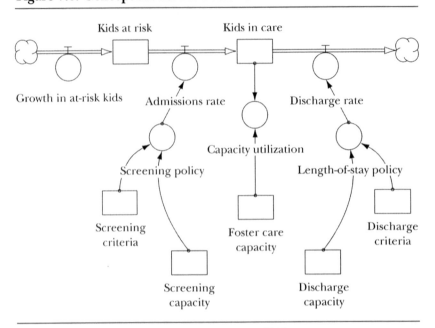

Source: Adapted from Richardson and Andersen, 1995.

A positive by-product can be the alignment of individual perspectives and internalized mental models.

Using these tools as facilitation techniques allows individuals to safely reveal their interpretations of the problem and its causes. It helps focus attention on interests rather than positions, and it allows differences in perception and values to become clear in a nonthreatening way. People can point to the visual diagram rather than at each other. Systems thinking tools have the added benefit of reducing destructive, vicious circles of negative emotions (Bryson and Finn, 1995).

Although systems thinking tools are relatively recent in addressing public problems, several concerns and caveats have emerged. First, complex diagrams and models can be more confusing than clarifying. Unless one "chunks" the insights embedded in the model, the insights can be lost in the complexity (Richardson, 1995). Catalysts must draw out insightful bits of the map as well as strategic implications. Second, working groups seldom end with finished maps or models. Instead, they develop snapshots that help them clarify the issue and develop effective strategies. In most cases, building the model is more important than the resulting model. The process of developing a shared mental model becomes a learning process about the issue. Eliciting ideas and deliberating and exploring varying perspectives are more important than completing a precise representation of the problem with all its causes and feedback loops.

The more simple cause-and-effect diagrams can be drafted in a few hours with the help of a facilitator. However, the complicated models and computer simulations require the expertise of systems modelers and process facilitators over several days. Developing computer simulations on such public programs as foster care, homelessness, mental health vocational placements, and probation and corrections are completed in the context of several one- or two-day group model-building workshops (Richardson, Andersen, Rohrbaugh, and Steinhurst, 1992; Vennix, Andersen, Richardson, and Rohrbaugh, 1992).

Public Leadership Summary

A key challenge for catalytic leaders is to think strategically and to encourage and nurture strategic thinking among key stakeholders. A wide variety of analytical techniques and tools can stimulate this conceptual process, including using data to show worsening conditions and troubling comparisons, sharing stories and metaphors that make an issue more real and salient, and framing strategic goals as desired outcomes.

A variety of systems thinking tools can reveal multiple aspects of problems, stimulating rich discussions on alternative action strategies. Analyzing issues and strategic responses with a systemic perspective can illuminate high-impact leverage points that can more effectively achieve sustained results. Systems thinking enhances the capacity to anticipate and evaluate the consequences of implementing specific action strategies, particularly the consideration of future consequences (including side-effects and surprise impacts). It involves envisioning beyond the present, and requires individuals to engage their frontal cortex to see multiple and overlapping interdependencies and to anticipate their potential impacts. Systems thinking tools can often be powerful catalysts for this activity.

Strategic thinking requires widening one's horizons, modifying underlying assumptions and beliefs, and seeing previously unnoticed interconnections and systemic linkages. It requires a catalyst to revise his or her thinking in light of fresh insights and revealed perspectives and interests. The catalyst must also synthesize ideas into a workable plan or set of strategies. Catalysts encourage collaborative planning processes that use strategic thinking tools to assist working group members and other key stakeholders to engage in strategic thinking. Although interconnected problems often require deeper levels of strategic thinking, one public leader commented, "I would even be happy with merely shallow strategic thinking."

Chapter Eight

Facilitating Productive Working Groups

It's easy to get key folks to a meeting. But gettin' them to work productively together, that's the hardest part.

Many people agree that society faces serious problems and ills, but few can agree on the right solutions. Most people, for example, believe that teenage pregnancy rates should go down, that the number of unemployed or dislocated workers should decline, and that the number of homeless families and individuals must be reduced. Beneath this agreement, there are varying and often conflicting values, interests, and proposed strategies to address these issues. Without sufficient agreement or consensus, problems may gain attention but remain unaddressed or addressed poorly, with attempts at quick and easy fixes.

We often hear the talk of collaboration and consensus, but we don't always know how to achieve it. Getting people to agree on a set of multiple strategies requires open-ended discussions of key issues, and even intense arguments and debates by opposing interests. Forging agreement is seldom as easy as the mayor of Austin, Texas, once bragged about its city manager, Camille Cates: "We tell her to bring all the interest groups together in a room and work out something . . . and she gets them all in there and they come out holding hands" (Ehrenhalt, 1990, p. 45).

A repertoire of process skills are used by people like Cates to build agreement and sustain implementation. The hub of these skills is facilitation, negotiation, and mediation. The governor of North Dakota noted that a unique set of skills are required to be an effective catalyst to forge agreement in public policy. The catalyst must understand the jargon, points of view, and stakes in the particular issue; draw truth out of poorly stated positions; synthesize statements; and actively integrate varied interests (Jones and Siegel, 1993). Public leaders must be catalysts for their productive working group, assisting it in reaching durable agreements on a set of strategies aimed at achieving a particular outcome. Catalysts are more than just traditional, neutral facilitators, however. They take an activist stance, energetically seeking agreements and tactfully moving stuck groups forward.

Facilitating the Group's Process: Leading from the Middle

Most research on group performance pertains to traditional teams, particularly working groups in organizational settings. Corporate leaders can develop a vision and inspire action because they have captive audiences of employees. Encouraging and stimulating a productive working group process, in which diverse and independent stakeholders have varying and often opposing views, requires a strong set of facilitation, negotiation, and mediation skills.

Although *facilitation* may be an overused word, the process is increasingly recognized as the preeminent skill of public leaders. It is not a style of being soft, or merely helping group members feel good about each other. On the contrary, facilitation requires skillful, direct, and strategic interventions in the working group's process. *Negotiation* is a bargaining process used when individuals have entrenched conflicts. Most often negotiation involves an intentional and structured process for resolving disputes when emotional or substantive polarization make the facilitation process difficult. *Mediation* is essentially a negotiation process that includes a neutral third party who helps individuals be more effective in their bargaining.

Being a catalyst for an effective public working group process is more similar to multiparty negotiation than to small-group leadership in an organization. Facilitating the group's process essentially involves four distinct challenges:

1. Generating fresh ideas and new insights
2. Coping with conflict

3. Getting a group unstuck and moving the debate forward
4. Forging multiple agreements

Catalysts are not passive facilitators. In difficult situations, they intervene more aggressively into the process, making or generating proposals. Instead of leading from the top, a catalyst provides leadership "from the middle."

Generating Fresh Ideas and New Insights

Stimulating strategic and sustained action on interconnected public problems demands new insights, systemic perspectives, and the consideration of multiple interests. This calls for action-oriented information gathering that is facilitated by postponing the evaluation of potential strategies until a sufficiently broad number have been considered, and by using questions to inquire and reveal information in the following key areas (Eden and Huxham, 1986):

• The general nature of the issue inherent in the outcome or desired result
• The reasons why it is an issue for each of the working group members, and his or her underlying interests
• Possible action strategies to achieve the outcome
• Possible impacts and ramifications of the action strategies
• Linkages with related problems and issues

Unfortunately, there is a natural tendency to approach public problems with an impoverished "option bag," bereft of good, fresh ideas (see Chapter Five). Members of working groups will often start discussing action strategies with a preconceived belief that they already know or have discovered the best solutions for the situation, and that all that is needed is to persuade everyone else into agreement—or into submission. It is natural for each working group member to focus on a particular way of seeing an issue. Individuals typically use only one mental map to understand the world. We tend to filter out contrary evidence, concentrating and storing information that supports our views or fits into a coherent story, while reshaping previously stored information to fit our perspectives. Individuals get comfortable in their ways of seeing the world and in their prescriptions for changing it.

In addition to these individual tendencies, working groups are further hampered by tendencies toward premature criticism and premature closure on the quick fix. These hinder a group's ability to generate fresh ideas. Without effective process leadership, groups may reject potentially effective options, fail to appreciate others' points of view, and be less likely to seek new insights or advice from outside sources. To counter these tendencies, leaders can generate fresh ideas and new insights in two ways:

1. Separating the generation of ideas from the evaluation of them
2. Using open-ended questions to inquire and reveal

Separating Idea Generation from Evaluation

It is easy for individuals to evaluate ideas immediately and discard ones that do not fit their preconceived mental model. However, an essential element in creative thinking is to separate thinking of possible options and strategies from selecting among them. Evaluative judgment inhibits imagination and creative thought. The more a group can separate the creative act from the evaluative act, the more inventive and fresh the ideas will be. Group norms that allow for and even encourage the postponement of critical evaluation help facilitate the generation and invention of multiple options. In addition to a set of nonevaluative norms, two group techniques greatly enhance a working group's potential to generate ideas while postponing critical evaluation and selection.

Brainstorming is a well-known group technique to generate a long list of creative or unique ideas and options for consideration. It is used effectively by a wide variety of problem-solving groups, work teams, and multiparty negotiation teams (Hirschhorn, 1991; Moore, 1986; Fisher, Kopelman, and Schneider, 1994). Brainstorming allows people to produce as many ideas as possible—based on a key question or issue—while postponing criticism, evaluation, and selection. In brainstorming sessions, no decisions are made. Four common ground rules are essential in generating creative ideas:

1. Generate as many ideas as possible by pursuing a quantity of ideas over quality
2. Refrain from judging or evaluating individual contributions until the brainstorming is over.
3. Avoid censoring one's thinking.
4. Build upon other's ideas by offering variations and additions to individuals' contributions.

Too often, when working groups most need to break free of cognitive ruts and frameworks, they are the least capable of brainstorming. Catalysts watch for signs that indicate the group needs to free its thinking. When brainstorming is used to respond to a group's immediate doldrums, rather than as a mechanical step in a formal group sequence, it has more salience and "bite" (Hirschhorn, 1991).

The *round-robin* is another common group technique. Like brainstorming, it effectively separates the generation of ideas from their evaluation and selection. The round-robin approach is commonly used in some form of the nominal group technique (NGT). Although more structured than brainstorming, round-robin discussions can generate many ideas about a particular problem in a short time period. Starting with a key question or issue, each member in turn adds an idea or item to the group's list of responses, giving everyone a chance to contribute. After three or four rounds of recording individuals' ideas on a flip chart, group members' ideas are fully exhausted and listed. This listing is followed by a more detailed discussion of items or subsets of ideas. While less spontaneous than brainstorming, the simple process of going around the table helps keep expressive and articulate members from monopolizing or dominating at the expense of more timid, unsure, or inarticulate members.

Questions That Inquire and Reveal

After using such techniques as brainstorming and round-robin discussions to start the group's work, conversations generally return to more natural ways of talking, working, and inquiring. By using questions in less-structured discussions, catalysts continue to stimulate the working group's collective "voyage of discovery." The most important question is, How can we achieve the results we want? Other questions need to be asked, but will fundamentally return to this basic question. The ability to ask the right questions is critical to elicit information, examine assumptions, clarify underlying interests, and reveal mental models. In fact, what makes facilitation work is asking the right questions, ones that can create moments of mutual understanding.

Psychological research is clear: people's minds are seldom changed once perspectives are well-formed. However, new perspectives and frameworks can be added and assimilated into existing mental models, gradually and incrementally, if stimulated by effective questions and with ongoing dialogue and reflection. Open-ended questions have a particularly strong catalytic effect on individuals and working groups. They expand members' perspectives and nudge working group members to deeper and more systemic views. What distinguishes catalytic leaders is that instead of having the right answer, they have the right questions. Catalysts shape the working group's journey of discovery by the questions they ask. They

- Ask questions that direct attention to desired future results, not past failures
- Uncover motives and reveal causal assumptions by asking *what* or *how*
- Ask questions that check for understanding and that clarify interests
- Ask questions that broaden options

It's natural for humans to inquire and to learn. Catalysts tap this natural interest through the sensitive use of questions. Not every question works, however. Questions can be productive or counterproductive. They can energize and inform, or they can drain and distract. They can be asked in ways that engage working group members and make them feel eager to answer or inquire further, or they can be asked in ways that make individuals feel intimidated, put on the spot, and reluctant to get engaged.

Asking questions effectively is more a function of the intention of the person asking than a specific set of guidelines being followed. The spirit of the inquiry distinguishes effective questions from ineffective ones, and it involves more than just digging for information (Oakley and Krug, 1991). The attitude of the questioner is also critical. Regardless of which words are used, questions have multiple levels of communication that individuals sense. In their essence, catalytic-type questions stimulate the discovery of new ideas, insights, perspectives, frames of reference, and areas of agreement. They focus the attention and energy of the working group on the results it wishes to achieve. As a result, the catalyst embodies a sense of inquiry or learning.

Questions That Direct Attention to Desired Future Results

Questions should focus on clarifying the outcomes or articulating ways to reach the desired result, such as, What do we need to do to get to where we want to be? Such questions direct group members' attention to action strategies. Questions that focus on results do not address such issues as, What are the reasons for failure? What's not working? What's wrong? Instead, questions will spotlight such things as, What do we want more of? What can be done to address this? What is already working that we can build on? Catalytic questions tend to encourage individuals to look forward, not backward.

Individual stakeholders can be driven by such questions as, What is my agency at risk of losing? How can I protect my resources? How can I defend my organization against past mistakes? These concerns must be shifted to a more forward-thinking direction on outcomes and how to reach them. This can be facilitated by asking questions that focus on desired future results. Even in the most difficult situations, the chances of accomplishing an outcome or achieving agreed-upon results are increased if questions are framed in a forward-looking way (Fisher, Kopelman, and Schneider, 1994).

Questions That Elicit Stories and Reveal Mental Models

Questions are perhaps the only way to get a snapshot of what is in someone's head. The better one understands internal mental models and assumptions of working group members, the easier it is to reach agreement on action strategies. Understanding does not necessarily mean agreement, but rather comprehension of how someone else sees a particular problem. Catalysts do this by seeing the world from another's point of view without necessarily fully agreeing with that perspective.

Good, open-ended questions successfully elicit stories by asking, for instance, What do you think we should do to reach this outcome? This can be followed by saying, "Tell me how this happens from your point of view." Sometimes revealing assumptions may be pursued by asking uncomfortable questions. Pursuing unfavorable inquiries can tease out assumed causal relationships, as in, How exactly would this help us reach our desired outcome? The catalyst should be aware when a question has created defensiveness so the question can be rephrased. The challenge is to be hard on the problem, not hard on the people who are gathered to work on the problem (Fisher and Ury, 1981). Effective, nondefensive questions are open-ended, giving individuals an opportunity to search for possible responses. Closed questions seek narrow yes or no answers or other brief answers, thus discouraging interactive communication among members and inhibiting creative thinking.

Catalytic questions ask *what* or *how* and encourage joint inquiry about what is to be achieved and how to do it, while lowering resistance or defensiveness. Moreover, questions that begin with *what* typically encourage multiple responses. Although questions that begin with *how* may elicit only single responses, they can be followed with *what else* questions to stimulate multiple answers. Asking more open-ended questions, such as How would that help us create the results we want? or What would be the outcome of that particular strategy? stimulates working group members to articulate internal mental models. As a result, assumptions about causal relationships can be more easily revealed and tested in nonthreatening ways.

Effective open-ended questions seldom ask *why*. *Why* questions can generate someone's assumptions about causes (we should do this because . . .) or can clarify someone's goal (we should do this to . . .). However, they can easily generate an excuse or encourage blaming about past events. Instead of focusing attention on the desired outcome and effective action strategies to reach the outcome, *why* questions can direct energy to the past and can generate resistance, defensiveness, or a sense of being challenged that can shut down a group member. For example, asking Why do you think that will work? can be interpreted as questioning one's logic or reasoning. A person may feel forced to justify his or her statement or belief.

By using *what* and *how* questions, individuals can more easily reveal underlying interests. Through such questioning, one can formulate, or help others formulate, action strategies that better fulfill their needs and interests, and the interests of other working group members. Individuals are not always aware of their underlying needs or motives. Asking about the results an individual hopes to achieve, rather than his or her particular position or project, can help the person clarify internalized needs not consciously considered or analyzed.

Questions That Check for Understanding and Clarify Interests

Clarifying questions provide the feedback necessary to check and verify that the intention of the person is being captured and that the essence of an individual's insights are understood. Clarifying questions can begin as, Let me see if I understand, or, Let me make sure I understand your interests. They can end with, Does this sound accurate? Is this what you mean? Have I understood you correctly? Further clarifying questions can be asked: Do you have other important interests that we haven't yet considered? This can lead to other questions that encourage individuals to expand or elaborate on the issue and help clarify ambiguities and broad generalizations.

Listening to an individual's explicit and implicit agenda is important. Clarifying questions are critical in illuminating needs and concerns that may be below the surface of the working group's discussions, revealing unstated interests. For example, questions can identify underlying interests shared by all working group members or complementary interests that may be overlooked by key stakeholders. Clarifying questions also invite individuals to expand or clarify an idea being expressed and ensure that people are speaking the same language.

Questions That Broaden and Multiply Options

Achieving sustainable improvements with interconnected problems requires multiple action strategies, not just one grand strategy. When addressing long-standing public problems, however, working groups can fail to consider sufficient options and may be tempted to jump too prematurely to a single solution or quick fix. It is not necessarily natural for individuals or groups to generate multiple options before selecting; yet it is clear that a multiplicity and variety of action strategies are required for success. The key is not looking for the one best answer, but to use questions to generate multiple options and a potential portfolio of strategies to address an interconnected problem.

Coping with Conflict

Conflict naturally exists while a working group is in the give and take of forging agreements. Conflict is not necessarily something to be avoided. Conflict can raise an issue to visibility and can ignite a working group to look at strategies more seriously. There will always be different perceptions, interpretations, preferred options, and strategies. Multiple views of an issue are natural and should be nurtured. The quality of decisions is enhanced when multiple, conflicting perspectives are brought to bear on the issue (Amason, 1996).

Moderate levels of conflict can be helpful. Conflict can jump-start the creative process and stimulate novel insights. However, unmanaged conflict can result in high levels of stress that reduces the potential for systematic and careful analyses by group members, that creates defensive behaviors, and that produces frantic searches for immediate relief (Nutt, 1989). Unmanaged conflict can also lead to emotional debates and lasting animosities among individuals that undermine the implementation of action strategies. Working group members must maintain a level of trust and positive relationships that allow them to sustain action. If working group members have strong negative sentiments toward one another or toward the group, they are less likely to participate in the implementation of any agreements (Amason, 1996).

Effective management of conflict—both preventing it and fostering it—leads to more successful working groups and networks. The Applegate Partnership—the unique partnership between the logging industry and environmentalists in southern Oregon—discovered that it was best to not focus on conflict during first meetings, but to focus on existing common ground. Once trust and rapport had begun to develop, group members used conflict to generate new insights. Unfortunately, individuals often avoid or suppress conflict even after trust is built. They either fear its divisiveness or they lack the necessary skills to cope with it constructively. Catalysts do not shy away from conflict; they embrace it. The challenge is to assist in its clear expression and transform it into conflict that enhances the quality of the working group's decisions, without weakening the ability or will of group members to continue to work together. It is difficult to distinguish between serious conflict and the normal give and take of a working group's discussions. The sharper the conflict, the more important that a public leader needs to engage in facilitation, negotiation, and mediation strategies.

The Most Common Sources of Conflict

Some public problems are more likely to promote disagreement than others. A catalyst's principle task is to help identify the central causes of a disagreement and to stimulate the group to manage the conflict in a way that produces an agreeable set of sustainable strategies. Once a working group agrees to the outcomes or desired results, disagreements will naturally emerge around the means for achieving these outcomes. Conflicts on action strategies are essentially ignited by four sources (Moore, 1986; also see Table 8.1):

1. Although diverse stakeholders may have come together to address a particular problem or issue, they may not have come together over common values (Waddock, 1991). Value differences create serious conflicts, but having shared values is not necessary for agreement on action strategies. If people feel their values are at least understood, they are more likely to stay at the table. Strong value conflict can tear a working group apart if it becomes the dominant focus. The goal is to seek shared interests, not shared values.

Possible interventions include

- Relying on a superordinate goal or outcome that all members share
- Avoiding defining criteria in terms of underlying values
- Not requiring divergent strategies to adhere to the same underlying values
- Seeking shared interests, not shared values

2. Differing interests and competition for scarce resources can easily ignite conflict over priorities. These can be significant, particularly when available resources are limited or when a win for one subgroup is seen as a loss for another. Such conflicts are stimulated by perceptions of scarcity and assumptions of a fixed, zero-sum pie (Cobb and Elder, 1983; Fisher and Ury, 1981).

Effective interventions include

- Facilitating interest-based bargaining
- Agreeing on criteria for selecting strategies

3. In convening groups to address public problems, interpersonal differences and style conflicts can lead to open or hidden interpersonal antagonism or distrust. Everyone wants to feel listened to and respected. If working group members feel their concerns are not acknowledged or taken seriously, mistrust and suspicion mount. In addition, there may be a history of unresolved conflicts that needs attention and that generates anger, fear, withholding information, and a general degeneration of the group process. These relationship or personal conflicts affect the relationships of the members and are as important to acknowledge and address as the more substantive ones (Fisher and Brown, 1988).

Successful interventions include

- Dealing with past relationship issues
- Controlling expression of negative emotions through procedural ground rules
- Allowing appropriate venting of emotions as part of the strategy development process
- Improving the quality and quantity of communications

4. Even something as "factual" as data can generate conflicts when addressing interconnected public problems. Data can be ambiguous, erroneous, or even conflicting. When this occurs, individuals most often refer to data that best fit their preconceived assumptions and internal mental maps. Further, as problems get more complex, individuals typically rely more on emotional arguments than on data-driven discussions.

Helpful interventions include

- Agreeing on what data are important
- Using third-party experts to gain outside opinions and clarify data interpretations

Approaches for Coping with Conflict

In addressing public problems, people often attempt to resolve disagreements through coercion and political compromise. While collaborative problem solving is frequently touted, it's practiced less often than preached. Yet research demonstrates that working groups that address public problems with a problem-solving approach create more committed and sustainable strategies (Bryson, Bromiley, and Jung, 1990; Moore, 1986). Unfortunately, no standard procedures or formal steps can guarantee the resolution of conflicts. Conflict resolution and negotiation are ancient arts that in the past were learned through personal experience. Today the field of conflict management is in a state of rapid growth, and several approaches have been proven useful to facilitate conflict management. Fisher and Ury's *Getting to Yes* (1981), for example, is the classic work that identifies four elements for effectively forging durable, mutually satisfactory agreements:

1. Direct the energies of the group members to the defeat of the issue, and not the defeat of each other, by separating the people from the problem.
2. Recognize and work with interests rather than positions, which redefines the public leadership role in terms of finding mutual interests rather than in terms of resolving conflicting positions.
3. Before committing to a set of strategies, generate a variety of options for joint gain based on shared or complementary interests.
4. Insist that agreements be based on objective criteria that can be mutually agreed to.

These guiding principles form a solid foundation for resolving conflict and agreeing on action strategies. Although leaders or members of working groups can use many specific and unique inter-

Table 8.1. Sources of Conflict on Action Strategies.

Source of Conflict	Typical Causes	Possible Interventions
Underlying value differences	Different ways of life, ideology, or religions	Rely on superordinate goal or outcome that all members share
	Strong emotional beliefs	Avoid defining criteria in terms of underlying values
		Do not require the divergent strategies to adhere to the same underlying values
		Seek shared interests, not shared values
Differing priorities	Perceived or actual competing interests	Facilitate interest-based bargaining
	"Zero-sum" or "fixed-pie" assumptions	Agree on criteria for selecting strategies
	Scarce resources will force the selection of only a few strategies to pursue	
Relationship issues	History created distrust	Deal with past relationship issues
	Stereotypes and misperceptions	Control expression of negative emotions through procedural ground rules
	Poor communication and listening	
		Allow appropriate venting of emotions as part of strategy-development process
		Improve the quality and quantity of communications
Data conflicts	Lack of information	Agree on what data are important
	Different interpretations of data	Use third-party experts to gain outside opinion and clarify data interpretations

Source: Adapted from Moore, 1986.

ventions to cope with conflict, the fundamental challenge is how to stimulate an interactive process that provokes the clarification and debate of different and opposing perspectives, while discouraging disruptive, even injurious types of interpersonal and relationship conflicts (Amason, 1996). Effective approaches to coping with conflict generally target each of these two areas: the cognitive, substantive conflicts around the policy issue, which typically revolve around differences in values, priorities, and data interpretation; and affective conflicts embedded in interpersonal relationship issues.

Catalytic Interventions to Cope with Conflict

Substantive Issue Focus	*Relationship Focus*
Keep the focus on the group's agreed-upon outcome.	Encourage understanding of others' viewpoints through "perspective taking."
Clarify and unbundle the differences.	Recognize emotions involved in forging agreement.
Don't assume a fixed pie.	Build trust, not suspicion.

Substantive Conflicts

Catalytic leaders need to keep the group focused on the desired outcome. During the course of the group's deliberations, the agreed-upon outcome becomes the magnet for collaboration that drives discussion on action strategies. When conflict erupts, especially disagreements that may disrupt or derail the group's process, the agreed-upon outcome becomes the superordinate goal or higher-order issue that can refocus collective attention.

When the Applegate Partnership stumbled into strong, emotional disagreements about saving trees versus saving jobs, group members would remind each other that they shared the same overarching goal—the vitality of their local community, including its job base and natural resources. This helped put the disagreement in perspective and calm emotional hot-buttons. Redirecting attention to the desired results helps focus the discussions on the problem, not on specific individuals. Instead of attacking people who are in disagreement, energy is directed to attacking the problem (Fisher and Ury, 1981; Fisher, Kopelman, and Schneider, 1994).

Public leaders need to clarify and unbundle differences. Conflict must be acknowledged and defined before it can be managed. The purpose in conflict management is not to end all differences, but to clarify those that block agreement. Sometimes it is easy to understand the conflict. It may be a matter of two differing perspectives. With interconnected and complex public issues, however, understanding the underlying conflict may not be so simple. It may require individuals to disaggregate and unbundle the underlying issues, making the differences concrete and specific in a way that sharpens the differences. Unbundling conflicts facilitates each individual's ability to work constructively on the disagreements.

There are many tools and techniques for disaggregating conflicts. Knowing which technique, or combination of techniques, to clarify and resolve a conflict comes from experience, common sense, and intuition. (See especially Fisher, Kopelman, and Schneider, 1994.) An important element in unbundling conflicts is uncovering underlying interests, both long-term and short-term. Individuals can get so locked into their positions and perceptions of what will work and what won't work that they forget their driving need, motive, or underlying interest behind that assertion. (More important, they may overlook that their interests can be met in other ways.) When people discover and talk about their personal and organizational interests, they can more clearly reveal differences in values and priorities. Beneath individuals' particular interests lie more basic values. Agreements do not require shared values within a working group of diverse stakeholders, but understanding differences in values can significantly improve the group's problem-solving process.

Even if the underlying interests and needs have been clearly identified, individuals often assume a "fixed pie," that more for one person means less for another, or that by pursuing one strategy another strategy is forgone. This assumption of scarcity creates a fear of losing resources if one "doesn't win." Forging "pie-expanding" agreements is the essence of negotiations and mediation. Many specific interventions have proven successful. (See especially Fisher, Kopelman, and Schneider, 1994; Moore, 1986.) Although there are true fiscal restraints that limit the expenditure of public and private resources to address a public problem, multiple strategies can be devised that are not necessarily constrained by resource scarcity or that can expand resources beyond financial considerations.

Relationship Issues

A second element in the unbundling process is to disentangle relationship issues from substantive issues. Working group processes are more productive when individual members establish trust and interdependence. When discussions are strained, it may be difficult to move the discussion forward. Individuals may need to set aside task considerations to work more directly on relationship issues. Establishing a sense of connectedness is part of the invisible work in facilitating and negotiating agreements (Kolb, 1995). It involves developing connections among working group members, establishing and reaffirming good working relationships, and maintaining a sense of shared purpose. Three general interventions are helpful in maintaining a sense of connectedness and in coping with relationship-oriented conflicts.

Perspective Taking. Public leaders need to take consideration of varying perspectives. People work together more easily and deal with conflict more successfully when they feel their concerns and perceptions are understood. The key to forging agreement among diverse stakeholders is not convincing others of what is right, but understanding other participants' mental models and inventing options in alignment with internalized assumptions. A catalyst's success often depends on his or her ability for such perspective taking.

To understand a conflict, it helps to observe the disagreement from at least three different points of view: another's, a neutral third-party's, and yours. Individuals skilled in conflict resolution are usually adept at jumping back and forth between perspectives. Seeing the situation or issue as others see it is one of the most important skills a catalyst can possess (Fisher and Brown, 1988; Fisher and Ury, 1981).

Catalysts also explore and understand others' feelings about the proposed action strategies. The more someone seems different, the more we are likely to have formed a stereotype, and the less likely we are to know what is important to him or her. To create a sense of connectedness, we need to demonstrate that we understand others' points of view, their perspectives, and their passions.

Catalysts use clarifying, open-ended questions such as the following to probe for more information, avoid jumping to interpretations, and test understanding:

- What would that strategy accomplish?
- How will this help us reach our desired outcome?
- What would the effects be if this was implemented?

The goal is to enhance understanding of different viewpoints by working to understand others' perceptions and underlying interests. Such perspective taking, although difficult, is crucial for revealing underlying interests and insights into where common ground exists, and for helping others reach sustainable agreements.

Recognition of Emotions Involved in Forging Agreement. Logic and strategic thinking alone are not sufficient to reach agreement. Emotions such as fear, anger, frustration, and even love are normal and often necessary to pursuing public problems. Emotions can act as a strong catalyst. They inspire people to action, mobilize resources, and convey important clues to individuals' underlying motivations and interests. To be effective in problem solving, particularly among diverse stakeholders, catalysts try to balance reason and emotion. They encourage analysis that is informed by emotions and feelings, and emotions that are guided by reason and systemic analysis (Fisher and Brown, 1988).

Catalysts use the expression of emotions as another way to identify underlying perceptions and interests. By exploring emotions, we can increase our understanding of others' mental models, interests, and assumptions. Once emotions are acknowledged, individuals can more easily move on to substantive issues. In addition, catalysts learn to use facilitative techniques to help group members vent. Venting is not the same as character assassination or direct personal attacks. Rather, productive venting is a less volatile expression of frustration related to issues, not people. Facilitators encourage emotional expression, but prevent destructive venting. Verbal aggression toward another tends to produce counteraggression, impedes getting at underlying issues, and can squelch group communication. In difficult conflict situations, such feelings can too easily drown out and overwhelm more deliberative processes. Facilitators and mediators attempt to neutralize negative emotions directed at individuals and enhance positive ones (Moore, 1986).

Building Trust. Coping with conflict requires the continuous development and nurturing of trust. Trust refers to an individual's capacity to depend on, or place confidence in, the honesty or accuracy of another person's statements or actions, and is usually over time. In working groups, trust is usually built incrementally through an increasing number of commitments and congruent actions that confirm the belief that the commitment is or will be carried out.

Dealing with disagreements is, of course, much easier when trust already exists. However, repeated national surveys show a clear yet unfortunate trend that social trust in the United States has been declining for more than a quarter-century (Putnam, 1995). The traditionally strong social networks have eroded, feeding a decline in community engagement and social trust. In addition, stereotypes of others further alienate working group members when they convene to attack a public problem. In public-private partnerships— some of the most difficult working groups to facilitate—research shows that trust is strengthened by two rather common behaviors: *producing the goods,* or doing what you have promised or committed to do, and *drinking together,* or sharing social time and developing social bonds or networks (Waddock, 1988).

Catalysts thus influence a working group's ability to build trust by clarifying commitments and by encouraging individuals to take them seriously. They also suggest and schedule social time or events that develop interpersonal connections and reduce stereotypes. Although social elements may appear unimportant, they are an important part of the underlying glue that builds connectedness and shared purpose as divergent stakeholders and antagonists jointly address a common problem.

Getting a Group Unstuck and Refocused

In addition to getting bogged down in fights and conflicts, working groups can flounder and get stuck in thinking ruts or avoid the task due to some fears of moving forward. Group members get stuck in thinking ruts when they consciously or unconsciously pursue one framework or way of thinking on a particular issue. Working groups tend to persist with an initial framework or approach to a problem, whether or not that particular approach proves to be productive over the course of several meetings. Once convened, working groups form a framework of givens about the issue that acts as a platform from which the group operates for much of its discussion. From its initial meetings, the approach to the task and the interaction in the group sets lasting precedents (Gersick, 1988).

Other thinking traps occur when groups rally behind a single answer to the premature exclusion of other options. By committing too early to a particular solution, groups do not have to think further about an issue. Such working groups are victims of what is commonly called "groupthink," in which groups seek to reach quick closure and agreement on one solution. Groupthink behavior involves hidden group pressures to conform and to support a particular option, while making it difficult for members to consider other alternatives. The result is that the group stops thinking and is trapped or captured by one particular solution.

Avoidance Tendencies

Some working groups become passive. Group members may get to a point where they want to avoid further movement forward in a debate or discussion, and seek to slow down or immobilize the group. This occurs for several reasons. First, there may be latent difficult questions or issues that people are too anxious or too afraid to discuss openly. They hesitate raising the issue or asking the real question because it may produce uncomfortable conflict. Unfortunately, important questions left unasked and unanswered can shape and color later discussions. Second, group members may be unclear about what is being asked of them in the working group or what their role in decision making is. They may be unsure how the decisions will be made or who is deciding. Third, they may be anxious about the status differences or power relationships in the working group, which may lead people to avoid participating for fear of stepping on others' turf. These confusions are not uncommon. When faced with uncertainty or confusion, group members become anxious, which causes them to clam up. These emotional responses can often lead to a common group response of withdrawing or fleeing from the task at hand.

At other times, a working group may develop a fight mentality, in which members attack the convener, the chair, or other participants as a way of avoiding the task. Fight and flight behaviors often emerge for similar reasons: working group members are afraid or unsure of the task at hand, unclear of decision-making responsibility, or are anxious about power relationships. The catalyst needs to bring the working group's attention back to the task, facilitating the group from a flight or fight mode to a work mode (see Table 8.2 for more details).

When productive working groups are creative, members feel free to think broadly and spontaneously, to challenge one another, to test underlying assumptions, and to piggyback on each others' ideas. However, overly spontaneous discussions can lead members to engage in distracting and irrelevant discussions. Floundering occurs when the process lacks focus or when deliberations and conversations are spontaneous and unfocused. The group may be focused on an irrelevant idea, pursuing a topic way off the group's intended task. Such discussions promote confusion and a sense of nondirection. They can be resented as a waste of valuable time by working group members.

Useful Interventions to Get a Group Unstuck

There are a wide variety interventions that can get a group unstuck. Catalysts help move a group through a state of inertia to a new level of activity and performance by stimulating a burst of energy to the point where fight or flight patterns are dropped, energy is renewed, and new perspectives are developed. Techniques include

- Making facilitating statements
- Dividing the issue into smaller manageable chunks or related topics and subgroups
- Introducing third parties into the agreement-building process (neutral facilitators, mediators, or outside experts)

Facilitating Statements
Facilitating statements help a working group reflect on its work, assessing where it has come from, where it is going, or why it is

Table 8.2. Characteristics of Fight and Flight Behavior, and Catalytic Interventions to Stimulate Work.

FIGHT	FLIGHT	WORK
Using energy against others or the group leaders	Draining energy out and diverting attention	Providing a catalyst for group members to address an issue

Giving Information, Opinions, Suggestions

1. Using emotion-laden words	1. Taking side trips, "chasing rabbits"	1. Suggesting group norms
2. Repeating points	2. Telling irrelevant stories	2. Providing relevent data to educate and inform
3. Making speeches	3. Playing down differences to avoid conflicts	3. Identifying underlying interests
4. Accusing, blaming	4. Intellectualizing	4. Suggesting workable options by linking different ideas together
5. Name-calling		5. Suggesting experiments
6. Taking fixed position		

Responding to Others' Suggestions, Opinions

1. Criticizing	1. Being unresponsive; giving no acknowledgment	1. Crediting others' ideas
2. Interrupting	2. Opting out of discussions	2. Piggybacking on others' ideas
3. Hairsplitting	3. Suppressing own feelings and reactions	3. Asking clarifying questions
4. Actively ignoring	4. Expressing futility, resignation, hopelessness	4. Exploring others' feelings and expressing own feelings
5. Categorizing	5. Deferring to others or the group leaders	5. Summarizing and reflecting back ideas
6. Selectively using and interpretating what was said		
7. Personally attacking someone's suggestion or interpretation		

Responding to Commonalities

1. Ignoring common ground and agreements	1. Agreeing with everything	1. Testing for agreements
2. Discounting agreements as unimportant or irrelevant	2. Agreeing prematurely to avoid conflict and other groupthink behaviors	2. Clarifying both shared interests and complementatry interests
3. Continuously returning to areas of disagreement	3. Agreeing on easy, quick fixes	3. Summarizing areas of common ground
		4. Building on areas of agreement
		5. Using agreement to move forward or dealing with more difficult conflicts

(continued)

Table 8.2. *(continued)*

Responding to Differences in Perspective and Values

1. Focusing only on differences	1. Smoothing over differences	1. Identifying and clarifying differences
2. Enlarging number or size of differences	2. Avoiding discussion of differences hoping they will go away	2. Clarifying underlying interests
3. Using differences as basis for stimulating conflict and rivalry	3. Using secrecy to avoid confrontation	3. Clarifying semantic confusion and misundertanding
4. Labeling and stereotyping others' ideas	4. Complying with, or submitting to, the strongest position of others	4. Using differences as basis for inventing new approaches and strategies
5. Using outside experts to bolster one's position		
6. Using power plays and coercive tactics to force one's perspective or values on the group		

Responding to Personal Criticism

1. Rebutting	1. Ignoring the attack	1. Asking for additional, clarifying information
2. Returning with a personal attack or insult	2. Using criticism as an excuse to "leave the table"	2. Shifting the focus off the person and back to the problem being addressed by the working group
3. Highlighting the criticism as further evidence for stalemate		3. Reframing from blaming about the past to future remedies
		4. Refocusing attention on common interests and shared goals

Managing the Group's Time

1. Arguing for tight deadlines that create stress	1. Ignoring deadlines	1. Using deadlines and other "temporal markers" as catalysts to move the group forward
2. Insisting on fixed timelines	2. Jumping to quick fixes or simple answers to avoid conflict	2. Segmenting the group's time and using milestones against which to measure progress
3. Fighting about whether deadlines are real or not		3. At a "half way" point, summarizing group agreements

(continued)

Table 8.2. *(continued)*

FIGHT Using energy against others or the group leaders	FLIGHT Draining energy out and diverting attention	WORK Providing a catalyst for group members to address an issue
Using Breaks and Time Between Meetings		
1. Gaining support from individuals for one's position 2. Mobilizing advocacy-coalition for battle	1. Escaping	1. Seeking outside input to stimulate deeper reflection on issues 2. Building cohesion within the work group or network 3. Healing wounds 4. Individual caucusing to clarify underlying interests and identify common ground
Using Questions		
1. Using questions to pin down or trap 2. Asking leading questions 3. Making personal attacks or critical statements masked as questions	1. Asking irrelevant questions	1. Asking questions that invite others to speak—"gatekeeping" 2. Asking information-seeking questions of *what* or how 3. Asking questions for reality testing 4. Asking for summarizing comments from each group member
Using Humor		
1. Using humor used to put others down 2. Using humor to call attention to self	1. Using clowning, distracting humor to avoid work	1. Using humor to provide perspective 2. Using humor to reduce dysfunctional tension

Source: Adapted from Shepard, 1979.

stuck. Facilitating statements can balance the important spontaneity of discussions with a direction of deliberations, without creating excessive dependence on one person's leadership or guidance (Hirschhorn, 1991). There are two types of facilitating statements made by catalysts: statements of time and scope, and process comments.

Statements of Time and Scope. A common facilitating statement of time and scope is simply to remind the working group of its primary purpose. One might say, "I think that we are a little off-track here. This is interesting information, but we need to stay focused on the key purpose of our discussion."

Setting or acknowledging temporal milestones, or time pacing, is another effective intervention, particularly when a group is pursuing a goal under time limits. Time constraints are important because groups adjust their rate of work and style of interaction in response to time constraints. Groups with less stringent time constraints work more slowly on tasks and give more attention to interpersonal matters. Groups with tight time pressures communicate at a faster rate and use a more fast-paced or autocratic decision-making process.

Catalysts use temporal milestones to break momentum, allowing opportunities for new perceptions of the situation to emerge, and to change directions in discussions and activities. Although time pacing occurs throughout the working group's process, working groups are more sensitive to standards of time and scope at a perceived midpoint in their deliberations. Midpoints in group processes provide unique windows for helping groups move forward. Recent research in group processes indicates that teams, task forces, and problem-solving working groups will persevere with the same cognitive approach to their task until some midpoint, when an "alarm clock" goes off. Groups allow themselves to persist with opening work patterns until the midpoint, which is not necessarily the completion of a specific amount of work. Then awareness of the deadline and feelings of urgency break the group's momentum and stimulate a renewed search for ideas (Gersick, 1990).

Midpoints are powerful opportunities for intervening to move a group forward. About halfway through problem solving—at a group's midpoint—the following three conditions emerge:

1. Groups are experienced with the issue, understand many of its various interrelationships with other issues, have enough information to generate new options, and are familiar with key stakeholders' interests.
2. They have used up enough of their time that they feel compelled to get on with the task; they experience a jolt of urgency.
3. There still is enough time left to change their approach while forging agreement on strategies, thus generating sufficient optimism to move forward in a focused way.

At the midpoint, group members are likely to make fundamental changes in their thinking about the issue, pull in new ideas, and reframe prior ideas in ways that allow them to jump forward. Until the midpoint, members may be unwilling and resistant to perceive truly different approaches to the issue, and interventions aimed at fundamentally altering the group's approach are bound to fall flat (Gersick, 1989).

Once the group is convened and is moving forward, attempts to change the way a group works may not be successful except in midpoint transition times. Therefore, interventions during the first half should be directed at helping the group gather more data relevant to its initial framework rather than at trying to change the group's approach to strategy development. A midpoint reminder of a deadline, however, can stimulate a deliberate and abrupt attentional shift in the group's efforts that closes the initial phase of strategy development and sets sights for a new set of tasks. If there are no externally imposed deadlines, or where deadlines are uncertain and shifting, then the leader must "hold steady" until the group reaches a stage when it feels stuck or compelled to take stock and move forward in new directions.

Process Comments. Process comments highlight how a working group may be getting off track, avoiding its work, or merely stuck. They can be observations on stymied group discussions or direct requests to individuals. They can be as simple as saying, "It looks like some people are withdrawing from the discussion. What are the underlying issues?" Or process comments can be more specific, such as saying, "Earlier Sue mentioned that we are a little off-track in our discussion and that we needed to stay focused and return to the key issue. I wonder if there is a basic confusion about the outcome we are focusing on. Or perhaps there is some other uncertainty or underlying issue that isn't being discussed?"

Some process statements are made as direct requests. When one member is obstructing the group's work, a process statement can limit the person's impact on the group, and a direct request can be the most effective. To a person who is monopolizing the airtime of the group, one could say, "Paul, you've stated your position very clearly, and now it would be helpful to hear what other working group members think." To a person who is trying to close down the debate prematurely, one might say, "Ann, your suggestion may close the discussion too quickly. I think it would be helpful for us to hear more about the different perspectives. After we have heard more about the differences, perhaps we can then see where we can come to agreement." In both cases, the individual is asked to step back in the interests of further work, not because the speaker is upset or angry. Process comments follow a common protocol of describing undesirable or unproductive behavior in a nonjudgmental, nonevaluative way, and then inviting further discussion by other group members.

Dividing the Issue into Related Subtopics

When a group is stuck, passive, or plagued with rabbit chasing, breaking the issue into smaller subtopics can move the group forward. Breaking the larger problem into separate problems and then subgrouping (forming smaller subgroups, each of which takes a smaller part of the larger problem) can provoke more focused, productive discussion. Although this intervention is not particularly revolutionary, it is an important catalytic technique. It gives the working group more safety to disagree and to think critically. It also builds closer ties and a sense of connectedness.

Facilitators, Mediators, and Outside Experts

There are times in all successful groups when an outside third party can improve the working group's process or increase its productivity. Although too easily seen as a sign of weakness, it is truly a sign of strength when the group agrees that an outside, external perspective is necessary to help reach sustainable agreements. Two distinctly different types of external third parties are commonly used: an outside facilitator or mediator who helps the group with its process and outside experts who can help with the substance.

Facilitation and mediation skills are increasingly used by successful public leaders. Yet as Moore (1986) states, outside facilitators or mediators often become necessary in a working group's process when

- The emotions of the group members are intense and are preventing agreements.
- Communication among the individuals, in quantity or quality, is poor, and the members can't change the situation on their own.
- Repetitive negative behaviors, such as blaming or stereotyping, are creating barriers and hindering a productive working group process (and facilitative statements by working group members are not successful in curbing them).
- Members disagree about the order in which they should first focus on multiple, interrelated issues of a problem.
- Group members are having difficulty reconciling real or imagined conflicting interests or value differences.
- The group is stuck, or individuals or subgroups have reached an impasse.

Outside technical experts are useful when there are serious, substantive disagreements. They can be used effectively to depoliticize discussions, particularly by helping to focus the debate on systemic or technical issues. They can educate group members by bringing a fresh awareness to the issue: suggesting and testing more realistic assumptions, and providing new perspectives. They provide "value-added" insights when they reveal new interconnections and leverage points for action strategies. They can also provide an "energizing reassurance" to working group members when doubts emerge.

To be successful, third parties need to be relatively unbiased, with no particular political agenda. An acceptable, outside facilitator or expert is impartial and neutral, with no authoritative decision-making power over the group or the issue. The facilitator or mediator does not favor or champion one strategy or subgroup over another, nor does he or she expect to gain any benefits or special favors from any of the members during the process. Although an outside party may have personal opinions about the issue, people who are perceived as being partisan or strongly ideological are not successful in playing a neutral facilitator or educator role.

Forging Multiple Agreements

Effective working groups do not seek agreement on a single, comprehensive answer or solution to the problem. Instead, they undergo the process of building multiple agreements and creating a set of strategies to which they can commit. It can be as simple as an agreement between two individuals or agencies within the working group, such as a county health department and a local school district agreeing to provide educational materials on teenage pregnancy prevention. Or it can be a full-group consensus on a portfolio of strategies and a public commitment by each individual or agency to implement it jointly, such as the establishment of a multicounty network, jointly funded and governed by several public and private agencies that pursue regional initiatives in a coordinated fashion.

Agreement is essential, whether on small initiatives or on a more comprehensive set of strategies. Concerted action on interconnected public problems requires specific commitments to action, usually commitments of resources. Commitment and agreement are intertwined and require both intellectual agreement and emotional resolution to be long-lasting (Yankelovich, 1992). Sustainable, durable agreements don't just happen; they must be actively sought, invented, negotiated, and forged. Sustainable and durable agreements

- Meet the legitimate interests of key stakeholder groups to the greatest extent possible
- Take larger community or public interests into account
- Target perceived high-leverage points in the system
- Improve (or at least do not damage) relationships among stakeholders

As catalysts for effective working group processes, public leaders assist in forging agreements in three specific ways: they work to develop a nonconfrontational agreement-building process for selecting multiple strategies; they build larger agreements from smaller ones; and they seek high levels of consensus among diverse stakeholders.

Nonconfrontational Agreement-Building Process

Effective catalysts ensure that group norms are established early in the process. Not only does the initial climate need to promote creative and strategic thinking, but forging agreement on a set of the most promising actions is facilitated by maintaining a continual process of dialogue and testing of ideas. An environment is created in which information is shared rather than withheld.

Establishing common ground about important concepts and searching for common interests lead to a gradual development of mutual understanding of the issue, which vastly increases the chances of forging agreement on strategies. Catalysts help to develop and nurture a climate of committed openness among group members (C. Stivers, personal communication, 1995).

In addressing interconnected problems, committed openness in working groups is characterized by the following beliefs:

- That fixating prematurely on early options or a quick-fix strategy is detrimental and should be avoided
- That there is more than one acceptable solution to a public problem
- That all working group members have important and valid needs and interests
- That any conflict can best be illuminated and managed by searching for underlying interests
- That they can recognize and acknowledge differences and maintain optimism that these differences can be worked out

Start with Small Agreements

Forging agreement on a set of strategies is a gradual process of building bigger agreements on a foundation of previous small, easy-to-reach agreements. Catalysts find and highlight agreements wherever they can, such as by backtracking to summarize earlier agreements or by taking straw polls to test for agreement on emerging ideas or strategies. Easy agreements are sought first before focusing on the more difficult agreements that will require careful bargaining and negotiation. As one community leader stated, "Agreements are like magnets. Put a little out there and it attracts other agreements." Another stated, "Pick the easy ones first. Pluck the fruit on the lower branches 'cuz they are the easiest to reach." If disagreements become the first thing working groups focus on, individuals will tend to focus on conflict most of the time and overlook existing areas of common ground.

Consensus Decisions

Using coercive means to force agreement on a particular strategy seldom leads to a sustainable or durable agreement among diverse stakeholders. In choosing action strategies, structured approaches based on problem solving and interest-based negotiation are more effective in stimulating committed and sustained action than are approaches using coercion or compromise (Bryson, Bromiley, and Jung, 1990; Fisher, Kopelman, and Schneider, 1994). Particularly when the problem is complex and interconnected, and successful implementation will require voluntary actions among diverse and interdependent groups, consensus decisions will improve the likelihood of implementation success.

Consensus, however, does not mean that every working group member enthusiastically supports or is equally passionate about the package of strategies. Several levels of agreement exist, and total agreement and enthusiasm are not necessary for consensus.

Levels of Agreement

1. An individual can give an unqualified and enthusiastic yes to an action strategy or set of strategies.
2. An individual finds the action strategy or set of strategies perfectly acceptable.
3. An individual can live with the action strategy or set of strategies, but is not especially enthusiastic.
4. An individual does not fully agree with the action strategy or set of strategies, but does not choose to block it.

A soft consensus occurs when there is a lack of strong objections, or there is no dissatisfaction strong enough to stop the effort. Working group members who feel high levels of agreement, or a strong consensus, will of course generate more energy and commitment to implement and sustain action, yet obtaining such a strong consensus is not always possible. The goal is to reach a sustainable consensus on strategies that move toward the desired outcome. Such consensus cannot be forced. It is a gradual, give-and-take process until agreement emerges or is negotiated to mutual satisfaction.

Public Leadership Summary

Over the course of many meetings, catalysts facilitate group communication to help diverse stakeholders identify and agree on a set of multiple strategies to achieve an outcome. When conflicts of interest and perspective become severe, more structured negotiation and mediation techniques are used to seek agreements seen as a joint gain, or at least where no one loses. This is done within a group process, sometimes in public meetings surrounded by reporters and with TV cameras going, and sometimes in more private venues behind closed doors. Regardless of the size and public visibility of the working group, effective public leadership assists diverse stakeholders to agree on and commit to a set of strategies.

A unique role for catalysts is conceiving ingenious solutions to conflicting interests. Rather than reacting solely to options proposed by the members, a catalyst can synthesize divergent interests and partisan concerns and formulate options that address the needs and interests of key stakeholders. Some community leaders have labeled this "the elegant third solution." It is crafted to satisfy and integrate diverse interests, and it seeks an innovative alternative solution not initially proposed by either side of the typical two-party conflict.

Public leaders thus act as catalysts to move a group to work together rather than engage in fight or flight behavior. They become facilitators and mediators to stimulate a productive working group process. They maintain focus on the desired outcome and help reveal underlying interests. They break up patterns of work avoidance and build agreements.

Some groups may become passive or seek to avoid their work. Such flight behavior can surface because of uncertainty about the task, doubt about the group's decision-making authority, or ambiguity about the status or power relationships within the group (Hirschhorn, 1991). Groups in a flight mode may deflect or assign responsibility for decision making to a dominant individual or an authority figure. Groups in the flight mode jump too prematurely to options without first considering other perspectives, interests, or systemic interrelationships. To avoid difficult choices, or to avoid unnerving conflict, they pursue quick, easy fixes.

A group in the fight mode uses energy to confront, attack, compete, and belittle. These behaviors may be the by-products of conscious choices by certain members to slow down or derail the group's productivity. Fear of loss of power or resources may motivate individuals to resort to fight behaviors. The fight mode can also be an unconscious way of avoiding the group's task. In other cases, it results from a lack of trust. Particularly in community conflicts, individuals who view themselves as victims may feel less willing to collaborate with others to shape a new set of strategies.

No matter which reasons spur group members to adopt fight or flight behaviors, catalysts continually intervene to return a group to the work mode. Effectively intervening requires the identification or diagnosis of when the group is working and when it is avoiding or fighting. Catalysts must undertake a constant diagnosis and intervention process. Groups are not stagnant, and new issues emerge that fuel heated fighting or avoidance. It becomes a continuous effort to facilitate a group into a productive work modality. Table 8.1, which appeared earlier in the chapter, provides a diagnostic framework that highlights key behaviors and interventions that catalysts frequently use.

Chapter Nine

Leading from Personal Passion and Strength of Character

To address interconnected public problems effectively, public leadership requires individuals to act as catalysts—convening and joining with a diverse group of individuals, forging sustainable agreements, setting into motion multiple strategies, and sustaining momentum over time. Such catalytic leadership, however, is more than a set of analytical skills and interpersonal competencies. It is also characterized by a common set of attitudes, traits, and habits.

Successful catalysts are often described as optimistic, persistent, good-humored, and energetic. At a time when cynicism seems rampant in the general population, a public leader's optimism creates a sense of "do-ability," engendering the belief that something can be done to deal with an issue. This optimism implies that workable strategies are possible, even when nothing at first would appear to have much impact. Enthusiasm and persistence in the face of complex interrelationships—a certain doggedness—also characterize the catalyst. In addition, a sense of humor is critical to maintain one's perspective in the heat of conflict that naturally arises when debating policy action options.

Strength of Character, Not Strength of Personality

At first glance, the traits and virtues of catalytic leaders do not seem much different from the qualities used to describe leaders for the last century. However, what seems to separate the catalyst from more traditional leaders is a difference in the underlying notion of strength. Historically, it was assumed that good leaders had strong personalities. They knew how to grab the reins, making decisions firmly and uniformly, pushing solutions forward, manipulating agreements among key power holders, and quickly getting things done. The desire for a strong leader was driven by an aggravating sense of frustration among followers. The leader's strength inspired confidence in followers seeking answers. In today's complex, interconnected environment, where no single agency or jurisdiction has sufficient authority or power to make things happen, such a strong leader is not capable of facilitating sustained collective action among independently minded and diverse partners. Relying on an individual with a strong personality often creates distrust and resistance, which can lead to inaction.

Does catalytic leadership mean weak leadership? No, successful catalysts exhibit a strength of character that establishes their credibility to convene diverse groups. They have the personal confidence to facilitate and mediate sometimes difficult agreements, and they possess a long-term perspective that helps focus and refocus group members' attention in the face of small defeats.

Definition of Character

The word *character* means more than a master virtue or the sum of individual, discrete personality traits such as optimism, persistence, and humor (Luke, 1993). Ancient philosophers to twentieth-century psychologists agree on what encompasses character. Plato described character as the real self after death, the naked soul stripped bare of external qualities of beauty, title, power, or wealth. Aristotle identified character as the enduring attitudes and sensibilities that resulted in certain habits or patterns of actions and feelings. More recent philosophers similarly defined character as a unification of a person's tendencies through time, and the expression of habitual tendencies or dominant patterns of conduct. From a psychological perspective, character was defined historically as patterns of behavior and actions consistent with an individual through time, motivated by internal dispositions that define the individual, particularly in contrast to other people.

Difference Between Character and Personality

Although character closely resembles personality, character is the deeper, more essential or fundamental part of the self. It is different from two other important personality aspects: personality traits and intellectual capacity. Psychologists now recognize that unlike personality, character contains moral overtones and qualities. They explain that one's character includes the "persisting patterns of attitudes and motives which produce a rather predictable kind and quality of moral behavior" (Peck and Havighurst, 1960, p. 164). One's character can thus be described as certain habits or patterns characteristic of a person, particularly one's style of thinking and acting in matters of importance.

For catalysts in an interconnected world, character is the spirit and intent of one's leadership actions to make a difference. Character provides an underlying foundation on which to build a sense of personal mastery. It infuses energy into the specific tasks and skills discussed in earlier chapters. Character is what lies behind one's conduct and encompasses the inner side: the will, dispositions, and inclinations. What distinguishes catalytic leadership is a strength of character based on three foundations: a continuous focusing on desired results, a sense of connectedness and relatedness, and exemplary personal integrity.

A Passion for Results

Being able to resist the urge for short-term, quick fixes requires one to plan beyond the moment and to think in the long term. American philosopher John Dewey called this quality the habit of greater thoughtfulness about the future—the "intelligent forethought of ends and resolute endeavor to achieve them" (Dewey and Tufts, 1925, p. 246). The setting of future intentions commits a public leader to long-term projects and relationships and provides a sense of direction and integrity to one's behavior over time. Analysis of presidential leadership reveals that long time frames, both forward and backward, are critical for success. Presidential advisors, for example, found it helpful to think in "time streams," using historical scenarios to help envision potential future scenarios that may evolve out of choices made in the present. A future focus is even considered a core element of strong character in the business community. A Touche Ross survey (1988) of key corporate leaders and deans of business identified a long-term perspective critical to ethics. In ranking the moral issues facing business, researchers considered the preoccupation with short-term earnings and profits one of the greatest threats to ethical leadership.

Developing a habit of taking the long view adds to one's strength of character. A long-term focus is the underlying basis for persistence and provides the perspective that reminds public leaders that dramatic changes can seldom be expected overnight. A rural community leader said, "You can't shoot all the rabbits in the first hunt." This longer-term perspective provides the necessary focus to sustain action when only small wins can be garnered. It also helps in marshaling enough motivation to continue in the face of the many small defeats that naturally occur when addressing interconnected problems.

Focusing and Refocusing on Desired Outcomes

More than just a future orientation distinguishes catalytic leadership. The commitment to attain a future outcome allows catalysts to respond to immediate concerns without losing focus on longer-term results. Catalysts maintain a focus on longer-term outcomes and results, and they continually remind others of the ultimate outcomes for which they are collectively striving.

Without continuously focusing and refocusing on desired outcomes, one's energy can easily get stretched. Distractions can become too tempting and strategic opportunities may be missed. The long-term outcome reveals important priorities in which immediate decisions can be made in terms of their longer-term impact. Where increasingly scarce resources force difficult choices, and when there is always more to be done than hours in the day, the long-term outcome becomes the filter by which immediate decisions can be made.

Sheer tenacity is commonly required: to lie in wait for a policy window to open, to convene groups of diverse interests, and to build the necessary trust to identify common interests and forge sustainable agreements. A great deal of time is needed to network, have lunch, give talks, attend meetings, testify before groups, all with the aim of pursuing a particular outcome. Such persistence is often more important than expertise or political skill (Kingdon, 1984). The essence of strategic opportunism is the ability to remain focused on long-term outcomes while staying flexible enough to respond to day-to-day difficulties (Isenberg, 1987). One must adjust activities to fit emerging conditions and take advantage of unexpected opportunities without getting distracted. Such persistence and tenacity can occur only when guided by a continual focusing on a future goal or desired result.

Seeing Multiple Interconnections and Ripple Effects

There are no silver bullets for any of today's public problems. As a result, catalysts must look for interconnections, assessing the strength of various linkages and seeking to find less-obvious high-leverage points to improve a situation. Peter Senge (1990) refers to this style of thinking as the "fifth discipline." Public problems are caught in webs of other related problems, and this systemic awareness strengthens the resolve of public leaders to seek multiple strategies, not just one grand solution.

Although it is impossible to understand fully all the interconnections involved with any particular problem, catalysts take time to consider the interrelationships of the diverse interests as well as the long-term consequences of various actions. This habit of thinking involves three perceptual lenses:

1. Thinking about impacts on future generations, or what the Iroquois Nation refers to as "the seventh generation"—considering the impacts of current decisions on the next seven generations
2. Thinking about geographical ripple effects and consequences beyond the immediate concern, called "externalities" by economists
3. Thinking in terms of issues and strategies that cross functions, specialties, and professional disciplines (such as medical doctors looking at the impact of gang violence on public health, or industrial development specialists reviewing the impact of educational performance of local school systems on the ability to attract new enterprises)

Using these three analytical lenses is not necessarily easy. A public official from one jurisdiction, for example, seldom thinks about the impacts of policies on neighboring jurisdictions. Public officials too often think of addressing issues internally and independently, not interdependently. Organizations and institutions don't reward such interjurisdictional awareness or action. Consequently, it takes strength and sensitivity for an individual to explore interconnections and potential impacts of an issue on other communities and agencies.

Passion Toward Outcomes

Focusing on outcomes doesn't mean that an individual becomes an expert at counting and measuring outcomes. Rather, it is the practice of articulating what the desired results are and why they are worth measuring. Catalysts have a stake in improving an immediate condition, such as reducing child abuse, reemploying dislocated workers, or reducing teen violence. Because the outcome will make the world a better place, it has immense significance for the catalyst. It becomes a continuous and passionate focus that involves an intellectual and emotional intensity. It is not a fanatical obsession; fanatics are commonly defined as individuals who redouble their efforts after losing sight of their aim. Rather, the outcome becomes the overarching purpose or goal that energizes and guides one's behavior over time.

Catalysts are not neutral; they care deeply about an outcome. They have a personal desire to bring about change and to make a difference. They merge reason and emotion into passionate convictions. In the corporate world, a compelling organizational vision provides inspiration; in public leadership, the desired result or outcome for the public good becomes the passionate focus and spark that energizes and mobilizes.

Unfortunately, many are reticent to engage their emotions and be passionate. There is a long tradition to avoid emotions, beginning with the founders of our country who rallied against the use of passion and emotions in politics. Public administrators are instructed to be nonpolitical and impartial and to avoid claims of bias or political favoritism. In business administration, engineering, and other professional programs, emotions are trained out of individuals for fear of reducing one's neutral analytical capabilities. In study after study of character development, philosophers and psychologists have concluded that intellect and emotion are essential components of virtue and character (Peck and Havighurst, 1960). Aristotle emphasized that action lacking feeling or emotion does not express virtue. Virtuous choices are propelled by feelings and emotions. Emotions are integral to moral response and directly influence what is determined morally relevant. Two millennia ago, Aristotle concluded that the person of character is emotionally engaged in pursuing the common good (Sherman, 1989).

It is not a passionate outburst that blindly sets off an emotional storm, nor is it a wild passion that sets loose the competing passions of individual self-interests. Rather, it is an emotional spark that mobilizes and sustains energy, and that creates a purposeful, contagious commitment. Passion and energetic commitment build support and trust in an interdependent web of diverse stakeholders. Two qualities distinguish passion that acts as a catalyst from passion that overwhelms or controls others.

First, the passion is directed toward a desired outcome, not toward a specific solution. Strength of feeling toward one favored solution easily blinds a public leader. When a public leader is passionate and committed to a particular solution, the process of choosing action strategies becomes an "either-or" debate rather than a "both-and" deliberation. Catalysts are intent about achieving a particular outcome, but they do not have a deep stake in how to get there. It takes an internal strength to realize there may not be one best way. Although catalysts feel strongly about reaching a particular result and have a personal desire to make a difference, they do not harbor a false sense of confidence that they have the right solution to get there. Rather, they encourage multiple, diverse strategies to achieve the goal. Second, this passion for reaching an outcome is softened by a committed openness that continually views action strategies as experiments rather than as definitive solutions.

Committed Openness

Because of the complexities and ripple effects of interconnected problems, catalysts understand that no project, program, or policy should be seen as final or definitive. In fact, changes are likely to be required. Unfortunately, public officials are under tremendous pressures to take decisive actions and to solve problems definitively. Individuals are reelected to public office if they are perceived as good problem solvers. Likewise, administrators are hired because they have a track record of solving problems. Interconnected public problems, however, are not amenable to immediate, technical fixes by single organizations. Such problems cannot be controlled and are seldom, if ever, solved permanently.

Catalytic leadership requires the strength to consider action strategies as "unfolding experiments," and the humility of continual experimentation (Michael, 1983; Coates, 1995). As one citizen said about a community leader, "What makes her so damn good is that she listens, learns, and integrates." A spirit of inquiry enables one to test new ideas, weave together various interests, develop strategies from meager resource bases, assess their impacts, and seize emerging strategic opportunities. The inquiry is not merely an intellectual exercise; it also involves emotions. Catalysts may debate passionately about particular policies and programs, but their primary concern is identifying the most promising set of strategies. Further, as implementation of action strategies proceeds, catalysts remain open to considerations that require revisions in earlier conclusions and decisions as plans are enacted.

This alertness and the spirit of inquiry form a committed openness—a passion or commitment to attaining certain results while remaining open to identifying and testing new and diverse ways to achieve those results. Such committed openness at first glance appears paradoxical and contradictory. In reality, it characterizes a novel attitude that enables public leaders to understand the nature of an issue by acting on it, assessing its impacts, seeing even better options, and then revising their thinking in light of these fresh insights.

Sense of Connectedness and Relatedness

In a world where interconnected problems must be addressed by collaborative alliances and cross-agency partnerships, catalytic leaders are forced to operate in the more fuzzy realms of relationships and emotions. Catalysts work within these networks of relationships, with individuals from different organizations and with different backgrounds who deal closely with one another on value-laden and emotion-filled issues. Emphasizing connectedness and interdependence, they strive to nurture trusting working relationships, a sense of shared interests, and some sense of shared fate (Kolb, 1995). They understand the need to be inclusive and interactive, working across systems and agencies, connecting with other efforts, and involving key networks, partners, and stakeholders to pursue outcomes.

When working in small groups, catalysts understand the natural tensions involved in group dynamics, are astute in recognizing the feelings and concerns of others, and handle conflicts by weaving self-interests into connected interests. They can adapt a facilitative style, but also know when an outside facilitator is necessary. They also develop and nurture thick informal networks (Kotter, 1991) and political connections, before they are needed, by cultivating good rapport and informal communication channels with people. One community leader emphasized, "I have lunch with people all the time, building and nurturing my network, so that when I need to call on any of them, I won't have to go out and start from scratch."

These interpersonal qualities have been described with a variety of labels, such as emotional intelligence, interpersonal polish, and people skills (Goleman, 1995). Too often, it is simply described as charisma. The traditional image of a charismatic leader is one who has uncommon eloquence, putting words "to the formless belongings and deeply felt needs of others" (Levinson, 1996, p. 160). Being a catalyst extends beyond the ability to give good speeches and to galvanize followers behind a personal vision. It requires deep listening. Catalysts recognize underlying interests and concerns of diverse, independent-minded stakeholders. They help them see and understand their interdependence in solving a problem and assist them in weaving diverse and sometimes conflicting interests together. Power is seen more as energy, not control, in connecting multiple interests together to address a common problem.

Seeing Multiple Perspectives

Much of the catalyst's interpersonal abilities rests on the habit of perspective taking. Perspective taking is the process by which an individual imagines the "ways another individual thinks about, feels in response to, or literally sees the world" (Kohn, 1990, p. 101). It is similar to empathy, or knowing how another feels, and is different from sympathy, or feeling for someone (Kohn, 1990). In catalytic leadership, this is critical. The better we understand another's concerns, the easier it is to find common interests. The key to any difficult conflict is to understand what is going on in the heads and hearts of the different group members. Understanding means comprehending, or seeing from another's perspective. Understanding does not necessarily mean agreement, however. This process of perspective taking, and then demonstrating that we understand others' concerns and perspectives, provides an important foundation of credibility for convening individuals, facilitating agreement, and sustaining action (Fisher, Kopelman, and Schneider, 1994).

Perspective taking is a process of putting oneself in another's place, even if that person is not present (Fisher, Kopelman, and Schneider, 1994). One of the greatest criticisms of interest-based negotiation with a small group of key stakeholders is that a larger public interest or collective good can be overlooked and sacrificed because the perspectives of those not at the table are not fully deliberated. In interconnected public problems, catalysts sometimes assume speaking on behalf of missing parties or perspectives. A key role of a catalyst is to ensure that agreements are implementable and endurable. Catalysts remind working groups or networks that certain perspectives or interests must be sufficiently discussed to ensure that, in the future, others will not organize coalitions to obstruct the agreed-on actions.

Concern for Others

Catalysts attempt to develop endurable and implementable strategies for achieving certain results for the public good. On one level, their underlying concern for others is manifested in seeking to weave together individual self-interests into agreements that are either a joint gain or at least where no one loses. Mediating individuals' self-interests to meet group needs is instrumental in arriving at sustainable agreements. On another level, there is a deeper, more substantive concern for the larger public good that always remains in the picture, a disposition to promote the welfare of others. This concern is different from the classic notion of benevolence.

Enlightenment philosophers focused on the virtues of benevolence and compassion to describe this larger concern for others. Unfortunately, these virtues have come to inherit a hierarchical quality of "caring over" someone. Benevolence implies a sense of separateness and altruism, a sympathy for another, and is reflected in a desire to help others who are less fortunate and need help. Confucius articulated a concern for others that better reflects an interdependence or sense of relatedness. He called it *jen*. The possession of *jen* manifests as a "caring about one's fellows" and is based on the understanding that all human lives are intertwined (Luke, 1993). It is a predisposition to help those "with whom we feel a personal connection for reasons that are neither egoistic nor altruistic" (Kohn, 1992, p. 266), an empathy based on interconnections, or a sense of connectedness with other people rather than an empathy of separate, autonomous individuals.

This sense of relatedness cannot occur without first shifting one's attention away from a preoccupation with oneself and toward looking outward to relationships and interpersonal networks. It means that when we act, we not only take in personal interests but also extend our focus to the interests and concerns of others. At the end of several years of studying character, noted psychiatrist Robert Coles remarked that character is what you decide to do for others, not just yourself (Coles, 1989).

Exemplary Personal Integrity

It is not enough to have the capacity to reason abstractly about systemic interconnections and ripple effects. Strong character requires caring about how the well-being of people is affected by one's actions. A two-sided portrait of character thus emerges: one that includes certain habits of thinking and one that has concern for relationships and others—empathy and perspective taking. This portrait of character rests on a strong sense of personal integrity. Habits of thinking and caring, together with an exemplary integrity, form the basis of the strength of character for a catalyst.

Definition of Integrity

The term *integrity* commonly describes someone who acts in accord with her or his principles or commitments when facing pressures or enticements of various sorts to do otherwise (Luke, 1998). It is also used to describe an ethical, honest person who has convictions and acts in ways consistent with his or her stated commitments, values, or beliefs. Another definition is the more classical meaning of being undivided or "out of one piece," and is similar to engineering uses of the word, as in referring to a building's structural integrity. The classical meaning depicts an important notion: to have integrity, a catalyst's internal commitments hold together in a coherent, integrated way. Integrity is manifested by a well-ordered and integrated set of commitments or beliefs that guides one's actions and shows consistency over time. Such integrity takes on a coherence, a fabric woven into one's character over a lifetime.

Lack of Integrity

A person's failure to act consistently with his or her commitments or promises generates the accusation that the individual lacks integrity. Not following through on agreements, giving into undue pressure, and inconsistencies between what one says and what one does are indicators that an individual lacks integrity. The self-indulgent behavior of a public leader who is unable or unwilling to resist temptation is also characteristic of one who lacks willpower and integrity.

The lack of integrity may stem from several things. First, a person may not yet have engaged in sufficient deliberation and reflection to develop an integrated, well-ordered set of commitments that can enable the focused action required by a public leader. The lack of such a coherence stems from a vacillating character in which different habits alternate with one another rather than embody one another. Instead of a collection of separate, isolated commitments and beliefs, integrity requires a well-ordered set of commitments developed from continual deliberation, choice, and reflection and then integrated into one's habit patterns.

Second, the lack of integrity can be explained as weakness of will, where the internal strength and resolve to act in accordance with prior commitments dissolves in the face of difficulties. The ability to adhere to commitments is at the core of integrity. The person of integrity must have the strength of will to hold true to commitments in the face of conflicts, pressures, enticements, and defeats. Moral courage or moral heroism may even be required for catalysts to maintain their commitments and moral convictions, particularly when conflict arises between their core commitments and existing laws (Hart, 1984). Noted philosopher Alaistair MacIntyre (1993) reminds us, however, that strength of character also requires a sense of alertness, or an openness to considerations that require revisions in earlier conclusions and decisions as strategies are enacted

A third explanation for the incongruity between words and actions is deception. In public deception, one's formal statement or proclamation is hollow or misleading. The person promises adherence to certain commitments or values while knowing there is no such commitment. Deception can also involve not being true to oneself. Lacking integrity, an individual may engage in personal deception, not reflecting or manifesting in public places what is genuinely in one's heart.

Inner Strength

Integrity requires that catalysts have an inner strength for sharing leadership, for emotional self-control, and for moral courage. Inner strength—referred to by psychologists as "ego-strength"—is not a kind of inflated ego that allows persons to bully, ignore, exclude, or disrespect others who disagree with them. Rather, inner strength provides the self-confidence to bring other people into the act and the inner strength to be aware of and deal with intense emotions that naturally arise while being a catalyst.

Ego-Strength That Allows for Sharing Leadership and Credit

One person alone seldom has the energy or requisite skills to provide the leadership for all four catalytic tasks. Leadership throughout the process is performed by many people. Effective catalysts stimulate a "leader-full" process rather than one driven by a single leader. Catalysts don't have the internal motivation to be in charge of everything. They step into and out of the leadership role as necessary to galvanize others and to stimulate action. They are passionately motivated by a larger goal or outcome. Individuals with an inner ego-strength are not driven to be in control (Peck and Havighurst, 1960). They recognize that an inability to control is not necessarily a sign of incompetence. Lack of ego-strength creates a basic insecurity and most often motivates individuals to control the discussion and group process tightly. Similarly, lack of ego-strength forces one to attempt to take credit, rather than give credit, for successes. With inner strength comes the willingness to share credit, which is crucial in forging agreements and sustaining action.

Catalytic leadership is an "egoless" process, a shared process based on a sense of inner strength, not abdication or abandonment. As one local leader said, "To be effective, I have to check my ego in at the door." This is fundamentally different from historical descriptions of leaders, where *leader* and *ego* have been synonymous with "taking charge." In fact, the ancient Greek word for *ego* also means "leader."

Core Commitments That Provide an Inner Compass

Integrity requires an "inner compass," an ongoing set of internal imperatives and commitments, rather than a reliance on external rules and controls, that orients and guides one's actions. Integrity requires the considered, consistent adherence to chosen core values, convictions, and commitments. A person with integrity has an inner strength to establish lines over which one will not step—lines that are sometimes difficult to define or predict in advance, but are nevertheless always present.

At its deepest level, the essence of inner strength is developing, pursuing, and holding commitments toward such things as principles, causes, ideas, and people. Core commitments are those that attain a privileged status in people's lives (Bluestein, 1991) and become identity-conferring commitments, that is, they contribute to one's identity (Taylor, 1985). Whatever the commitment, a catalyst is someone who cares deeply about a public problem. Indifference is incompatible with the possession of strong commitments. One who lacks identity-conferring commitments generally has only very tentative loyalties to most things: public issues, causes, even relationships (Kupperman, 1991).

Emotional Self-Regulation and Impulse Control

As stated earlier, emotions are crucial in catalytic leadership. Passion for outcomes helps sustain efforts in the face of conflict and barriers, and feelings can arouse attention when dry logic doesn't work. But strong emotions can override complex issues and can undermine sensitive network relationships. Inner strength provides the psychological support for managing emotions and for impulse control.

Emotional self-regulation, or channeling emotions toward a productive end, is considered the master aptitude of emotional intelligence (Goleman, 1995). Emotional self-regulation does not mean tuning out or ignoring emotions. The goal is balance, not emotional suppression, to be neither a slave to passion nor detached and indifferent.

Inner strength also allows a person to assert a form of self-control. The person holds in check immediate impulses and then examines, reflects, and considers the consequences of potential actions. Self-control is the practice of deferring gratification, of being more concerned with long-term impacts of conduct than with immediate pressures or enticements. A person of weak character is likely to be impulsive, yield to temptations quickly, and be more easily enticed or prompted to act contrary to previous commitments. Someone without inner strength will tend to be an extreme conformist who habitually does what others expect. Inner strength provides a stronger sense of self that frees one from arbitrary external pressures, generating an inner strength often necessary to be consistent in pursuing long-term goals and commitments, and to be firm in advancing the public interest in the face of increasing pressures to do otherwise.

Strength of Conscience

Persons with integrity feel a strength of conscience that exhibits a firm, but not necessarily rigid, internalized set of moral principles that guide one's behavior and action. Persons with integrity have traversed what are considered four qualitatively different forms of conscience, beginning with the most primitive—a set of crude, basic rules of what not to do. The next level of conscience is rule conformity, with authority residing outside of oneself. Third is a conscience that consists of an organized body of internalized moral rules, influenced by others' rules, yet incapable of being internally questioned or tested. The fourth level of conscience, the kind exhibited in persons with integrity, is characterized by a core set of internalized commitments and beliefs, accessible to examination and weighing. The set can change and deepen as new commitments are made and new action is tested. Consequences are then assessed and reflected into one's future actions (Peck and Havighurst, 1960).

Moral Courage

Moral courage is needed to convene people, to face conflict, and to disagree publicly on issues integral to one's commitments or values. Acting with integrity can sometimes be disruptive to the status quo. Inner strength provides the basis for moral heroism that may be required to push the envelope. Further, moral courage fosters inner strength that allows catalysts to engage in honest self-reflection and to modify and change "identity-conferring commitments" that may need to be altered. In other words, it provides the inner strength and courage often necessary to revise old ways of thinking.

Trust and Exemplary Integrity

Integrity requires acting consistently with a well-ordered set of commitments and beliefs. It is the foundation upon which interpersonal trust and credibility rest. Following through on commitments and agreements is critical in developing interpersonal trust and is the foundation for effective working relationships. Trust is thus a fundamental ingredient in public leadership. By all accounts, it is the underlying foundation for cooperative, collaborative, and collective efforts to address interconnected public problems. (In fact, trust and integrity are fundamental to all forms of social interaction. The importance of trust has been documented in areas such as interpersonal communication, Giffin, 1971; public-private partnerships, Waddock, 1988; effective negotiation, Bazerman, 1994; interorganizational cooperation, Ring and Van de Ven, 1992; implementation of self-managing teams, Lawler, 1992; and the perception of public risks, Slovic, 1993.)

A high level of interpersonal trust has important impacts on the catalytic leadership process. When raising an issue to the public's attention, information is seen as reliable and valid when presented by someone trusted. Likewise, the way an issue is defined will seem more reasonable if framed by someone trusted. The catalytic spark provided by the public leader in convening a working group is dependent on the credibility of his or her relationships. Conveners perceived as evenhanded and trustworthy can more successfully motivate diverse stakeholders to commit time and energy to addressing an issue. Once a group is convened, trust allows working group members to stay outcome-focused. With high levels of trust, there is less discomfort at revealing personal interests, confronting disagreements, and acknowledging errors. There is greater ease for the group to learn, to adjust, and to self-correct as they negotiate action strategies. Finally, next to having sufficient funding, the development of strong bonds of trust is the key to sustaining an implementation network. Implementation relies more on trust than on monitoring and control capabilities (Ring and Van de Ven, 1994). The real strength of multiorganizational implementation networks lies in the supportive relationships that develop among partners in the network. The network grows and contracts as the levels of trust increase or decline.

When individuals are not highly trusted, suspicions run rampant when they try to raise an issue to public visibility. Data are seen as suspect, tainted, or exaggerated. The issue may be perceived as being too narrowly focused. Further, convening a working group will be impossible, or at best will take considerably more time, if people suspect the agenda of the convener, if trust is low, or if the convener has no previous track record. Past relationships and collaborations among group members may have resulted in low trust levels, creating baggage that exacerbates fight or flight behaviors in the group. Facilitation and negotiation of agreements are especially hard to forge when distrust prevails. The absence of trust easily diverts the energy of the working group onto other, often more personal issues. Working group members must also maintain a level of trust and positive relationships that allows them to sustain action during implementation. If working group members have strong negative sentiments toward one another or toward the working group, they are less likely to commit to the implementation of any agreements.

Although it is a continuous struggle, catalysts build and nurture trust within networks and groups in many ways (see Chapter Eight). Trust is built by making and keeping promises and agreements, and by being open and sensitive to group members' needs, values, and interests. Full trust within a working group or network may never be achieved or, once achieved, may be temporary. Therefore, successful groups foster an interactive process characterized by a spiral of rising trust.

Characteristics of Being Trustworthy

- One's conduct shows consistency over time and is not unpredictable or erratic. There are no surprises.
- A person takes personal commitments seriously and scrupulously keeps promises. Agreements are followed through. One's actions are consistent with one's words. No false promises are given.
- A person is honest, which does not necessarily mean full disclosure. However, greater disclosure of personal interests and underlying needs facilitates finding agreements. (However, even small amounts of dishonesty create a large amount of distrust.)
- Perceived competence or ability is critical if a person is to be trusted. If one does not have the necessary ability or skills in a particular area, the individual may not generate sufficient credibility to be trusted to convene a working group or to conduct certain activities.
- A person must exhibit goodwill, or the degree to which he or she is believed to want to do good for another or for a larger common good. The individual's intentions and motives are not driven solely by self-interest (Mayer, Davis, and Schoorman, 1995; Fisher and Brown, 1988).

The individual catalyst's conduct must generate trustworthiness. The term *trust* usually refers to an individual's capacity to depend on, or place confidence in, the honesty or accuracy of another person's statements or actions. Trust implies a sense of certainty of relationships among people. Interpersonal trust is based not only on confidence in the predictability of another's actions, but also on one's confidence in the moral integrity or goodwill of another (Ring and Van de Ven, 1994). An analysis of the development of the Law of the Sea Treaty, for example, shows that the trustworthiness of a particular subcommittee chair, Tommy Koh of Singapore, led directly to the successful completion of one key part of the treaty. Koh nurtured a strong sense of trust by being even-handed yet persistent in challenging ways, so that conflicting parties could come to him and openly discuss their country's interests and concerns. Because he had the trust of many of the country's representatives, he could craft and test—publicly and privately—alternative options that addressed the needs of different parties (Tanner, 1991).

Unfortunately, trust is created very slowly and is easily destroyed by a single mistake. The perception of being trustworthy is hard to acquire and easy to lose (Slovic, 1993). Trustworthiness emerges slowly from involvements and interactions with one another—involvements that create and reveal a history of consistency, honesty, and goodwill.

Ethical Conduct and Right Behavior

Catalytic leadership embodies a strength of character that comes from the development of a set of habits of thinking and caring built on a foundation of personal integrity. It is leadership that aims at service rather than dominance, stimulating strategic thinking and facilitating collective action among diverse individuals and organizations. As a result, the moral dilemmas and choices facing catalysts require considerably more reflection, deliberation, and continual learning than encompassed in any one professional code of ethics or set of rules. (Even if there were an ethical code of conduct, blind obedience to such codes and rigid, nonreflective behavior typically inhibits the growth of strong character.)

Ethical Conduct

Determining what is right or wrong, good or bad, is the essence of moral or ethical judgment. For catalysts, right conduct is not guided by following a general principle, rule, or specific code of ethics. Instead, they exhibit three levels of ethical deliberation that distinguish them as individuals of exemplary integrity (Luke, 1993)

- Familiarity with rules and established norms of proper conduct and behavior unique to the particular organization, community, society, or culture

- Reasoned judgment concerning these rules of proper conduct when applied to changing circumstances or conflicting moral requirements
- The embodiment of a deep concern for the well-being of humanity

Locally Accepted Norms and Customary Rules of Conduct

The catalyst is skillful in managing his or her conduct in accord with the accepted rules or norms established by a group, community, or particular profession. Effective working groups establish behavioral norms and procedural guidelines that offer ground rules for appropriate conduct. In addition, requirements of accepted ethical practices by professional groups provide a set of formal prescriptions and rules for behavior. Although the customary rules of proper conduct vary by professional group, community, or working group, they provide the first level of ethical conduct.

Reasoned Judgment

Catalysts easily acquire the minimum mastery of accepted norms and practices. In addition, they have a flexible attitude—a reasonableness to deal with exigent cases and changing circumstances. Persons of strong character are differentiated from others in their use of reasoned judgment. This judgment is required either when the environment changes so that no specific rule applies or when individuals experience a conflict of principles or obligations. Being ethically responsible as a catalyst cannot be reduced to a hierarchy of rules for all cases and exceptions. Too much variability exists in the contexts in which catalysts work. Settings range from rural timber communities to growing agricultural valleys to hemorrhaging urban metropolises; from neighborhoods, school districts, communities, and regions to states, provinces, and countries. The settings are far too richly textured and varied to capture a common set of rules of conduct that can be applied in all circumstances at all stages of a group's or network's development.

Moral Concern for Others

With catalysts, reasoned judgment is primarily guided by an extensive concern for others. Ethical action revolves around the interdependence between personal well-being and societal well-being, which leads to a sense of shared destiny with others. To have this concern for others is to understand the importance of being a member of a larger moral community and provides the broadest theme for right conduct. A broad concern for societal well-being adds a deeper dimension to ethical behavior. In an environment where everything is connected to everything else, catalysts are forced to reflect more seriously on the impacts and ripple effects of public actions. Interconnectedness leads to increased moral complexity, and with it comes increasing moral obligations and the consideration of policy ethics (Luke, 1991; Jonas, 1984).

Policy Ethics

Catalysts not only consider the immediate costs and benefits of proposed action strategies, they also consider the delayed consequences and the less-visible costs passed onto others who may not have any direct recourse. Discussions around ethics, however, are too often preoccupied with the behavioral ethics of personal conduct. Discussions of ethical conduct must also extend to the long-term implications of action strategies and their ripple effects over time and geography. Such a "policy ethic" is necessary because

- Scientific discoveries and technological advancements have created new opportunities and threats that create unintended side effects on the interconnected systems in which public problems exist.
- Potential effects of today's strategic actions have lasting impacts on future generations that can either enhance or harm their quality of life.

Although a debate continues on whether or not these long-lasting conditions create an ethical obligation, moral horizons still need to be broadened when trying to assess proper conduct. Several guiding principles have emerged from the fields of bioethics and environmental ethics that provide starting points for deliberating policy ethics (Attfield, 1983; Jonas, 1984). First, the ethic of stewardship implies that the current generation has a unique role as custodian or steward for the existing natural system, as well as a creative role in improving it while simultaneously participating in it. Second, discussions of right conduct are expanded to include intergenerational ethics and a responsibility toward future generations. In an interconnected and technologically advanced world, it is increasingly within the power of those living to affect seriously the quality of life of those yet unborn. Bringing a better future into being requires a focus on, and responsibility for, the welfare of future generations.

Public Leadership Summary

Character of Catalysts

- Passion for results
- Sense of connectedness and relatedness
- Exemplary personal integrity

Catalytic leadership is not mysterious or new. But as one catalyst stated, "It is not easy. It is frustrating. It is tiring. It is risky. It is too slow." Certain core characteristics, however, appear more salient than those qualities associated with past leaders. These include specific commitments or habits that help one make a difference: focusing on results while welcoming divergent strategies to reach the outcome; caring about connections and relationships; and recognizing and nurturing the networks and webs in which things are accomplished. Personal integrity and trust are built on the bedrock of core commitments, inner strength, and a commitment to right conduct. These form the basis for a strength of character that energizes catalytic leadership.

Developing these habits occurs through a refinement of perception, reflection, feeling, and action through repeated efforts. It is a nonmechanical repetition, one more like the virtuosity of a craftsperson or musician than that of an assembly-line worker. Such actions become second nature—effortless, but careful and attentive (Hardie, 1980). A perfect state of strong character and exemplary integrity, however, may be unreachable. Developing exemplary integrity is a process of self-cultivation that continues throughout one's life. Underlying or perhaps motivating this life-long process of character formation is a well-considered moral commitment. Aristotle's person of good character finds pleasure in the thought and the passionate pursuit of noble ends. Catalytic leaders have a sincere commitment to the ideal and a spirit of inquiry, which involves regular examination of the ethical impact of one's actions. This spirit of inquiry is propelled by a constant and unending process of self-cultivation that transforms the catalyst's conduct throughout life.

Establishing Criteria Based on Desired Outcomes

Much of the political process in working groups revolves around advancing preferred courses of action. Using evaluation criteria can significantly reduce dependence on political bargaining and can lead to improved working group decisions. Although identifying criteria may not seem controversial, when criteria are explicitly discussed, conflict around individual values and interests and questions of fairness may arise.

Types of Criteria

Criteria used to compare and contrast multiple alternatives emerge from the desired outcome to be achieved. With the focus on reaching the desired outcome, evaluation criteria typically fall into the following four interdependent categories: systemic, interest-based, resource, and political. Most individuals focus on one criterion to the exclusion of the other three. Competing criteria do not necessarily have to be reconciled for agreement, and neither must working group members be equally enthusiastic for each criterion. Strongest commitment is gained, however, with strategies that meet more than one of these criteria.

Systemic or Strategic Criteria

Interconnected problems have multiple linkages and are nested within a network of other issues. Although there are multiple linkages and multiple causes, not all are equal in influencing the problem. Systemically, there are a few causes that are more impactful and influential in addressing the problem. Some strategies will more effectively achieve the outcome over the long run because of their more direct causal linkage. The key evaluative question: Are these strategies addressing the underlying core problems or are they merely pushing on the symptoms? This criterion seeks to assess whether a set of strategies strategically pinpoints and leverages change over the long run. It can stimulate such related questions as

- Are these high-leverage options that target the systemic causes of the problem, or are they low-leverage actions?
- Will these strategies create "cascading effects" throughout the system?
- Will these strategies have a long-lasting effect?

Interest-Based Criteria

Successful strategies are those in which individual stakeholders feel their personal and organizational interests will be met. Strategies based on common or similar interests will generate sufficient commitment to ensure implementation. Even when interests are not common or similar, they may be complementary and non-competing. When interests are truly in conflict, there are also strategies in which stakeholders trade or barter things that are valued differently, trading less important items for more important ones (Susskind and Cruikshank, 1987). Multiple and diverging interests can be accommodated within a broad portfolio of inter-related strategies and can provide the building blocks for actions to which an increasing number of members can support and commit. Research shows that in multinational efforts to address boundary-crossing problems, sustainable initiatives are characterized by a sense that no one loses. The key evaluation criterion here is, Do these strategies meet our individual and collective interests? The following questions can help the group ascertain if this criterion is met:

- Do key stakeholders all gain? (an "all-gain" portfolio)
- Do any stakeholders lose? (a "no-one-loses" portfolio)

- Are the varied interests of the working group reflected in the strategies?
- Do these strategies meet the most important underlying concerns?
- Are conflicting interests apparent and, if so, are they integrated into new, more inventive strategies?

Resource Criteria

Financial resources are always a primary criterion. There are seldom sufficient funds available to implement all potentially effective strategies. Resources in this context extend beyond finances. They include information, expertise, funding, time, personnel, and competencies. Resource criteria are too often used as an initial feasibility sieve to eliminate effective strategies prematurely because they do not appear realistic. However, only marginal improvements will result unless the effort reaches beyond current capabilities and resources. The key question is, Can sufficient resources be generated or reallocated to stimulate a catalytic effect? Other potential resource evaluation questions include

- Are the resources readily available? If not, are they obtainable?
- Can existing resources be reallocated to align agencies better to achieve the desired outcomes?
- Are there sufficient staff competencies and technical know-how within the implementation agencies?

Public Acceptance and Political Criteria

Strategies to address public problems garner varying levels of public acceptance and political support. Public acceptance requires both intellectual and emotional acceptance (Yankelovich, 1992). Acceptance by elected officials is enhanced when the proposed actions satisfy their constituents, improve reelection prospects, and, from their perspective, are good public policy (Kingdon, 1984). Quite often, general acceptance can be characterized when a strategy or set of strategies is considered in common currency or in season. Unfortunately, these acceptable strategies may not necessarily meet the preceding systemic, interest-based, or resource criteria. Nevertheless, evaluative criteria must consider the important question, Will these strategies, taken together, be acceptable politically and publicly? Related questions to tease out this acceptance include

- Which strategies will have the greatest level of public acceptance?
- Which strategies will have the greatest level of political acceptance?
- Which strategies will satisfy the greatest number of key decision makers?

Bibliography

Ackoff, R. *Creating the Corporate Future.* New York: Wiley, 1981.

Agranoff, R. "Human Services Integration: Past and Present Challenges in Public Administration." *Public Administration Review,* 1991, *51*(6), 533–542.

Amason, A. C. "Distinguishing the Effects of Functional and Dysfunctional Conflict on Strategic Decision Making: Resolving a Paradox for Top Management Teams." *Academy of Management Journal,* 1996, *39*(1), 123–148.

Annie E. Casey Foundation. *The Path of Most Resistance: Reflections on Lessons Learned from New Futures.* Baltimore: Casey Foundation, 1996.

Associated General Contractors of America. *America's Infrastructure: A Plan to Rebuild.* Washington, D.C.: Associated General Contractors of America, 1983.

Attfield, R. *The Ethics of Environmental Concern.* New York: Columbia University Press, 1983.

Aufderheide, P., and Chester, J. *Talk Radio: Who's Talking? Who's Listening?* Washington, D.C.: Benton Foundation, 1990.

Barnard, C. *The Functions of the Executive.* Cambridge, Mass.: Harvard University Press, 1938.

Bass, B. M. *Leadership and Performance Beyond Expectations.* New York: Free Press, 1985.

Bass, B. M. "From Transactional to Transformational Leadership: Learning to Share the Vision." *Organizational Dynamics,* 1990, *18,* 19–31.

Bass, B., and Avolio, B. J. "The Implications of Transactional and Transformational Leadership for Individual, Team, and Organizational Development." *Research in Organizational Change and Development,* 1990, *4,* 231–272.

Batten, J. D. *Tough-Minded Leadership.* New York: American Management Association, 1989.

Baumgartner, F. R., and Jones, B. D. *Agendas and Instability in American Politics.* Chicago: University of Illinois Press, 1993.

Bazerman, M. H. *Judgement in Managerial Decision Making.* New York: Wiley, 1994.

Behn, R. "The Big Questions of Public Management." *Public Administration Review,* 1995, *55*(4), 313–324.

Bellone, C. "The Public Interest: Discussing the Public Good in Space and Time." *Administrative Theory and Praxis,* 1994, *16*(2), 223–233.

Bennis, W. "The Four Competencies of Leadership." *Training and Development Journal,* Aug. 1984.

Bennis, W., and Nanus, B. *Leaders: The Strategies for Taking Charge.* New York: HarperCollins, 1985.

Berlew, D. E. "Leadership and Organizational Excitement." *California Management Review,* 1974, *17,* 21–30.

Bigelow, B., Fahey, L., and Mahon, J. "A Typology of Issue Evolution." *Business and Society,* Spring 1993, pp. 18–29.

Birch, D. *The Job Generation Process.* Cambridge: Massachusetts Institute of Technology, Program on Neighborhood and Regional Change, 1979.

Blank, M. J., and Lombardi, J. "Towards Improved Services for Children and Families: Forging New Relationships Through Collaboration." Policy brief based on the *Eighth Annual Symposium of the A. L. Mailman Family Foundation,* The Institute for Educational Leadership, 1992.

Bloomquist, W., and Ostrom, E. "Institutional Capacity and the Resolution of a Commons Dilemma." *Policy Studies Review,* 1985, *5*(2), 383–393.

Bluestein, J. *Care and Commitment: Taking the Personal View.* New York: Oxford University Press, 1991.

Blumbaugh, D. "Changing Role of Public Administrators," *Public Management,* 1987, *69*(6), 8–11.

Bridges, W. *Transitions: Making Sense of Life's Changes.* Reading, Mass.: Addison-Wesley, 1980.

Bridges, W. *Surviving Corporate Transitions.* New York: Doubleday, 1988.

Brinkerhoff, D., and Goldsmith, A. "Promoting the Sustainability of Development Institutions: A Framework for Strategy." *World Development,* 1992, *20*(3), 369–383.

Bryman, A. *Charisma and Leadership in Organizations.* Thousand Oaks, Calif.: Sage, 1992.

Bryson, J. *Strategic Planning in Public and Nonprofit Organizations.* (2nd ed.) San Francisco: Jossey-Bass, 1995.

Bryson, J., Bromiley, P., and Jung, Y. S. "Influences of Context and Process on Project Planning Success." *Journal of Planning Education and Research,* 1990, *9*(3), 183–195.

Bryson, J., and Crosby, B. *Leadership for the Common Good: Tackling Public Problems for the Common Good.* San Francisco: Jossey-Bass, 1992.

Bryson, J., and Einsweiler, R. (eds.). *Shared Power.* Lanham, Md.: University Press of America, 1991.

Bryson, J., and Finn, C. "Creating the Future Together: Developing and Using Shared Strategy Maps." In A. Halchmi and G. Bouckaert (eds.), *The Enduring Challenges of Public Management.* San Francisco: Jossey Bass, 1995.

Buffum, S. *The Applegate Partnership: A Case Study.* Eugene: University of Oregon, Department of Planning, Public Policy, and Management, 1993.

Burns, J. M. *Leadership.* New York: HarperCollins, 1978.

Campbell, J. E., Copple, B., Clooney, N. J. Jr., Marcus, L. B., and Spear, T. D. *Funding for the 21st Century: Building Funding Capacity for CSAP Partnerships and Other Community-Based Coalitions.* Washington, D.C.: Community Anti-Drug Coalitions of America, Center for Substance Abuse Prevention, 1994.

Carnegie Foundation. *A Nation at Risk.* New York: Carnegie Foundation, 1983.

Carpenter, S. *Solving Community Problems by Consensus.* Washington, D.C.: Program for Community Problem Solving, 1992.

Carpenter, S., and Kennedy, W.J.D. *Managing Public Disputes.* San Francisco: Jossey-Bass, 1988.

Cayer, J., and Weschler, L. *Public Administration: Social Change and Adaptive Management.* New York: St. Martins Press, 1991.

Centers for Disease Control and Prevention. *Homicide Among Males Aged Fifteen to Twenty-Four.* Washington, D.C.: Centers for Disease Control and Prevention, 1996.

Checkland, P. "Soft Systems Methodology." In J. Rosenhead (ed.), *Rational Analysis for a Problematic World.* Chichester, UK: Wiley, 1989.

Child, J., and Smith, C. "The Context and Process of Organizational Transformation: Cadbury Limited in Its Sector." *Journal of Management Studies,* 1987, *24,* 565–593.

Chrislip, D., and Larson, C. *Collaborative Leadership: How Citizens and Civic Leaders Can Work Together.* San Francisco: Jossey-Bass, 1994.

Cleveland, H. *The Knowledge Executive: Leadership in an Innovative Society.* New York: NAL/Dutton, 1985.

Cleveland, H. *Birth of a New World: An Open Moment for International Leadership.* San Francisco: Jossey Bass, 1993.

Coates, J. F. "Impacts We Will Be Assessing in the Twenty-First Century." *Impact Assessment Bulletin,* 1991, *9*(4), 8–25.

Coates, J. F. "Why Is It So Difficult to Do Anything?" *Technological Forecasting and Social Change,* 1992, *42,* 413–417.

Coates, J. "What to Do When You Don't Know What You Are Doing." *Technological Forecasting and Social Change,* 1995, *50,* 167–170.

Cobb, R., and Elder, C. *Participation in American Politics: The Dynamics of Agenda Building*. Baltimore: Johns Hopkins University Press, 1983.

Coe, B. "Open Focus: A Model of Community Development." *Journal of the Community Development Society*, 1990, *21*(2), 18–37.

Coles, R. "On the Nature of Character: Field Notes." In C. Sommers and F. Sommers (eds.), *Vice and Virtue in Everyday Life*. Orlando, Fla.: Harcourt Brace, 1989.

Conger, J. A., and Kanungo, R. N. "Toward a Behavioral Theory of Charismatic Leadership in Organizational Settings." *Academy of Management Review*, 1987, *12*, 637–647.

Conger, J. A., Kanungo, R. N., and Associates. *Charismatic Leadership: The Elusive Factor in Organizational Effectiveness*. San Francisco: Jossey-Bass, 1988.

Copple, J. E., and others. *Funding for the Twenty-First Century: Building Funding Capacity for CSAP Partnerships and Other Community-Based Coalitions*. Washington, D.C.: Community Anti-Drug Coalitions of America, Center for Substance Abuse Prevention, 1993.

Council of State Planning Agencies. *Global Interdependence and American States*. Working Paper for the annual Council of State Planning Agencies Conference, 1989.

Covello, V., von Winterfeldt, D., and Slovic, P. "Risk Communication: A Review of the Literature." *Risk Abstracts*, 1986, *3*, 171–182.

Crosby, B. *Policy Implementation and Strategic Management: The Challenge of Implementing Policy Change*. Washington, D.C.: Management Systems International, 1995.

Cua, A. S. "Competence, Concern, and the Role of the Paradigmatic Individuals (chun-tzu) in Moral Education." *Philosophy East and West*, 1992, *42*(1), 49–68.

Cuban, L. "Reforming, Again, Again, and Again." *Educational Observer*, 1990, *19*(1) 3–13.

Dahl, R. *The New American Political (Dis)order*. Berkeley: Institute for Governmental Services, 1994.

de Geus, A. P. "Planning as Learning." *Harvard Business Review*, Mar.–Apr. 1988, pp. 70–74.

Dewey, J., and Tufts, J. H. *Ethics*. New York: Henry Holt, 1925.

Downs, A. "Up and Down with Ecology: The Issue Attention Cycle." *Public Interest*, 1972, *12*, 38–50.

Drucker, P. *Managing in Turbulent Times*. Portsmouth, N.H.: Heinemann, 1980.

Dumaine, B. "Times Are Good? Create a Crisis." *Fortune*, June 28, 1993, pp. 123–130.

DuPraw, M. E., and Potupchuk, W. R.. *Collaborative Transportation Planning: Guidelines for Implementing ISTEA and the CAAA.* Washington, D.C.: Program for Community Problem Solving Working Paper, April 1993.

Eden, C. "Using Cognitive Mapping for Strategic Options Development and Analysis (SODA)." In J. Rosenhead (ed.), *Rational Analysis for a Problematic World.* New York: Wiley, 1989.

Eden, C. "Strategic Thinking with Computers." *Long Range Planning,* 1990, *23*(6), 33–43.

Eden, C., and Huxham, C. "Action-Oriented Strategic Management." *Journal of the Operational Research Society,* 1986, *39,* 889–899.

Eden, C., and Radford, J. *Tackling Strategic Problems.* Thousand Oaks, Calif.: Sage, 1990.

Eden, C., and Simpson, P. "SODA and Cognitive Mapping in Practice." In J. Rosenhead (ed.), *Rational Analysis for a Problematic World.* New York: Wiley, 1989.

Ehrenhalt, A. "The City Manager Myth." *Governing,* 1990, *3*(12), 40–46.

Etzioni, A. *Studies in Social Change.* Austin, Tex.: Holt, Rinehart and Winston, 1966.

Etzioni, A. *A Responsive Society: Collected Essays on Guiding Deliberate Social Change.* San Francisco: Jossey-Bass, 1991.

Etzioni, A. "Incorrigible: Bringing Social Hope and Political Rhetoric into Instructive Contact with What It Means to Be Human." *Atlantic Monthly,* July 1994, pp. 14–15.

Festinger, L. *A Theory of Cognitive Dissonance.* Stanford, Calif., Stanford University Press, 1968.

Fischoff, B. "Strategic Policy Preferences: A Behavioral Decision Theory Perspective." *Journal of Social Issues,* 1983, *39*(1) 133–160.

Fischoff, B. "Managing Risk Perception." *Issues in Science and Technology,* 1985, *2,* 83–96.

Fisher, R., and Brown, S. *Getting Together: Building a Relationship That Gets to Yes.* Boston: Houghton Mifflin, 1988

Fisher, R., Kopelman, E., Schneider, A. *Beyond Machiavelli: Tools for Coping with Conflict.* Cambridge: Harvard Press, 1994

Fisher, R., and Ury, W. *Getting to Yes.* New York: Penguin Books, 1981.

Fleisher, C. S. "Using an Agency-Based Approach to Analyze Collaborative Federated Interorganizational Relationships." *Journal of Applied Behavioral Science,* 1991, *27*(1), 116–130.

Forrester, J. W. "Policies, Decisions, and Information Sources for Modeling." *European Journal of Operational Research,* 1992, *59,* 42–63.

Frederickson, H. G. "Can Public Officials Correctly Be Said to Have Obligations to Future Generations?" *Public Administration Review,* 1994, *54*(5).

Freeman, E. *Strategic Management: A Stakeholder Approach.* Boston: Pitman, 1984.

Freeman, E., and Evan, W. "Industrial Policy, Full Employment Policy and a Stakeholder Theory of the Firm." In J. Bryson and R. Einsweiler (eds.), *Shared Power.* Lanham, Md.: University Press of America, 1991.

Gardner, H. *Leading Minds.* New York: HarperCollins, 1995.

Gawthrop, L. "Images of the Common Good." *Public Administration Review,* 1993, *53*(6), 510–516.

Gersick, C. "Time and Transition in Work Teams: Toward a New Model of Group Development." *Academy of Management Journal,* 1988, *31*(1), 9–41.

Gersick, C. "Marking Time: Predictable Transitions in Task Groups." *Academy of Management Journal,* 1989, *32*(2), 274–309.

Gersick, C., and Davis-Sacks, M. "Summary: Task Forces." In J. R. Hackman (ed.), *Groups That Work (and Those That Don't): Creating Conditions for Effective Teamwork.* San Francisco: Jossey-Bass, 1990.

Gettys, C. F., and others. "An Evaluation of Human Act Generation Performance." *Organizational Behavior and Human Decision Processes,* 1987, *39,* 23–51.

Giffin, K., and Patton, B. R. *Fundamentals of Interpersonal Communication.* New York: Harper & Row, 1971.

Glazer, N. "How Social Problems Are Born." *The Public Interest,* 1994, *115.*

Goleman, D. *Emotional Intelligence.* New York: Bantam Books, 1995.

Grady, D., and Chi, K. "Formulating and Implementing Public Sector Innovations: The Political Environment of State Government Innovators." *Public Administration Quarterly,* 1994, *17*(4).

Gray, B. "Conditions Facilitating Interorganizational Collaboration." *Human Relations,* 1985, *38*(10), 911–936.

Gray, B. *Collaborating: Finding Common Ground for Multiparty Problems.* San Francisco: Jossey-Bass, 1989.

Gray, B., and Hay, T. M. "Political Limits to Interorganizational Consensus and Change." *The Journal of Applied Behavioral Science,* 1986, *22*(2), 95–112.

Gray, B., and Wood, D. "Collaborative Alliances: Moving from Practice to Theory." *Journal of Applied Behavioral Science,* June 1991, *27*(2).

Greenleaf, R. *Servant Leadership: A Journey into the Nature of Legitimate Power and Greatness.* Mahwah, N.J.: Paulist Press, 1977.

Guttmacher Institute. *Annual Survey of Teen Births.* Baltimore, Md.: Guttmacher Institute, 1996.

Hackman, J. R. (ed.). *Groups That Work (And Those That Don't): Creating Conditions for Effective Teamwork.* San Francisco: Jossey-Bass, 1990.

Hall, J., and Weschler. L. "The Phoenix Futures Forum: Creating Vision, Implanting Community." *National Civic Review,* Spring 1991, pp. 135–157.

Hardie, W.F.R. *Aristotle's Ethical Theory.* Oxford: Clarendon Press, 1980.

Hart, D. K. "The Virtuous Citizen, the Honorable Bureaucrat, and 'Public' Administration." *Public Administration Review,* 1984, *44,* 111–119.

Hart, D. K. "The Moral Exemplar in an Organizational Society." In T. L. Cooper and N. D. Wright (eds.), *Exemplary Public Administrators.* San Francisco: Jossey-Bass, 1992.

Harwood Group. *Citizens and Politics: A View from Main Street America.* Dayton, Ohio: Kettering Foundation, 1993a.

Harwood Group. *Meaningful Chaos: How People Form Relationships with Public Concerns.* Dayton, Ohio: Kettering Foundation, 1993b.

Hatry, H. *Monitoring the Outcomes of Economic Development Programs.* Washington, D.C.: Urban Institute Press, 1993.

Hatry, H., Liner, B., and Rossman, S. *Measuring Progress of Estuary Programs.* Washington, D.C.: Urban Institute, 1995.

Hawkins, J. D., and Catalano, R. F. *Communities That Care.* San Francisco: Jossey-Bass, 1992.

Heifetz, R. *Leadership Without Easy Answers.* Cambridge, Mass.: Belknap Press, 1995.

Hendrick, R. "An Informative Infrastructure for Innovative Management of Government." *Public Administration Review,* 1994, *54*(6), 543–550.

Henry, G. T., and Dickey, K. C. "Implementing Performance Monitoring: A Research and Development Approach." *Public Administration Review,* 1993, *53*(3), 203–211.

Henton, D., and others. *Building Economic Community: How Civic Entrepreneurs Are Transforming America.* San Francisco: Jossey-Bass, 1997.

Hibbard, M. "Community Beliefs and the Failure of Community Economic Development." *Social Service Review,* 1986.

Hirschhorn, L. *Managing in the New Team Environment,* Reading, Mass.: Addison Wesley, 1991

Holsti, O. R. "Limitation of Cognitive Abilities in the Face of Crisis." In C. F. Smart and W. T. Stanbury (eds.), *Studies in Crisis Management.* Toronto: 1978, pp. 35–55.

Hood, J., Logsdon, J., and Thompson, J. "Collaboration for Social Problem-Solving: A Process Model." *Business and Society,* 1993, *32*(1).

House, R. J. "A 1976 Theory of Charismatic Leadership." In J. G. Hunt and L. L. Larson (eds.), *Leadership: The Cutting Edge.* Carbondale: Southern Illinois University Press, 1977.

Howell, J. M., and Avolio, B. J. "The Ethics of Charismatic Leadership." *Academy of Management Journal,* 1992, *6*(2), 43–54.

Hull, C., and Hjern, B. *Helping Small Firms Grow.* London: Croom Helm, 1987.

Hutt, M. D., Walker, B., and Frankwick, G. "Hurdle the Cross-Functional Barriers to Strategic Change." *Sloan Management Review,* Spring 1995, 22–30.

Huxham, C. "Facilitating Collaboration: Issues in Multiorganizational Group Decision Support in Voluntary, Informal Collaborative Settings. *Journal of the Operational Research Society,* 1991, *42*(12), 1037–1045.

Ingvar, D. H. "'Memory of the Future': An Essay on the Temporal Organization of Conscious Awareness." *Human Neurobiology,* 1985, *4,* 127–136.

Innes, J. E. "Group Processes and the Social Construction of Growth Management." *Journal of the American Planning Association,* 1992, *58*(4), 440–453.

International Institute for Management Development. *World Competitiveness Yearbook.* Lausanne, Switzerland: International Institute for Management Development, 1996.

Isenberg, D. J. "How Senior Managers Think." *Harvard Business Review,* Nov./Dec. 1984.

Isenberg, D. J. "The Tactics of Strategic Opportunism." *Harvard Business Review,* Mar.–Apr. 1987, pp. 92–97.

Jennings, E. T. "Building Bridges in the Intergovernmental Arena: Coordinating Employment and Training Programs in the American States." *Public Administration Review,* 1994, *54*(1), 52–60.

Jonas, H. *The Imperative of Responsibility.* Chicago: University of Chicago Press, 1984.

Jones, S., and Siegel, M. *Public Will: Its Connection to Public Policy and Philanthropy.* Washington, D.C.: The Union Institute, 1993.

Kanter, R. M. *The Change Masters.* New York: Simon & Schuster, 1983.

Kaplan, M. "Infrastructure Policy: Repetitive Studies, Uneven Response, Next Steps." *Urban Affairs Quarterly,* 1990, *25*(3), 371–388.

Keohane, R., and Nye, J. S. *Power and Interdependence.* New York: Little, Brown, 1977.

Kettner, P. M., Daley, J. M., and Nichols, A. W. *Initiating Change in Organizations and Communities: A Macro Practice Model.* Pacific Grove, Calif.: Brooks/Cole, 1985.

Kierkegaard, S. *The Present Age* (A. Dru, trans.). New York: HarperCollins, 1962.

Kim, D. H. *Systems Thinking Tools: A User's Reference Guide.* Cambridge, Mass.: Pegasus Communications, 1994.

King, W. R. "Integrating Strategic Issues into Strategic Management." *OMEGA: The International Journal of Management Science,* 1984, *12,* 529–538.

Kingdon, J. *Agendas, Alternatives and Public Policy.* New York: Little, Brown, 1984.

Kirlin, J. "Policy Responses: Creating the Conditions for Devising Reasonable and Regional Solutions." In J. DiMento and L. Graymer (eds.), *Confronting Regional Challenges.* Cambridge, Mass.: Lincoln Institute of Land Policy, 1991.

Kohn, A. *The Brighter Side of Human Nature: Altruism and Empathy in Everyday Life.* New York: Basic Books, 1992.

Kolb, D. M. "The Love for Three Oranges or What Did We Miss About Ms. Follett in the Library?" *Negotiation Journal,* 1995, *11*(4), 339–348.

Kolb, D. M., and Putnam, L. L. *The Multiple Faces of Conflict in Organizations.* Program on Negotiation at Harvard Law School, Working Paper Series 91–8, October 1991.

Koren, G., and Klein, N. "Bias Against Negative Studies in Newspaper Reports of Medical Research." *Journal of the American Medical Association,* 1991, *266,* 1824–1826.

Korten, D. C. "Community Organization and Rural Development: A Learning Process Approach." *Public Administration Review,* 1980, *40*(5), 480–511.

Kotter, J. P. *A Force for Change: How Leadership Differs from Management.* New York: Free Press, 1991.

Kouzes, J. M., and Posner, B. *What Followers Expect from Leaders: How to Meet People's Expectations and Build Credibility.* San Francisco: Jossey-Bass, 1988.

Kuhn, T. *The Structure of Scientific Revolutions.* Chicago: University of Chicago Press, 1970.

Kupperman, J. J. *Character.* New York: Oxford University Press, 1991.

Lane, D. C. "Modeling as Learning: A Consultancy Methodology for Enhancing Learning in Management Teams." *European Journal of Operational Research,* 1992, *59,* 64–84.

Larmore, C. E. *Patterns of Moral Complexity.* Cambridge: Cambridge University Press, 1987.

Larson, C. E., and LaFasto, F.M.J. *Teamwork: What Must Go Right and What Can Go Wrong.* Thousand Oaks, Calif.: Sage, 1989.

Laumann, E., and Knoke, D. "The Increasingly Organizational State." *Society,* 1988, *25*(2), 21–28.

Lawler, E. *The Ultimate Advantage: Creating the High-Involvement Organization.* San Francisco: Jossey-Bass, 1992.

Leavitt, H. J., and Lipman-Blumen, J. "Hot Groups." *Harvard Business Review,* Jul.–Aug. 1995, pp. 109–116.

Levi, B.T, and Spears, L. "Breaking Gridlock: The North Dakota Consensus Council." In *Northwest Report.* St. Paul: Northwest Area Foundation, Feb. 1995.

Levinson, H. "The Leader as Analyst." *Harvard Business Review,* Jan.–Feb. 1996, pp. 158–160.

Lindbloom, C. *Inquiry and Change.* New Haven, Conn.: Yale University Press, 1990.

Linden, E. "Burned by Warming." *Time,* Mar. 14, 1994, p. 74.

Linsky, M. *Impact: How the Press Affects Federal Policymaking.* New York: Norton, 1986.

Lipnack, J., and Stamps, J. *The Teamnet Factor: Bringing the Power of Boundary Crossing into the Heart of Your Business.* Essex Junction, Vt.: Oliver Wright Publications, 1993.

Lipset, S., and Schneider, W. *The Confidence Gap: Business, Labor, and Government in the Public Mind.* (rev. ed.) Baltimore: Johns Hopkins University Press, 1987.

Logsdon, J. "Interests and Interdependence in the Formation of Social Problem-Solving Collaborations." *Journal of Applied Behavioral Science,* June 1991, *27*(2), 23–37.

Lorenzoni, G., and Baden-Fuller, C. "Creating a Strategic Center to Manage a Web of Partners." *California Management Review,* 1995, *37*(3), 146–163.

Louisiana Department of Environmental Quality. *Leap to 2000: Louisiana's Environmental Action Plan. Project Report: Vision Statement and Negotiated Single Text of the Policy Advisory and Steering Committees.* Baton Rouge: Louisiana Department of Environmental Quality, 1991.

Lowery, S. A., and De Fleur, M. L. *Milestones in Mass Communication Research.* (2nd. ed.) New York: Longman, 1988.

Luke, J. S. "Finishing the Decade: Local Government to 1990." *State and Local Government Review,* Fall 1986a, pp. 132–137.

Luke, J. S. *A Preliminary Study of the Homeless in Omaha, Douglas County.* Omaha, Neb.: Center for Applied Urban Research, 1986b.

Luke, J. S. "From Managerial Ethics to Policy Ethics: New Leadership Requirements for Public Administrators." In J. Bowman (ed.), *Ethical Frontiers in Public Management.* San Francisco: Jossey-Bass, 1991.

Luke, J. S. "Character and Conduct in Public Affairs." In T. Cooper (ed.), *Handbook on Administrative Ethics.* New York: Dekker, 1993.

Luke, J. S. "Personal Integrity in Public Service." *International Encyclopedia of Public Policy and Administration.* Boulder, CO: Westview Press, 1998.

Luke J. S., and Caiden, G. "Coping with Global Interdependence." In J. Perry (ed.), *Handbook of Public Administration.* San Francisco: Jossey-Bass, 1989.

Luke, J. S., and Neville, K. *Teenage Pregnancy Reduction: A Case Study of the Tillamook County Experience.* Eugene: University of Oregon, Department of Planning, Public Policy and Management, 1996.

Luke, J. S., Ventriss, C., Reed, B. J., and Reed, C. *Managing Economic Development: A Guide for State and Local Government Leadership Strategies.* San Francisco: Jossey Bass, 1988.

Luria, A. R. *The Higher Cortical Functions in Man.* New York: Basic Books, 1980.

Lyles, M. A., and Thomas, H. "Strategic Problem Formulation: Biases and Assumptions Embedded in Alternative Decision-Making Models." *Journal of Management Studies,* 1988, *25*(2), 131–142.

MacIntyre, A. "Is Akratic Action Always Irrational?" In O. Flanagan and A. Rorty (eds.), *Identity, Character, and Morality.* Cambridge, Mass.: MIT Press, 1993.

Mandel, M. "Application of Network Analysis to the Implementation of a Complex Project." *Human Relations,* 1984, *37*(8), 659–679.

Martin, A. *Collaborative Technologies to Support Organizational Change.* Menlo Park, Calif.: SRI International, 1993.

Mason, R., and Mitroff, I. *Challenging Strategic Planning Assumptions.* New York: Wiley, 1981.

Mathews, D., and McAfee, N. *Community Politics.* Dayton, Ohio: Kettering Foundation, 1995.

Matland, R. "Synthesizing the Implementation Literature: The Ambiguity-Conflict Model of Policy Implementation." *Journal of Public Administration Research and Theory,* 1995, *5*(2), 145–174.

Mayer, R. C., Davis, J. H., and Schoorman, F. D. "An Integrative Model of Organizational Trust." *Academy of Management Review,* 1995, *20*(3), 709–734.

McCall, M. W. Jr., and Kaplan, R. E. *Whatever It Takes: Decision Makers at Work.* Englewood Cliffs, N.J.: Prentice Hall, 1985.

McCombs, M. "Explorers and Surveyors: Expanding Strategies for Agenda Setting Research." *Journalism Quarterly,* 1992, *69*(4).

McKinley, J. B. "From 'Promising Report' to 'Standard Procedure': Seven Stages in the Career of a Medical Innovation." *Milbank Memorial Fund Quarterly,* 1981, *59*(3), 374–411.

Melaville, A. I., and Blank, M. J. *What It Takes: Structuring Interagency Partnerships to Connect Children and Families with Comprehensive Services.* Washington, D.C.: Education and Human Services Consortium, 1991.

Melaville, A. I., Blank, M. J., and Asayesh, G. *Together We Can: A Guide for Crafting a Profamily System of Education and Human Services.* Washington, D.C.: U.S. Government Printing Office, 1993.

Michael, D. "Competence and Compassion in an Age of Uncertainty." *World Future Society Bulletin,* 1983, *17*(1), 1–5.

Milward, H. B. "Interorganizational Policy Systems and Research on Public Organizations, *Administration and Society,* February 1982, *13*(4), 457–478

Miner, J. "The Uncertain Future of the Leadership Concept." *Journal of Applied Behavioral Science,* 1982, *18*(3), 293–307.

Mintzberg, H. "The Pitfalls of Strategic Planning." *California Management Review,* 1993, *36*(1), 32–47.

Mintzberg, H., Raisinghani, D., and Teoret, A. "The Structure of Unstructured Decision Processes." *Administrative Sciences Quarterly,* 1976, *21,* 227–245.

Mitroff, I. I. *Stakeholders of the Organizational Mind.* San Francisco: Jossey-Bass, 1983.

Mitroff, I. I., and Linstone, H. A. *The Unbounded Mind: Breaking the Chains of Traditional Business Thinking.* New York: Oxford University Press, 1993.

Mohrman, A. M. Jr., and Associates. *Large-Scale Organizational Change.* San Francisco: Jossey-Bass, 1989.

Moore, C. W. *The Mediation Process: Practical Strategies for Resolving Conflict.* San Francisco: Jossey-Bass, 1986.

Morecraft, J.D.W. "Executive Knowledge, Models, and Learning." *European Journal of Operational Research,* 1992, *59,* 9–27.

Myrtle, R. C., and Wilber, K. H. "Designing Service Delivery Systems: Lessons from the Development of Community-Based Systems of Care for the Elderly." *Public Administration Review,* 1994, *54*(3), 245–252.

Nadler, D. A., and Tushman, M. L. "Beyond the Charismatic Leader: Leadership and Organizational Change." *California Management Review,* 1990, *32,* 77–97.

Nalbandian, J. "Reflections of a 'Pracademic' on the Logic of Politics and Administration." *Public Administration Review,* 1994, *54*(6), 531–536.

National Alliance of Business. *A Blueprint for Business on Restructuring Education.* Washington D.C.: National Alliance of Business, 1989.

National Civic League. "Where Americans Place Their Confidence." Denver: National Civic League, 1994.

Neustadt, R. E., and May, E. R. *Thinking in Time: The Uses of History for Decision Makers.* New York: Free Press, 1986.

Newell, A., and Simon, H. *Human Problem Solving.* Englewood Cliffs, N.J.: Prentice Hall, 1972.

Nutt, P. *Making Tough Decisions.* San Francisco: Jossey-Bass, 1989.

Nutt, P. C., and Backoff, R. W. *Strategic Management of Public and Third Sector Organizations: A Handbook for Leaders.* San Francisco: Jossey-Bass, 1992.

Nutt, P. C., and Backoff, R. W. "The Dance of What and How: Creating and Sustaining Organizational Transformation." In A. Halachmi and G. Bouckaert (eds.), *The Enduring Challenges in Public Management.* San Francisco: Jossey-Bass, 1995.

Oakley, E., and Krug, D. *Enlightened Leadership.* Denver: StoneTree, 1991.

Olshfski, D. "Public Sector Executives." *Public Productivity and Management Review,* 1990, *13*(3), 223–243.

Oregon Progress Board. *Oregon Shines.* Salem: Oregon Progress Board, 1989.

Oregon Progress Board. *Oregon Benchmarks.* Salem: Oregon Progress Board, 1991.

Oregon Progress Board. *Oregon Shines II.* Salem: Oregon Progress Board, 1996.

O'Toole, L. J. "Multiorganizational Implementation: Comparative Analysis for Wastewater Treatment." In R. Gage and M. Mandel (eds.), *Strategies for Managing Intergovernmental Policies and Networks.* New York: Praeger, 1990.

O'Toole, L. J. "Rational Choice and Policy Implementation: Implications for Interorganizational Network Management." *American Review of Public Administration,* 1995, *25*(1), 43–57.

Otway, H., and Von Winterfeldt, D. "Beyond Acceptable Risk: On the Social Acceptability of Technologies." *Policy Sciences, 14,* 247–256.

Ozawa, C. P. *Transformative Mediation Techniques: Improving Public Participation in Environmental Decision Making.* Working Paper Series 91–7. Program on Negotiation at Harvard Law School, Sept. 1991.

Pasquero, J. "Superorganizational Collaboration: The Canadian Environmental Experiment." *Journal of Applied Behavioral Science,* June 1991, *27*(2), 38–64.

Peach, J. D. "The International Dimensions of Domestic Programs." *GAO Journal,* Summer/Fall 1991, pp. 43–52.

Peck, R. F., and Havighurst, R. J. *The Psychology of Character Development.* New York: Wiley, 1960.

Peters, T. J., and Waterman, R. H. Jr. *In Search of Excellence: Lessons from America's Best-Run Companies.* New York: HarperCollins, 1982.

Pitz, G. F., Sachs, N. J., and Heerboth, J. "Procedures for Eliciting Choices in the Analysis of Individual Decisions." *Organizational Behavior and Human Performance,* 1980, *26,* 396–408.

Popper, D., and Popper, F. "The Storytellers." *Planning,* 1996, *62*(10), 18–19.

Potupchuk, W. R., and Polk, C. G. *Building the Collaborative Community.* Washington D.C.: National Institute for Dispute Resolution, 1994.

Provan, K. G., and Milward, H. B. "Institutional Norms and Organizational Involvement in a Service Implementation Network." *Journal of Public Administration Research and Theory,* 1991, *1*(4), 391–417.

Putnam, R. D. "The Prosperous Community: Social Capital and Public Life." *The American Prospect,* 1993, *13,* 35–42.

Putnam, R. D. "Bowling Alone: America's Declining Social Capital." *Journal of Democracy,* 1995, *6*(1), 65–78.

Radford, J. "The Analysis and Resolution of Decision Situations with Interacting Participants." In C. Eden and J. Radford (eds.), *Tackling Strategic Problems: The Role of Group Decision Support.* Thousand Oaks, Calif.: Sage, 1990.

Rauch, T. *Demosclerosis: A Hardening of the Democratic Arteries.* Occasional Paper Series. Denver: University of Denver, Center for Public Policy, 1994.

Reed, C., Reed, B. J., and Luke, J. "Assessing Readiness for Economic Development Strategic Planning." *Journal of the American Planning Association,* Autumn 1987, pp. 521–530.

Reischauer, R. D. "Welfare Reform: Will Consensus Be Enough?" *The Brookings Review,* Summer 1987, pp. 3–8.

Richardson, G. P. "Problems with Causal-Loop Diagrams." *System Dynamics Review 2,* Summer 1986, pp. 158–170.

Richardson, G. P. "System Dynamics: Simulation for Policy Analysis from a Feedback Perspective." In A. Fishwick and P. A. Luker (eds.), *Qualitative Simulation Modeling and Analysis.* New York: Springer-Verlag, 1991.

Richardson, G. P., and Andersen, D. F. "Teamwork in Group Modeling Building." *System Dynamics Review,* Summer 1995, *11*(2).

Richardson, G. P., Andersen, D. F., Maxwell, T. A., and Stewart, T. R. *Foundations of Mental Model Research.* Albany: Center for Policy Research, Nelson A. Rockefeller College of Public Affairs and Policy, State University of New York, March 1994.

Richardson, G. P., Andersen, D. F., Rohrbaugh, J., Steinhurst, W. "Group Model Building." Proceedings of the 1992 International System Dynamics Conference, Utrecht, The Netherlands, 1992.

Ring, P., and Van de Ven, A. "Developmental Processes of Cooperative Interorganizational Relationships." *Strategic Management Review,* 1992, *13*(7), 483–498.

Ring, P., and Van de Ven, A. "Structuring Cooperative Relationships Between Organizations." *Academy of Management Review,* 1994, *19*(1), 90–118.

Rittel, H., and Webber, M. "Dilemmas in a General Theory of Planning." *Policy Sciences,* 1973, *4,* 155–169.

Roberts, N. "Transforming Leadership: A Process of Collective Action." *Human Relations,* 1985, *38*(11), 1023–1046.

Roberts, N., and Bradley, R. T. "Stakeholder Collaboration and Innovation: A Study of Public Policy Initiation at the State Level." *Journal of Applied Behavioral Science,* June 1991, *27*(2), 209–227.

Roberts, N., and King, P. "Policy Entrepreneurs: Catalysts for Innovative Public Policy." In F. Hoy (ed.), *Best Paper Proceedings.* New York: Academy of Management, 1989a.

Roberts, N., and King, P. "Stakeholder Audit Goes Public." *Organizational Dynamics,* Winter 1989b, 63–79.

Rocha, E. "Contemporary Poor People's Movements: The Case of Homeless Empowerment." Chicago: Paper presented at the Annual Meeting of the Association of Geographers, 1995.

Rochefort, D. A., and Cobb, R. W. (eds.). *The Politics of Problem Definition.* Lawrence: University Press of Kansas, 1994.

Rogers, E., and Dearing, J. "Agenda-Setting Research: Where Has It Been? Where Is It Going?" In J. Anderson (ed.), *Communication Yearbook.* Thousand Oaks, Calif.: Sage, 1988.

Sabatier, P. A. "An Advocacy Coalition Framework of Policy Change." *Policy Sciences,* 1988, *21*(3), 129–168.

Sabatier, P. A. "Towards Better Theories of the Policy Process." *Political Science and Politics,* 1991, *24*(2), 147–156.

Sarason, S. "The Nature of Problem Solving in Social Action." *American Psychologist,* April 1978, pp. 370–380.

Saxenian, A. *Regional Advantage: Culture and Competition in Silicon Valley and Route 128.* Cambridge, Mass.: Harvard University Press, 1994.

Schactel, W. *Metamorphosis.* New York: Basic Books, 1959.

Scheberle, D. "Radon and Asbestos: A Study of Agenda Setting and Causal Stories." *Policy Studies Journal,* 1994, *22*(1), pp. 74–86.

Schön, D. *Beyond the Stable State.* New York: Norton, 1971.

Schwartz, P. *Art of the Long View.* New York: Doubleday, 1991.

Schwarz, R. M. *The Skilled Facilitator: Practical Wisdom for Developing Effective Groups.* San Francisco: Jossey-Bass, 1994.

Selsky, J. "Lessons in Community Development: An Activist Approach to Stimulating Interorganizational Collaboration." *Journal of Applied Behavioral Science,* June 1991, *27*(2), 91–115.

Senge, P. M. *The Fifth Discipline: The Art and Practice of the Learning Organization.* New York: Doubleday, 1990.

Shepard, H. "Fight, Work, Flight Behaviors." Mimeograph, 1979.

Sherman, N. *The Fabric of Character: Aristotle's Theory of Virtue.* Oxford: Clarendon Press, 1989.

Sherman, S. "How Tomorrow's Best Leaders Are Learning Their Stuff." *Fortune,* Nov. 27, 1995, p. 92.

Simon, H. A. "Political Research: The Decision-Making Framework." In D. Easton (ed.), *Varieties of Political Theory.* Englewood Cliffs, N.J.: Prentice Hall, 1966.

Simon, H. A. *The Architecture of Complexity.* (2nd ed.) Cambridge, Mass: MIT Press, 1981.

Sinclair, U. *The Jungle.* New York: Doubleday, 1906.

Slovic, P. "Perceptions of Risk." *Science,* 1987, *236,* 280–285.

Slovic, P. "Perceived Risk, Trust, and Democracy." *Risk Analysis,* 1993, *13*(6), 675–682.

Slovic, P., Fischhoff, B., and Lichtenstein, S. "Behavioral Decision Theory." *Annual Review of Psychology,* 1977, *28,* 1–39.

Southern Willamette Private Industry Council. "Stakeholders Map." 1991.

State of California. "Memorandum of Understanding: Agreement on Biological Diversity." Aug. 14, 1991.

Stewart, T. "Managing in a Wired Company." *Fortune,* July 11, 1994, pp. 44–56.

Stone, C. N. "Efficiency Versus Social Learning: A Reconsideration of the Implementation Process." *Policy Studies Review,* 1985, *4*(3), 484–496.

Stone, D. A. "Causal Stories and the Formation of Policy Agendas." *Political Science Quarterly,* 1989, *104*(2), 281–300.

Susskind, L., and Cruikshank, J. *Breaking the Impasse: Consensual Approaches to Resolving Public Disputes.* New York: Basic Books, 1987

Sustainable Seattle. *Indicators of Sustainable Community: A Report to Citizens on Long-Term Trends in Our Community.* Seattle, Wash.: Sustainable Seattle, 1993.

Swanson, S. "The Sensual Speech." *The Toastmaster,* June 1986, pp. 21–23.

Tanner, K. L. *Leadership in Multilateral Negotiations: A Case Study of Tommy Koh and the Financial Arrangements Negotiations with the Law of the Sea Conference.* Working Paper Series 91–1, Program on Negotiation at Harvard Law School, Jan. 1991.

Taylor, G. *Shame and Guilt.* Oxford: Clarendon Press, 1985.

Taylor, S., and Novelli, L. Jr. "Telling a Story About Innovation." *Issue and Observations,* 1991, *11*(1), 6–9.

Thomas, C. S., and Hrebenar, R. J. "Interest Groups Grow but Their Power Wanes in State Government." In *Points West Chronicle.* Denver: Center for the New West, 1994.

Tichy, N. M., and Devanna, M. A. *The Transformational Leader.* New York: Wiley, 1986.

Touche Ross. *Ethics in American Business: A Special Report.* New York: Touche Ross, 1988.

Tuckman, B., and Jensen, M. "Stages of Small-Group Development." *Group and Organizational Studies,* 1977, *2,* 419–427.

Tversky, A., and Kahneman, D. "The Framing of Decisions and the Psychology of Choice." *Science,* 1981, *211,* 435–458.

Ury, W. L. *Getting Past No.* New York: Bantam Books, 1991.

Ury, W. L., Brett, J. M., and Goldberg, S. B.. *Getting Disputes Resolved.* San Francisco: Jossey-Bass, 1988.

U.S. Advisory Commission on Intergovernmental Relations. *Emerging Issues in American Federalism.* Washington, D.C.: Advisory Commission on Intergovernmental Relations, 1981.

U.S. Advisory Commission on Intergovernmental Relations. *Changing Public Attitudes on Governments and Taxes: 1990.* Washington, D.C.: U.S. Government Printing Office, 1991.

U.S. Department of Health and Human Services. *Report on Child Care in South Carolina.* Washington, D.C.: U.S. Department of Health and Human Services, Inspector General's Office, 1993.

U.S. Government Accounting Office. *Managing for Results.* GAO/GGO-95–22. Washington, D.C.: U.S. Government Printing Office, Dec. 21, 1994.

Van de Ven, A. "Suggestions for Studying the Strategy Process: A Research Note." *Strategic Management Journal,* 1992, *13,* 169–188.

Van de Ven, A., and Walker, G. "The Dynamics of Interorganizational Coordination." *Administrative Sciences Quarterly,* 1984, *29,* 598–621.

Vennix, J.A.M., Andersen, D. F., Richardson, G. P., and Rohrbaugh, J. "Model-Building for Group Decision Support: Issues and Alternatives in Knowledge Elicitation." *European Journal of Operational Research,* 1992, *59,* 28–41.

Vennix, J.A.M., and Gubbels, J. W. "Knowledge Elicitation in Conceptual Model Building: A Case Study in Modeling a Regional Dutch Health Care System." *European Journal of Operational Research,* 1992, *59,* 85–100.

Ventriss, C., and Luke, J. "Organizational Learning and Public Policy: Toward a Substantive Perspective." *American Review of Public Administration,* Dec. 1988, pp. 337–357.

View, V. A., and Amos, K. *Living and Testing the Collaborative Process: A Case Study of Community Based Services Integration.* Arlington, Va.: National Center for Clinical Infant Programs, 1994.

Volkema, R. J. "Problem Formulation in Planning and Design." *Management Science,* 1983, *29*(6), 639–652.

Volkema, R. J. "Problem Formulation as a Purpose Activity." *Strategic Management Journal,* 1986, *7,* 267–279.

Waddock, S. A. "Building Successful Social Partnerships." *Sloane Management Review,* Summer 1988, pp. 17–23.

Waddock, S. A. "Understanding Social Partnerships: An Evolutionary Model of Partnership Organizations." *Administration and Society,* 1989, *21*(1), 78–100.

Waddock, S. A. "A Typology of Social Partnerships." *Administration and Society."* 1991, *22*(4), 480–515.

Waldo, D. (ed.). *Public Administration in a Time of Turbulence.* Scranton, Pa.: Chandler, 1971.

Walker, L. J., and others. "Moral Stages and Moral Orientation in Real-Life and Hypothetical Dilemmas." *Child Development,* 1987, *58,* 842–858.

Walters, J. "How to Tame the Press." *Governing,* Jan. 1994, pp. 30–35.

Weick, K. E. "Small Wins: Redefining the Scale of Social Problems." *American Psychologist,* Jan. 1984, *39*(1), 40–49.

Weisbord, M. *Discovering Common Ground.* San Francisco: Berrett-Koehler, 1992.

Westley, F., and Mintzberg, H. "Visionary Leadership and Strategic Management." *Strategic Management Journal,* 1989, *10,* 17–32.

Westley, F., and Vredenburg, H. "Strategic Bridging: The Collaboration Between Environmentalists and Business in the Marketing of Green Products." *Journal of Applied Behavioral Science,* 1991, *27*(1), 65–90.

Wildavsky, A. *Speaking Truth to Power: The Art and Craft of Policy Analysis.* New York: Little, Brown, 1979.

Wilson, J. Q. *Bureaucracy: What Government Agencies Do and Why They Do It.* New York: Basic Books, 1989.

Wood, D., and Gray, B. "Toward a Comprehensive Theory of Collaboration." *Journal of Applied Behavioral Science,* June 1991, *27*(2), 139–162.

Yankelovich, D. *Coming to Public Judgment: Making Democracy Work in a Complex World.* Syracuse, N.Y.: Syracuse University Press, 1991.

Yankelovich, D. "How Public Opinion Really Works." *Fortune,* Oct. 5, 1992.

Zand, D. *The Leadership Triad.* New York: Oxford University Press, 1997.

Index

A

Absolute numbers, communicating data as, 160, 161
Accidents, as attentional triggers, 55–56
"Action detailing," 124
Activist groups, 16
Activities, of working groups, 86–87
Acts, of catalytic leaders, 26–27
Adaptive learning, 137–138, 145
Advocacy coalitions, 129–131
Affinity diagrams, 110
Agenda setting, 42
Agreement: emotions in forging, 202–203; on framing and reframing problems, 99–100; among group members, 91–92, 93; interorganizational, 134; levels of, 215–216; multiple, 213–216; nonconfrontational, 214; "pie-expanding," 200–201. *See also* Consensus
Air pollution problem, 157, 159
Alertness, of catalytic leaders, 225
Alternatives, criteria for comparing multiple, 241–244
Ambiguous group visions, 93–94
Anagenesis, social, 6
Analogies, in strategic thinking, 161, 164
Analysis, 151; in strategic thinking, 152
Anecdotes: problem awareness through, 48, 105–106; in strategic thinking, 162–165
Anger, strategic thinking and, 154–155
Annie E. Casey Foundation, 60 "New Futures Program" of, 100–101

Applegate Partnership: conflict management in, 194–195; first meetings of, 82–83
Arizona Strategic Planning for Economic Development (ASPED), 102
Attentional triggers, prioritization of issues by, 54–61
Authority: flow of influence from, 30–31; fragmentation of, 15–18; interconnected problems and, 32–35
Avoidance techniques, 204–205

B

Barnard, Chester, 30
"Battered-Child Syndrome," 65
Benchmark measures, 141
Benchmarks, 140–141; creation of, 138
Birch, David, 58
Blame, strategic thinking and, 154–155
Blocking of implementations, 74, 123. *See also* Sustaining action
Boston Compact, 134
"Both-and" deliberations, 224
Boundary crossing, of public problems, 7–15
Bounded problems, 11–12
Brain, analytical centers of, 152–153
Brainstorming, 188–189
Bureaucracy, formation of, 136
Bureaucrats, 18
Burns, James MacGregor, 25

C

Catalytic interventions, 205–213
Catalytic leadership, 4; conflict maintenance by, 194–203; convening

meetings and, 67–68; in core working groups, 77–78; expanding options with, 114–115; formulating intermediate outcomes by, 102–103; foundational skills for, 149–150; four essential tasks of, 33–35, 37–39; framing and reframing of problems by, 156–159; goals of, 120–122; at initial working-group meetings, 81; mutual learning sparked by, 95–96; organizing working groups by, 78–81; personal characteristics of, 218–239; in public arenas, 32–35; raising awareness of problems through, 41–42, 45–47; solving interconnected problems with, 19–21; strategies created by, 89; tasks of, 65–66; working-group facilitation by, 216–217

Catalytic questions, 189–194

Cates, Camille, 185

Causal diagrams, 176–180

Causal loop diagrams, 176, 181

Causal responsibility, 12

Cause-and-effect diagrams, 176, 180, 183

Champions, 129

Changing the Odds, 58

Character: of catalytic leaders, 218–239; defined, 219; personality versus, 220

Character assassination, 202

Charisma, 26, 28; in public leaders, 18–19

Charismatic leadership, 23, 28–29; common themes in, 29–32

Chlorofluorocarbons (CFCs), 71–72

"Circle of prosperity," 176, 181

Citizen groups, 16

Citizens, 23

Clarification, of core issues, 112–113

Clean Air Act of 1970, 60

Cleveland, Harlan, 73

Cleveland, Ohio, default of, 60–61

Coalition-building, 68

Cognitive biases, 153–154

Cognitive maps. *See* Mental models

Collaboration: achieving, 185–186; end-outcomes and, 92–93

Collective action, enabling mechanisms for, 132–141

Commitment: generating, 116, 119–120, 146; from key decision makers, 128–132; of resources, 131–132

Common ground, 106–107, 107–108, 117–118, 214. *See also* Agreement; Consensus finding

Communication, in strategic thinking, 159–162

Communication barriers, 127

Communication linkages, 97

Communication networks, 142–143; facilitators for, 143–146

Communication technologies, 16

Community forums, as attentional triggers, 56–58

Community politics, attentional triggering through, 57–58

Comparisons, in strategic thinking, 160–162

Complexity, management of, 109

Computer-aided simulations, 177

Computers, modeling public problems with, 111, 180–182

Conceptual models, 177

Concern for others, among catalytic leaders, 227–228, 237–238

Conditions: focusing public attention on adverse, 43–51; public problems as adverse, 42–43

Conduct, rules of, 237

Conflict: coping with, 194–203; mutual learning through, 96; personal, 196, 201–203; resolving through leadership, 216–217; sources of, 195–197, 198

Conflict management, 197–203

Connectedness. *See* Interconnectedness

Connectivity, power and, 74

Consciences, of catalytic leaders, 232–233

Consensus: achieving, 185–186, 215–216; end-outcomes and, 167–169; in interconnected problems, 13. *See also* Agreement

Constituent support, 129–131

Constraints, in public problems, 15–19

Consultative forums, 77

Continuous feedback, 137–139

Convergent thinking, 153

Cooperation, 146

Cooperative networks, 134

Core group members, 69, 90, 91; number of, 75–78; personal goals of, 126; reassessment of, 103–104

Core issues, clarification and redefinition of, 112–113

Core working groups, 75–78, 81–87; organization of, 76–77. *See also* Working groups

Corporate alliances, analysis of, 142

Corporation for Enterprise Development, 60

Countable problems, 45

"Courageous patience," 28

Creating strategies, 89–122; approaches to, 117–118; collaboration in, 92–93; for effective working groups, 90–91, 120–122; essential tasks in, 99; generating options in, 101–102; group agreement in, 91–92, 93–94; mental models in, 109–112; mutual learning in, 95–98; "ongoingness" in, 102–103; reassessment of working-group membership in, 103–104. *See also* Multiple strategies

Creative thinking, option invention through, 114–115

Credibility: of government sources, 46; of knowledgeholders, 80–81; of stakeholders, 74, 80–81

Crises, instilling urgency into, 52–53

Criteria, for comparing multiple alternatives, 241–244

Critical judgment, inhibitory nature of, 114–115

Cross-boundary networks, communication linkages in, 97

Cross-functional teams: analysis of, 142; shared leadership of, 96–97

Customary rules of conduct, 237

"Cycle of prosperity," 109

Cyclicity, in interorganizational enabling mechanisms, 133

D

Data: attentional triggering with, 58–61; communication of, 159–160, 162; conflicts generated by, 196–197; interpretation of, 46–47. *See also* Information

"Data junkies," 139

Deception, 230

Decision makers, garnering support from, 128–132

Decision-making, by working groups, 84

Deliberative interaction, 95–98

"Demosclerosis," 17

Denial, strategic thinking and, 154–155

Dewey, John, 220

Diagrams. *See* Affinity diagrams; Causal diagrams; Graphic facilitation techniques; Mental models; Word-and-arrow diagrams

Disasters, as attentional triggers, 55–56, 72

Divergent thinking, 153

Diversity, in working groups, 76

Douglas, Marjory, 163

Dramatic events, as attentional triggers, 55–56

E

East Palo Alto, California, decline in homicide rate of, 20

Economy at Risk, An, 58

"Ecotourism," 159

Effective champions, 129

Effective working groups, creating, 90–99, 120–122

Ego, described, 231

Egoless process, public leadership as, 231

Ego-strength, 230–231

"Either-or" debates, 224

Electronic communication linkages, 97

Emotional concern: generated by accidents and disasters, 55–56; problem awareness through, 49–51

Emotional self-regulation, of catalytic leaders, 232

Emotions: of catalytic leaders, 223–224, 232; conflicts and, 202–203

Employees, 23

Enabling legislation, 73

Enabling mechanisms, lack of, 127

"Endings," sense of, 27

End-outcomes, 92; collaboration and, 92–93; eliminating ambiguous visions by focusing on, 94; intermediate outcomes and, 168–170

Energy, of catalytic leaders, 218, 223–224. See also Negative energy, Positive energy

Enthusiasm, of catalytic leaders, 218

Ethical conduct, 236–238

Ethical leadership, threats to, 221

Evaluations: as attentional triggers, 58–61; of ideas and options, 188–189

Everglades, The: River of Grass (Douglas), 163

F

Face-to-face contact, 97

Facilitating statements, 205–211

Facilitators, 73; coping with personal conflict by, 202–203; network, 143–146, 146–147; of productive working groups, 185–217; refocusing working groups with, 211–213

Feedback, strategic implementation and, 136–140. See also Spiraling back

Feedback loops, 99, 122

Feedback systems, 139–140

"Feed-forward" loops, 99

"Feeling gathering," 104–105

"Felt needs," 27; urgency of, 52

Fidelity approach, 124

"Fifth discipline," 222

Fight behaviors, 205, 206–208

"Fixed pie," 200

Flight behaviors, 205, 206–208

Focusing events, 45; as attentional triggers, 56–57

"Folk heroes," leadership talents of, 24

Followers: of charismatic leaders, 28–29; leaders and, 22–23, 30–32; of transactional leaders, 25; of transformational leaders, 25–27; of visionary leaders, 27–28

Forced compliance: consensus and, 215; of stakeholders and knowledgeholders, 79

Formative evaluation, 137–138

Forming working groups, 67–88

Foster care caseloads, model of, 182

Four tasks of catalytic leadership, 33–35, 37–39. See also Creating strategies; Forming working groups; Raising awareness; Sustaining action

Fragmentation of authority, 15–18

"Frame-breaking" insights, 70–71; persons with, 75

Framing and reframing problems; group agreement on, 99–100; prioritization of issues by, 63–65; in strategic thinking, 155–165

Frequencies, communicating data as, 160, 161

Frohnmayer, David, 108

Functional interdependency, 9–10

Funding, obtaining, 131–132

Funding opportunities, as attentional triggers, 57–58

Future scenarios, in strategic thinking, 164–165

G

Geographical interdependencies, 9
Getting to Yes (Fisher & Ury), 197
Global problems, local problems versus, 9
Global warming, 71–72
Goals: dangers of ambiguous, 93–94; personal, 126; setting of, 92–93; of stakeholders, 172–174. *See also* Outcomes
Good humor, of catalytic leaders, 218
Government, outcome information demanded by, 138–139
Government leadership: institutionalization of, 4–5; interconnected problems and, 15–19; public distrust of, 18–19
Grand strategies, 115
Graphic facilitation techniques: for analyzing mental models, 110–111; catalytic effects of, 111–112
Greenhouse effect, 71–72
Gridlock, 17, 32
Ground rules, of working groups, 84–85
Group dynamics, 226
Group immobilization, 204–205
Group processes: working groups; facilitating, 186–187; management of, 89; in strategy development, 98–99. *See also* Special-interest groups
Groupthink, 204
Guidance mechanisms, 93

H

Habitual thinking, 152
Health and Human Services, U.S. Department of, 59–60
Healthy babies problem, 168, 169
"Heritage travel," 159
Hierarchical authority; group cohesion through, 93; leadership and, 22–23
Higher-order needs, transformational leadership and, 25–26

High-leverage points, 117, 118
Homelessness, 9
Homicides, decline in, 20
Honesty, 235–236
Hope, in priority issues, 53
"Hot-groups," 90
How questions, 192, 193
Humility, of catalytic leaders, 225
"Hyper-pluralism," 17

I

Ideas, generating fresh, 187–194
Images, problem awareness through, 49
Imagination, option invention through, 114–115
Immediate outcomes, 170
Immediate results, pressure for, 128
Impact network analysis, 176
Implementation: blocking of, 74, 123; collective and interorganizational, 132–141; commitment and support for, 128–132; common barriers to, 126–128; communication networks for, 142–143; network facilitators for, 143–146; of strategies, 124–126. *See also* Sustaining action
Implementation champions, 129
Impoverished option bag, 114, 187
Impulse control, of catalytic leaders, 232
Individualized consideration, by leaders, 26
Individual mental models, 109–111
Influence, of leaders, 30–31
Information: feedback of, 137–140; insights and, 104–105; personal interpretations of, 105–106; sharing of, 107–108, 136–137, 137–140. *See also* Data
Information-gathering; networks for, 142–143; results of, 112–113
Information revolution, 16
"Info-structure," 139–140
Inner compass, 231
Inner strength, 230–233

Innovators, 75

Inputs, increased, 167–168

Inquiry, spirit of, 225

Insights: "frame-breaking," 70–71, 75; gaining shared, 104–113, 121–122; generating new, 187–194; need for, 104–105; "pattern-breaking," 70–71; personal, 105–106; "value-added," 212. *See also* Anecdotes; Stories

Inspiration, from leaders, 26

Institutionalization: of government leadership, 4–5; of organizational structures, 27

Insurance industry, as stakeholder in global-warming issue, 72

Integrity, 228–236; of catalytic leaders, 228; defined, 229; inner strength through, 230–233; lack of, 229–230; trust and, 233–236

Intellectual stimulation, by leaders, 26

Intentional focusing events, as attentional triggers, 56–57

Interactions: deliberative, 95–98; among group members, 90

Interconnectedness: catalytic leadership and, 19–21; causes and effects of problems stemming from, 10–15; comprehension of, 112–113; developing a sense of, 225–228; diagramming, 176–180; functional, 9–10; generational, 10; geographical, 9; leadership and, 32–35; multiple strategies and, 115–117; public leadership and, 5–7; of public problems, 3–21; ripple effects from, 222–223; shared power and, 15–19; in strategic thinking, 174–183; strategic thinking and, 151–152

Interdependence, organizing working groups through perceived, 79–81

Interest-based criteria, 242–243

Interests: special-interest groups; Stakeholders; questions that clarify, 193. *See also* Self-interest

Intergenerational interdependencies, 10

Intermediate outcomes: end-outcomes and, 168–170, 171; formulating, 102–103

Interorganizational enabling mechanisms, 132–141

Interpersonal qualities, of catalytic leaders, 226

Intuitive thinking, 153–154

Issue attention cycles, 42–43, 44

Issue definition, 155–156

Issues. *See* Core issues; Priority issues; Public issues; Relationship issues

Issue salience, 47–49, 61; media and, 61–63

Issue timing, 61

Issue urgency, 52–53; media and, 61–63

Issue windows, 61

ithink software, 180

J

Jen, 228

Joint initiatives, analysis of, 142

Joint power agreements, 134

Joint Venture: Silicon Valley, 134

Judgment, of catalytic leaders, 237

Jungle, The (Sinclair), 162

K

Kempe, C. Henry, 65

Kettering Foundation, 57

Key decision makers, garnering support from, 128–132

Key individuals, in working groups, 78–81

Kids Count, 60

Knowledgeholders: at meetings, 69, 70–71; proliferation of, 15–16; reassessment of, 103–104; recruitment of, 78–81; sharing of information from, 107–108; and stakeholders at meetings, 73–74; in strategic thinking, 172; in working groups, 77

Koh, Tommy, 236
Kuhn, Thomas, 75

L

Lange, Dorothea, 49
Language barriers, 127
Large solutions, 115
Latent concerns: adverse social conditions as, 43–45; public problems as, 42–43
Leadership: catalytic, 4; charismatic, 18–19, 23, 28–29; contemporary approaches to, 23–25; described, 231; disadvantages of limited, 128; flow of influence from, 30–31; interconnectedness and, 32–35; "from the middle," 186–187; organizational, 22–25; personal characteristics of catalytic, 218–239; power and, 74; public versus public-sector, 4–7; required to solve public problems, 3–4; themes in contemporary definitions of, 29–32; transactional, 25; transformational, 22, 23, 25–27; visionary, 1–2, 23, 26, 27–28. *See also* Government leadership; Public leadership; Public-sector leadership
Leadership-followership dichotomy, 22–23, 31–32
Leap to 2000, 92
Learning: adaptive, 137–138, 145; mutual, 95–96; during strategy implementation, 125–126
Legitimacy, of working groups, 83–87
Limited leadership, 128
Lobbying, 73
Local problems, global problems versus, 9
"Lock-ins," 82
Long-term thinking, 220–221
Love Canal problem, 157–158

M

"Magnet for collaboration," 92–93
Making the Grade: The Development Report Card for the States, 60

Malpractice insurance problem, 118
"Many hands" problem, 15–19
Media: framing and reframing problems and, 64–65; prioritization of issues by, 61–63
Mediation, 186; refocusing working groups with, 211–213
Meetings: addressing problems at, 67–68; choosing participants for, 69–78; convening initial, 81–87; key participants at, 78–81
Memoranda of understanding (MOUs), 134
Mental models, 12–14, 109–112, 176; catalytic impact of articulating, 111–112; individual, 109–110; questions revealing, 191–193; shared, 110–111, 117; of teenage pregnancies, 179
Metaphors, in strategic thinking, 161–165
Midpoints, 209–210
Milestones. *See* Benchmarks
Minutes, 84
Mobilization, at meetings, 68
Moral concern, of catalytic leaders, 237–238
Moral courage, of catalytic leaders, 233
Moral gaps, problem awareness through, 50–51
Motivation, by vision, 27
Multilateral brokers, 143
Multiple agreements, 213–216
Multiple alternatives, criteria for comparing, 241–244
Multiple benchmarks, 140–141
Multiple strategies, 104–113; commitment to, 119–120; criteria for selecting, 241–244; generation of, 114–118
Mutual dependence, in public problems, 7
Mutual learning, 95–96
Myers Briggs Type Indicator (MBTI), 153–154

N

Narrative analysis, in strategic thinking, 163–164

National summits, as attentional triggers, 57

Negative energy, 74

Negotiation, 186

Network facilitators, 143–146, 146–147

Networks: communication, 142–143; interorganizational, 133–136; structure of, 134–135. *See also* Cross-boundary networks

Neutral locations, for initial working-group meetings, 82–83

"New Futures Program," 100–101

New York State, malpractice insurance problem in, 118

Nonconfrontational agreement-building, 214

Nonhierarchical guidance mechanisms, 93

Norms: social, 237; of working groups, 84–85

North Dakota Consensus Council: mutual learning enhanced by, 95–96; safe space provided by, 82

Novel perspectives, of knowledge-holders, 70–71

"Ongoingness," 102–103

Open-ended questions, 192

Openness, among catalytic leaders, 224–225

Opportunities, problem awareness through, 50

Optimism: of catalytic leaders, 218; framing and reframing problems and, 64; in priority issues, 53

Option evaluation, 114–115

Option generation, 101–102; multiple, 104–113, 114–118. *See also* Insights

Option invention, 114–115; for inter-organizational enabling mechanisms, 133–136

Options, questions that multiply, 193–194

Oregon Benchmarks, 58, 175

Organizational leadership: flow of influence from, 30–31; followers and, 31–32; models of, 22–23; shift to public leadership from, 23–25

Organizational leadership models, 22–23

Outcome-based information and feedback systems, 139–140

Outcome-based monitoring systems, 137

Outcomes: catalytic leaders' passion toward, 223–224; defined, 165; desired by catalytic leaders, 221–222; desired by working groups, 99–104, 121, 241–244; formulating intermediate, 102–103; problems defined as, 100–102; results and, 167; in strategic thinking, 165–170; successfully reaching, 124–125. *See also* End-outcomes; Goals; Results; Small successes; Successful implementation

Outside experts, refocusing working groups with, 211–213

Ozone hole, 71–72

P

Paradigm shifts, 75

"Parent talk," 159

Passion, 223–224

"Pattern-making" insights, 70–71

Percentages, communicating data as, 160, 161

Persistence, of catalytic leaders, 218, 221–222

Personal communication linkages, 97

Personal contact, 97

Personal experiences: problem awareness through, 48, 105–106, 106–107; in strategic thinking, 162–165

Personal integrity, of catalytic leaders, 228–236

Personality, character versus, 220

Perspectives: difficulty of changing, 116–117; multiple, 117–118, 226–227; taking, 201–202. *See also* Novel perspectives

Perspective taking, 227
Pessimism, strategic thinking and, 154–155
Photographs, problem awareness through, 49
"Pie-expanding" agreements, 200–201
Pierce, Neal, 58
"Pierce Report," 58
Pilot programs, solving interconnected problems with, 13
Policy agenda, 42; placing issues on, 42–43, 65–66; priority issues on, 52–53
Policy ethics, of catalytic leaders, 238
Policy learning, 125–126, 138
Policy-planning groups, 59
Policy structure models, 177
Political criteria, 243–244
Poor intellectual habits, 152
Positive energy, 74
Power, 74. *See also* Shared power
Power holders, identifying, 130
Power structure, dissipation of traditional, 16
Pragmatic thinking, 153
Prefrontal lobe, 152–153
Pregnancy, teenage, 6–7, 20, 45–46, 158, 178, 179
Priority issues, transforming problems into, 51–53
Problem "elites," 15–16; in core working groups, 76–77
"Problem-solution pairs," catalytic leadership and, 35
Procedural ground rules, of working groups, 84–85
Process comments, 210–211
Proxies, 84
Psychological biases and preferences, 153–154; catalytic questions affecting, 190
Public acceptance criteria, 243–244
Public agenda, 42; placing issues on, 42–43, 44–45, 46–47; priority issues on, 51–53
Public distrust, 18–19, 46–47, 233–236. *See also* Trust

Public Interest, The (Birch), 59
Public issues: dividing into subtopics, 211; meetings to address, 68; raising awareness of, 41–42, 43–51, 51–53
Public leadership, 4–7, 22–35; addressing public problems with, 19–21; analysis in, 151; character of catalysts in, 239; conflict management in, 199–203; as egoless process, 231; emergence of, 22–23; facilitating productive working groups by, 185–186; foundational skills for, 149–150; four essential tasks of, 33–35, 37–39; framing and reframing problems and, 64; interconnectedness and, 5–6, 8; media shaping of, 62–63; mediation skills in, 211–213; nurturing of champions by, 129; from organizational leadership to, 23–25; organization of working groups by, 78–81; raising of awareness of public issues by, 41–42, 43–51, 51–53; shared power and, 32–35; strategic thinking in, 183–184; strategies created by, 89; sustaining action by, 123, 146–147; tasks of, 65–66; working-group facilitation by, 216–217
Public opinion, media shaping of, 62
Public policy arenas, shared power and authority in, 32–35
Public-private collaborations, shared leadership of, 96–97
Public problems: attentional triggers for, 54–61; boundary-crossing nature of, 7–15; conducting meetings to address, 67–68; creating priority issues from, 51–53; defined as outcomes, 100–102; expansion of perspectives on, 112–113; framing and reframing of, 63–65; interconnectedness of, 3–21; intractability of, 14–15, 19–21; mental models of, 12–14; multiple causes of, 14–15; multiple definitions of, 13–14; natural termination of,

14–15; public leadership and, 19–21; realistic solution of, 14–15; results and, 166–168; social definition of, 11–12, 155–156; software for modeling, 111

Public programs, interorganizational enabling mechanisms for, 132–141

Public-sector leadership, 4–5

Purposes, of working groups, 83–84, 90, 91–94

Q

Questions, catalytic, 189–194

"Quick fixes." *See* Short-term fixes

R

Raising awareness, 41–66; common strategies for, 54–65; issue attention cycles in, 42–43; by public leaders, 41–42; transforming conditions into problems by, 43–51; transforming problems into priority issues by, 51–53

Rapid feedback, 137–139

Reasoned judgment, of catalytic leaders, 237

Record keeping, 84

Recruitment, into working groups, 78–81

Redefining Economic Development for the 1990s, 58

Redefinition, of core issues, 112–113

Reframing problems. *See* Framing and reframing problems

Relatedness, developing a sense of, 225–228

Relationship issues, conflict and, 201–203

Reports, as attentional triggers, 58–61

Representation, in working groups, 84

Resource criteria, 243

Resources, gaining commitment of, 131–132

Results: benchmarks for, 140; catalytic questions focusing on, 191; desired,166–168; dissemination of, 142–143; outcomes and, 167; passion of catalytic leaders for, 220–225; pressure for immediate, 128; problems defined as, 100–102. *See also* Goals; Outcomes

Right behavior, 236–238

Ripple effects, 10–11; interconnections and, 222–223

Ripple-effect stakeholders, 71–72; in strategic thinking, 172

Roadblocks, to strategy implementation, 123

Roles, of working groups, 85–86

Round-robin technique, 189

S

Safe spaces, for initial working-group meetings, 82–83

Salience. *See* Issue salience

Scenarios, in strategic thinking, 161–165

Scientific analyses, 107–108

Scientists. *See* Knowledgeholders

"Seed" funding, 131

Self-control, of catalytic leaders, 232

Self-indulgence, 229

Self-interest, 106–107

Self-organizing groups, 120; formation of, 135–136

Self-reflection, mutual learning through, 95–96

Self-regard, 28

Senge, Peter, 222

Shalala, Donna, 59

Shared knowledge, 107–108

Shared leadership: communication linkages and, 97; mutual learning and, 95; of working groups, 96–97

Shared mental models, 109–112

Shared power, interconnected problems and, 15–19, 32–35

Shared understanding, of issues, 104

Short-term fixes, 13, 35; resisting, 114; strategic thinking and, 155

Sizes, of working groups, 75–78, 91

Skills, foundational, 149–150. *See also* Analysis

Small agreements, 214–215

Small-group leadership theories, 24–25

Small successes, value of, 144–145

Social norms, 237

Soft consensus, 215

Software, for modeling public problems, 111

Solution-advocacy approach, 68

Southern Willamette Private Industry Council stakeholder map, 173

Special-interest groups, diminished influence of, 17–18. *See also* Activist groups; Citizen groups; Knowledgeholders; Stakeholders

Spiraling back, 146. *See also* Feedback

Staff support, for working groups, 86

Stakeholder analyses, 69–70; identifying stakeholders in, 170–174

Stakeholder maps, 170, 173

Stakeholders: avoiding quick fixes by, 114–115; concerted problem-solving by, 19–21; conflict among, 195–197; defined, 170; forging agreements among, 213–216; goals of, 172–174; in interconnected problems, 11, 12–13, 32; interest-based criteria and, 242–243; interests of, 106–107; and knowledgeholders at meetings, 73–74; at meetings, 67–68, 69–70, 71–72; outcomes and, 101, 164–165; power of, 74; proliferation of, 15–16; reassessment of, 103–104; recruitment of, 78–81; relationships among, 125; in working groups, 77, 89

Statements of time and scope, 209–210

Stein, Beverly, 92

STELLA software, 180

Stopping rule, 14

Stories: problem awareness through, 48, 105–106; questions eliciting,

191–193; in strategic thinking, 162–165

Strategic levers, 117; identifying, 174–183

Strategic maps, 180

Strategic network centers, 135

Strategic thinking, 151–184; analysis as a component of, 152; catalytic leadership and, 156–159; data communication for, 159–162; defined, 151–152; framing issues for, 155–165; interconnectedness and, 174–183; outcomes of, 165–170; prefrontal lobe and, 152–153; psychology of, 153–154; resistance to, 154–155; stakeholders in, 170–174; stories, metaphors, and scenarios in, 162–165; tools to stimulate, 176–177

Strategies. *See* Creating strategies; Implementation; Multiple strategies; Sustaining action

Strength of conscience, of catalytic leaders, 232–233

Strong consensus, 215

Structural options, 133–136

Studies, as attentional triggers, 58–61

Substantive conflicts, 199–201

Subtopics, dividing issues into, 211

Successful implementation: barriers to, 126–128; indicators of, 124–126; of interorganizational strategies, 144–146

Supervisory leadership theories, 24–25

Support: of constituents, 129–131; from key decision makers, 128–132; political, 146

Suspicion, 234

Sustaining action, 123–147; benchmarks in, 140–141; crafting strategies for, 116–117; feedback and, 137–139, 139–140; need for, 123; by public leadership, 146–147; during strategy implementation, 128–146; successful strategy implementation and, 124–128

Systemic criteria, 241–242

Systems thinking, 175; benefits of and cautions against, 180–183; visual maps in, 175–180. *See also* Strategic thinking

T

"Take-charge" leadership, 4

Tampa Bay water quality problem, 168–170, 171

Task groups, in core working groups, 77–78

Taxpaying, lack of results from, 18

Teams, leaders and followers in, 31–32

Technical analyses, 70, 107–108

Technical experts. *See* Knowledge-holders

Teenagers: educational problems of, 100–101; pregnancy among, 6–7, 20, 45–46, 158, 178, 179; public problems among, 3

Temporal milestones, 209

Tenacity, of catalytic leaders, 221–222

Thinking traps, 203–204

Think tanks, 59

Threats, problem awareness through, 50

Tillamook County, Oregon, teenage pregnancies in, 20, 45–46, 158, 178, 179

Time constraints, 209–210

Time pacing, 209

"Time streams," 220–221

Timing. *See* Issue timing

Transactional leadership, 25

Transformational leadership, 22, 23, 25–27; common themes in, 29–32

"Trouble down the road," avoiding, 62

Trust: in catalytic leaders, 233–236; conflicts and, 203; defined, 235; establishment of, 97–98; in interorganizational communication, 144. *See also* Public distrust

Trustworthiness, 235–236

Turf barriers, 126–127

U

Unbounded problems, 12

Unbundling; of differences, 200, 201; of outcomes, 102–103; through mathematical modeling, 110–111

Understanding, questions that check for, 193. *See also* Ideas; Insights; Memoranda of understanding (MOUs); Shared understanding

"Unfolding experiments," 225

United States: economic competitiveness of, 3; governance in, 4; public problems in, 3–4

Urban Strategies Council of Oakland (USCO), 58

Urgency. *See* Issue urgency

V

"Value-added" insights, 212

Venting, 202

Verbal aggression, 202

Verbal descriptions, of mental models, 110–111

Visionary leadership, 23, 26, 27–28; ambiguous, 93–94; of charismatic leaders, 28–29; common themes in, 29–32

Visions, dangers of ambiguous, 93–94

Visualization, of mental models, 110–111, 111–112

Visual mapping techniques: for analyzing mental models, 110–111; catalytic effects of, 111–112; in strategic thinking, 175–180

"Vital cycle," 109

"Voyage of discovery," 190

W

"Wake-up calls," 41

Welfare reform problem, 158

What else questions, 192

"What-if" thinking style, 153

What questions, 192, 193

Wheel metaphor, 116

Why questions, 192

Willpower, lack of, 229–230

Windows. *See* Issue windows

Withdrawal, strategic thinking and, 154–155

Word-and-arrow diagrams, 110

Word-of-mouth communication, problem awareness through, 48, 105–106

Working groups: activities of, 86–87; communication linkages in, 97; conditions for effective, 90–99; conflict within, 195–197, 197–203; desired results defined by, 167–168; establishment of trust in, 97–98; facilitating productive, 185–217; formation of, 67–88, 120–122; gaining commitment of, 118–120; ground rules of, 84–85; initial meetings of, 81–87; key individuals in, 78–81; legitimacy of, 83–87; optimal sizes of, 75–78; purposes of, 83–84; refocusing, 203–213; roles of, 85–86; staff support for, 86; structural options for, 133–136

Y

Youth. *See* Teenagers